Conceiving Masculinity

Conceiving Masculinity

MALE INFERTILITY, MEDICINE, AND IDENTITY

Liberty Walther Barnes

Temple University Press
Philadelphia

TEMPLE UNIVERSITY PRESS
Philadelphia, Pennsylvania 19122
www.temple.edu/tempress

Library of Congress Cataloging-in-Publication Data

Barnes, Liberty Walther, 1975–
  Conceiving masculinity : male infertility, medicine, and identity / Liberty
Walther Barnes.
      pages cm
  Includes bibliographical references and index.
  ISBN 978-1-4399-1041-2 (cloth : alk. paper) — ISBN 978-1-4399-1042-9
(pbk. : alk. paper) — ISBN 978-1-4399-1043-6 (e-book)   1. Infertility, Male—
Psychological aspects.   2. Masculinity in popular culture.   3. Human
reproduction—Political aspects.   I. Title.
  RC889.B37 2014
  616.6′921—dc23   •
                                                       2013042591

♾ The paper used in this publication meets the requirements of the American
National Standard for Information Sciences—Permanence of Paper for Printed
Library Materials, ANSI Z39.48-1992

Printed in the United States of America

2 4 6 8 9 7 5 3 1

In loving memory of
Earmalee Trusty Hiersche

Contents

Acknowledgments   ix

Prologue   xiii

1 Preconceived Notions   1

2 Seminal Work   20

3 Doctors Doing Gender   51

4 Just a Medical Condition   82

5 Taking Control   121

6 The Politics of Reproduction   155

Appendix A: Research Participant List   165

Appendix B: Interview Guide   167

Notes   171

Glossary   187

References   189

Index   201

Acknowledgments

Professor Rebecca Klatch ranks at the top of a long list of people I would like to thank for their help with this book. As my dissertation advisor at the University of California at San Diego (UCSD), Rebecca was my loyal advocate. She taught me the sociology of gender, encouraged me in my fieldwork, helped me to focus my ideas, treated me to lunches at the Faculty Club, believed in me, adored my children, and cheered me on to earn my Ph.D. If this book, which is based on my dissertation, is my baby, Rebecca is the intelligent, compassionate, indefatigable delivering midwife.

I extend heartfelt appreciation to the scientists and physicians who sacrificed many hours of their busy professional and personal lives to educate me, answer my questions, and allow me to observe their work. I thank Doctors Donald Evenson, Marc Goldstein, Larry Lipschultz, Cathy Naughton, Robert Oates, Dana Ohl, Gianpiero Palermo, Peter Schlegel, Aaron Spitz, Paul Turek, and Philip Werthman for their deep commitment to education and research and for so graciously sharing their time, knowledge, insights, and experiences with me. They have blessed many lives with their expertise—mine included. I owe a special thank-you to Dr. Cappy Rothman, a legendary male infertility specialist, who instilled confidence in a young graduate student and whose inspiration and connections made this research possible. Additional thanks are due to the office staff, nurses, medical assistants, and laboratory technicians who hosted me and let me take part in their work.

The research for this book was sponsored by the Intel Corporation, where I conducted two internships with the Digital Home and Digital Health groups in 2006 and 2007. I thank my manager, John Sherry, for his generous support of my unusual work. My mentors, Sue Faulkner, Margie Morris, Nancy Vuckovic, and Alexandra Zafiroglu, were incredible examples of dedicated researchers and helped me to formulate my research questions early on.

I express deep gratitude to the many professors and counselors at UCSD who prepared me so well. I am indebted to Christena Turner for office hours that stretched into late-night talks and for gently guiding me and allowing me to bask in her brilliance. I thank Lisa Cartwright, Steve Epstein, and Deborah Wingard, whose invaluable feedback on my doctoral dissertation helped me to see the possibilities of my data and refine my ideas; Maria Charles, who taught me the sociological principles of social inequality and the skills for designing research; and Gershon Shafir, who gave me the right nudge, at a critical moment, to pursue this research. I sing the praises of two typically behind-the-scenes unsung heroes, Rafael Acevedo and Manny dela Paz, for their motivational counsel and professional guidance. I also express warm appreciation to Dean Duncan and Sharon Swenson, two of my undergraduate professors at Brigham Young University, who inspired my passion to think and write critically and instilled in me a strong ethic of love for my informants.

I prayed for an editor who would have both sincere enthusiasm for this project and patience with a first-time author, and God gave me Mick Gusinde-Duffy. I thank Mick for his diligent care, soft voice, and steady encouragement. I also thank Micah Kleit, the faculty reviewers, and the staff at Temple University Press for their hard work in seeing this book through to completion. I am grateful to the many people who read various chapters of the book at different stages of manuscript development and who willingly offered their time, personal insights, and ideas for improvement, including Rene Almeling, Erin Cech, Miriam Clark, Erin Curtis, Zakiya Luna, Jennifer Nations, Marel Stock, Alexandra Vinson, and Katie Walther. A million thanks go to Sarah Franklin and Zeynep Gürtin at the University of Cambridge for their feedback on the full manuscript and for welcoming me into the ReproSoc family. I am eternally indebted to Arthur L.

(Larry) Greil, who read multiple drafts of the manuscript and provided excellent feedback. He is a selfless man with a benevolent heart. I will never be able to repay him for his generosity, but I hope I can one day pay the debt forward by guiding another aspiring scholar.

I thank Miriam Clark for summers of superb child care and year-round daily phone chats; Kara Eads, whose hospitality made so much of my work possible; Charlotte Barnes, research assistant extraordinaire, who organized my office, my files, and my life; Dana Edvalson, whose unwavering faith in everything good restores sanity to my soul; Raymond Hiersche, for ninety years of sacrifice and his unconditional love; and my beloved parents, Larry Walther and Katie Walther, for providing every opportunity the world had to offer and the love, support, encouragement, and confidence to do it all. *Thanks for believing in the little girl who spent too much time staring out the window and loving me for it.*

I would have no story to tell without the anonymous men and women who freely shared their infertility experiences with me and whose voices fill this book. *Wherever you are, please know that for many years now, in the privacy of my office, I have listened to your interviews, pored over your words in transcription, mourned your heartaches, laughed at your jokes, and celebrated your successes. I know your courage and sacrifice, your foibles and fears, your faith and commitment, and I have—in short—completely fallen in love with you. Thank you for allowing an absolute stranger to share in your lives.* The shortcomings of this book are mine, but its best parts I credit to these men and women.

Finally, I thank my best friend, Levi Barnes, whose abiding love came in the form of constant encouragement, technical support, airplane tickets to conferences, long philosophical discussions, midnight baby feedings, romantic lunch dates, and astounding flexibility. My love and appreciation are beyond words. *And thank you Lily, Gideon, Jairus, and Ben.* WE DID IT!

Prologue

In 1997 I was living in Bulgaria—a young, single adult with no children. Whenever I showed off photographs of the white, middle-class American family in which I had grown up, my Bulgarian friends became astonished, confused, or giddy with excitement: *Five children! Your mother has five children?* A few middle-aged Bulgarian women asked me privately whether the rumors were true: *Can women in America really have as many children as they want?* They confided that they had always wanted lots of children, but as I eventually came to understand, they had raised their families during the Communist era, when that desire conflicted with the interests of the state. Many Bulgarian women settled into careers that they had not chosen, raising one or two children but wishing for more. Limited access to basic contraception meant that many women relied on abortion as their primary means of birth control.

As social scientists are aware, sometimes we cannot see the social norms of our own culture until someone outside the culture points them out to us. In the United States most political discussions about reproduction focus on limiting reproduction—that is, on women's rights and access to contraception and abortion. From my interactions with Bulgarian women, I realized that I had never given much thought to unlimited reproduction as a right or a privilege. Can American women have as many children as they want? The United

States is a free country, right? Yet there are social, economic, and po-litical forces that shape women's ideas about childbearing and prevent women from having "too many kids." Not long after returning to the States, I discovered that there can also be biological barriers to the realization of procreative desires. When people ask what sparked my interest in the sociology of reproduction, I always answer, "Bulgaria." However, it was a subsequent experience in an infertility clinic that drove my interest toward infertility.

After years of an irregular menstrual cycle and nearly two years of unprotected sex without conceiving, I went to an infertility doctor, who prescribed for me five small doses of clomiphene citrate to in-duce ovulation. For the next three weeks, my bathroom was stocked with ovulation test kits, and I made multiple trips to the infertility clinic to monitor my swelling ovaries via ultrasound. Before long, an ultrasound revealed one ripe ovarian follicle ready to burst and re-lease one glorious, healthy egg. The clinic scheduled me for artificial insemination two days later, the following Saturday.

As luck would have it, my husband came down with the flu on Friday night. Saturday morning, we arrived at the clinic, where my husband—bleary-eyed, achy, and feverish—passed his semen collec-tion cup to the front desk staff. After a short wait in the doctor's of-fice, a nurse relayed bad news: "You have lots of sperm, but they're dead. Most of the ones that were alive died in the wash." (Before in-trauterine insemination, semen is put into a machine that "washes" the sperm, separating the sperm from seminal fluid and cellular debris via centrifugation.) I had to see this for myself, so the nurse escorted me to the laboratory. There, I peered into the microscope and watched a few lonely survivor sperm maneuver through a waste-land of motionless sperm corpses. With no other options, we moved forward with the insemination, using a syringe full of mostly dead sperm. "It only takes one," chirped the nurse, while I cried on the table with my feet in the stirrups. Two weeks later, a pregnancy test confirmed that my one prized egg had slipped away unfertilized.

The attending nurse (and, later, our doctor) told us quite incor-rectly that my husband's fever could not have killed the sperm. The staff gently reassured my husband that it was just a fluke, that his sperm would look better the next time around, and reiterated to me that conception requires only one sperm. I felt responsible for our in-ability to conceive, as if my egg had willfully refused to be fertilized.

There is no denying that serious issues of my own had once impeded my ability to conceive, but when my husband's sperm was dead and I had a live egg in the queue, infertility was still somehow my problem.

I never intended to become an expert on penises, testicles, semen, and sperm. Initially, I set out to study women's experiences with infertility, but I soon discovered that dozens of smart books were already devoted to the topic. My own personal experience brought to light something curious about infertility research: Men were missing. Men's experiences with infertility were peripheral to the infertility research I was studying. The memory of translucent dead sperm floating under a microscope made me wonder about the larger story of men and fertility. If dead sperm does not qualify as male infertility, what does? And where are all the infertile men?

As a medical sociologist, I am trained to poke at medical science—to test its resilience, detect its soft spots, and map the contours of its borders—to figure out what science can tell us about our social world and to understand how prevailing cultural ideas influence scientific pursuits and knowledge. This study is not an exposé of the infertility industry, and my goal is not to unveil a new infertility science. Rather, I examine the social framing of infertility, asking the following questions: What do infertility definitions and practices tell us about women and men and about masculinity and femininity? How do ideas about gender, including women's reproductive responsibilities and the fragility of masculinity, become enmeshed in medical knowledge and practices? In the age of advanced reproductive technologies, how do couples respond to the challenges posed by infertility? And what do these responses tell us about the flexibility of common gender beliefs? What follows are some answers to these seedling questions.

Preconceived Notions

Surely I was lost. When I arrived at a multistory building with a large sign that read, "Women's Health Center," I was certain I had come to the wrong place. I double-checked the address in my notebook, scratched my head, and wandered inside. "I'm looking for Dr. Bradley, the male infertility specialist," I repeated to several passersby. Someone suggested the third floor, where I came upon a receptionist who directed me to the seventh floor. I stepped off the elevator there and into a hallway lined with locked doors. I explained my plight to a man rushing by in a white coat. He keyed in a pass code, opened a door, and sent me inside. A nurse said that she was expecting me, handed me a set of hospital-issue scrubs, led me to a dressing room, and directed me to change. I deferentially obeyed. This was my first day of fieldwork.

Dr. Bradley soon arrived, accompanied by a younger doctor, a fellow in training. The three of us introduced ourselves and chatted briefly. Decked out in scrubs, a hairnet, and a face mask, I followed the two men into an outpatient surgery room. On the operating table I saw the silhouette of a human form covered from head to toe in blue surgical tissue paper. In the center of the room, equidistant from all four walls, a circular hole cut in that tissue paper exposed the patient's genitals. The scrotum, painted with yellow iodine, fluoresced under the lights. The penis lay flaccid. With no prior medical experience under my belt, I first learned here about scalpels and cauterization, varicoceles and hydroceles, and one of the best kept secrets in America: the prospect of restoring male fertility and repairing masculinity.

This book puts the world of male infertility under the microscope, magnifying the textures and contours, traffic and beats, colors and details of a dimension of our society that is often invisible and disregarded. To paint a full picture of this world, I provide two levels of analysis: institutional and individual. On the first level, I investigate the rugged history and development of male infertility science and medicine and explore the present-day institutions, institutional authorities, and practices that have been designed to address male infertility. On the second, I examine how infertile men see their lives, their futures, and themselves in a society that prizes male fertility and virility. Together, these institutional and individual perspectives tell a sociological story about all of the ways in which preconceived notions regarding men, women, masculinity, femininity, fatherhood, motherhood, and reproduction shape our understanding of male infertility today. Throughout this book I argue that the social process of constructing gender is tightly intertwined with the social process of constructing disease. The purpose of this book is to examine how culturally pervasive notions of gender shape our understanding of disease and how, in turn, disease impacts our personal ideas about gender. Male infertility provides a helpful case study for exploring the relationship between disease and gender.

A Sociological Approach

In modern American culture, *gender* is often considered a hard-wired, essential, and fixed part of our personal identities, and *medicine* is believed to be hard science, evidence-based, objective, and true. Sociologists, however, do not define gender or medicine in such rigid terms. Instead, we see gender as a *social* category: It is how we choose to express our sex assignment. Gender entails a set of social norms and culturally specific prescriptions about how men and women should look, act, perceive themselves, and engage with their social world. Gender is best described as an ideology, flexible and fluid, with the capacity to change over time and across space. Sociologists see medicine as another socially constructed category. The science of modern biomedicine is influenced by many social actors, including medical professionals and laboratory scientists; pharmaceutical corporations and health insurance providers; political groups, governments, and lawmakers; various environmental, humanitarian, and religious organizations; and the individuals whose everyday lives are affected by health issues. The job of medical sociologists is to untangle the social history of a disease, sorting out how authorities have been legitimized, how social institutions have been created, and how patients interpret their disease experience. In this space we discover society's deepest values, beliefs, and ideas. Our taken-for-granted assumptions and preconceived notions come to light, and we see how they have shaped our scientific understanding and treatment of disease. As the case of male infertility illustrates, sometimes medical science has to bend to accommodate society's gender ideals.

This book is not just a story about conceiving babies. It is a story about how we conceive of people—how we conceptualize men and women. Its aim is to uncover, unravel, and shake out all of society's preconceived notions about men and women that have influenced how we scientifically interpret and medically treat a couple's inability to get pregnant. Notions of gender inherited from earlier generations have influenced the development and organization of male infertility medicine over the past century and help explain how we conceptualize and understand male infertility today. According to the World Health Organization, male factor infertility affects no fewer than half of all infertile couples, and according to the American Society for Reproductive Medicine (ASRM), infertility is equally common in men and women.[1] Nonetheless, we often think of infertility as a women's issue, the wife's problem, a female disorder. Women are more likely to bear the social stigma of childlessness[2] and are more likely to undergo medical treatments, even in cases of male infertility.[3]

The National Center for Health Statistics (NCHS) of the Centers for Disease Control and Prevention (CDC) reports that 7.3 million American women have used infertility services.[4] Fertility surveys have closely monitored fertility rates, fertility status, and use of infertility services among women in the United States since 1955.[5] Yet the NCHS National Survey for Family Growth did not begin tracking male infertility until the twenty-first century, so less information is available on male infertility than on female infertility.[6] Infertility is an estimated $3 billion industry in the United States,[7] and specialists who treat women dominate the market. Internet sites, books, and magazines devoted to helping couples combat infertility provide long checklists for women: fertility signs they should watch for throughout their menstrual cycles, diets and vitamins that will improve their fertility, questions they should ask their doctors. Articles and books by psychologists, social workers, and social scientists focus primarily on the grief, frustration, and depression suffered by infertile women. Despite the fact men are just as likely to be responsible for a couple's inability to conceive, the notion that women are primarily responsible for infertility still prevails in much of the world today.[8] Where are all of the infertile men? How have they slipped so easily under the radar?

Masculinity and Virility in the Cultural Milieu

Some men "shoot blanks." This popular idiomatic expression, used to describe male infertility, invokes the image of a pulled trigger, a firing gun, but no ammunition discharging to hit the intended target. The metaphorical gunman is powerless and ineffective; his equipment is inadequate. Compare the idea of "shooting blanks" to other colloquial jargon, such as "grow a pair" and "that takes balls." These fragments of language illustrate the prevailing cultural belief that healthy testicles producing potent sperm are symbols of strength, courage, power, manliness, and masculinity. Throughout history and across cultures, the ideal macho man is depicted as virile and potent. A real man can get the sex he wants and impregnate a woman when he so desires. Certainly there are life stages and circumstances in which men do not want to achieve pregnancy. But as William, a businessman in his late thirties and one of the two dozen infertile men interviewed for this book, described the cultural expectations of masculinity, "Men should be able to gush sperm all over the place."

Sociologist Lisa Jean Moore, author of *Sperm Counts: Overcome by Man's Most Precious Fluid,* has written extensively on representations of sperm and semen in a variety of "seminal enterprises," including the donor sperm market, pornography, forensics, and fatherhood rights. On the basis of her wide-ranging research, Moore concludes that "men are clearly invested in the representations of semen as inherently linked to their sense of selfhood. . . . The more masculine the man, the more manly his semen and vice versa."[9] When I tell people that I study the social experiences of infertile men, I frequently hear responses such as "Oh, those poor guys" and "That must be so difficult for men" or my favorite, "Being able to get your wife pregnant is like the whole point of being a man." The general consensus is that real men gush sperm. Male infertility destabilizes the presumed fundamental basis of masculinity, disrupts traditional gender roles, and hits personal masculine identities right where it counts.

In 1992 researchers in Denmark announced an international fertility crisis: Over the previous fifty years, sperm counts had dropped more than 40 percent worldwide.[10] The report was met with panic and denial in both the scientific community and the media.[11] Over the next decade smaller studies of male fertility among various nationalities proliferated. Sperm counts were believed to provide not only a window into a nation's health but also a measure of national masculinity. As political scientist Cynthia Daniels humorously noted in her book *Exposing Men: The Science and Politics of Male Reproduction,* as the results of geographically specific studies were released, sperm counts of nations were being compared in Olympic competition terms. Some countries flaunted the masculinity of their men: "The mighty men of Finland are walking tall these days." Other reports, like one from Scotland, worried about declining sperm counts producing a "lack of national virility."[12] Some news coverage depicted sperm as tiny soldiers or rockets at war with toxic threats. One report suggested a link between the increase of women in workplaces and colleges and decreasing sperm counts, implying that women's rise in the public sphere was emasculating and feminizing men.[13] The media coverage of sperm count research highlighted the threat of rising female power, the cultural value of virility, and the centrality of virility to masculine ideals.

Infertility can cause men to question their ideas about masculinity, marriage, sex, and fatherhood and to think about their gendered bodies and body parts in ways they had not before. Throughout this book, I draw on a variety of sociological theories of gender to explain how male infertility doctors and infertile men construct notions of masculinity and conceptualize infertility. Fortunately, sociologists Cecilia Ridgeway and Shelley Correll have combined several prominent social theories of gender to develop a very concise gender system as a theoretical framework for examining and explaining how gender is constructed in our social world.[14] According to the gender system theory, gender ideology operates at three discrete levels: in the broad culture, within institutions, and among individuals. Sociologists do not subscribe to biologically essentialist explanations of gender but also cannot deny that gender ideology is annoyingly pervasive, durable, and enduring. According to Ridgeway and Correll, the stubborn resilience of the gender system is due to the constant interaction and interplay between culture, institutions, and individuals.[15] Cultural ideas about gender shape social institutions and get embedded in institutional practices. Sometimes society's ugliest ideas about gender, including assumptions that men are superior, more capable, and more competent than women, inculcate our social institutions. In other words, some social institutions are the nasty sausage factories of gender stereotypes, propagating outdated, inaccurate, and damaging ideas about men and women. As individuals we interact daily with social institutions, consciously or unconsciously accepting or rejecting these popular notions of gender.

Ridgeway and Correll employ the gender system theory to examine and explain gender discrimination in education, the workplace, and the home. The gender system also provides a nice framework for examining male infertility. My analysis uses the three basic levels of the gender system to look at how cultural ideas of male reproduction and masculinity have shaped the development of male reproductive medicine and are built into medical practices. I also consider how individuals conceptualize gender and how the interactions between medical institutions and patients reinforce or reconceptualize aspects of gender.

Contemporary gender theorists point out that over the life course, men and women are continuously exploring and deciding what gender means and how to enact it.[16] Of course, people do not randomly dream up new ideas about masculinity and femininity to embody and portray; we are all active participants in a highly interconnected social world. We have inherited a long history of culturally defined gender norms, and we can see how our access to opportunities, resources, and relationships requires us to enact certain culturally prescribed masculine or feminine traits in various situations. When an individual does not, cannot, or chooses not to adhere strictly to prevailing cultural norms of gender, he or she may discover that being different requires a lot of gender work. Gender work entails mentally and emotionally processing how personal ideas about gender fit in or clash with ubiquitous cultural ideals of gender. Gender work requires digging deep, reconsidering personal values, and weighing the social and economic benefits and costs of conforming to society's expectations or going against the grain.

Gender studies frequently focus on the experiences of women, which, as sociologist Judith Wajcman observes, reinforces "the perception that gender is only an issue where the research subjects are female," ignoring the fact that men's experiences are also shaped by gender beliefs.[17] While most feminist scholarship examines women's experiences with male dominance, over the past two decades a growing number of gender scholars have shifted their focus to men and masculinities, exploring the nuanced power relationships among men. Sociologist R. W. Connell argues that the hierarchy of gender is more complex than basic men-dominate-women models suggest, because men also strive to dominate other men.[18] A hierarchy of men exists in which salient aspects of identity, such as race, class, sexual orientation, age, and ability, grant men access to different forms of power and resources, networks, and women. In its most culturally understood hegemonic form, masculinity is achieved and portrayed through whiteness, wealth, education, intelligence, attractiveness, strength, athleticism, fatherhood, and heterosexual prowess.[19] Sociologist Michael Kimmel argues that manhood is equated with and defined by power.[20] In reality, the achievement of perfect manhood and masculinity is possible for only a small, privileged minority. As a result, most men suffer from feelings of powerlessness and inadequacy.[21]

There are multiple forms of masculinity, because masculine ideals change over time and across cultures, and the ways in which people enact masculinity vary by race, ethnicity, sexual orientation, socioeconomic class, and age. In other words, masculinity is a slippery topic of study. If we look across cultures, we can see empirical evidence that masculine preferences, hobbies, and interests are not connected to sex identity and that behaviors that one man may engage in to demonstrate his manliness another man may avoid for the same purpose. Forms of work, communication styles, and emotional expressions that are considered masculine in one culture or subculture may be deemed feminine in another. If masculinity is so dynamic, how can we isolate it under the sociological lens?

Sociologist Adele Clarke, author of *Disciplining Reproduction: Modernity, American Life Sciences, and "the Problems of Sex,"* observes, "It is difficult to conceive of a more sex- and gender-constructing and maintaining discipline and set of practices and discourses than those of the reproductive sciences."[22] We can debate which hobbies, interests, skills, sports, disciplines, careers, or art forms are gendered masculine or feminine. But male reproduction, entailing the ability to have an erection, penetrate a woman, produce sperm, ejaculate, and fertilize an egg, is quintessentially masculine. (Even if someday this function can be performed by women, I am willing to bet that we will still think of it as a masculine act.) In other words, a study of male infertility can't *not* be a study of gender and masculinity. Male infertility provides a useful case study for exploring masculine themes because infertility prevents men from accomplishing the most hegemonic form of masculinity. When women face infertility, their self-perceptions begin to fray. They are forced to engage in gender work, reconsidering their personal ideas about femininity and how to live up to them.[23] The personal stories recounted in this book capture how *men* reassess their values, make sense of their world, and reaffirm their personal masculine identities as compassionate husbands and responsible fathers-to-be as they come to terms with their inability to perform one of the most basic masculine functions.

Too often, gender scholarship that strives to examine men's gendered life experiences is reduced to trivial comparisons of men and women. Such studies often emphasize gender difference, inadvertently supporting biological determinist explanations of gender, reinforcing a strict gender binary, and perpetuating the gender stereotypes that are used to justify gender inequality. Though women experience infertility, this is not a comparative look at the sexes. And although wives play important supporting roles in the stories presented, this is a book about men. It examines how infertile men grapple with a very distinct, traditional, salient notion of masculinity that has emerged from a strict gender system. To be clear, I do not endorse a gender binary or stereotypes of masculinity; rather, I show how infertile men must negotiate the rigid walls of the modern American gender system. As the stories in this book demonstrate, people are resilient and creative when it comes to gender.

The Invention of Infertility

In 2010 British biologist Robert G. Edwards won the Nobel Prize in Medicine and Physiology for the development of in vitro fertilization, the procedure commonly known as IVF. This technological innovation, pregnant with possibilities, breathed new life into the term "infertility."[24] Just over thirty years ago, in a cotton-milling town in England, under the direction of Dr. Edwards, the conception and birth of Louise Brown sparked hope in couples around the globe that their days of childlessness were over. Louise was the first "test tube baby." Since her celebrated arrival an estimated 5 million children have been born worldwide thanks to IVF techniques. Though Dr. Edwards will go down in history as the scientist who helped put an end to infertility, it may be more accurate to say that he started it.

Throughout human history, couples have suffered from one condition known by different names: barrenness, sterility, involuntary childlessness, and—as it is known today—infertility. The term "infertility" captures the marriage between involuntary childlessness and the active pursuit of medical intervention. The prevalent use of the word hinges on an important social expectation: that people who want a baby and cannot conceive should take advantage of the medical opportunities that are available for expediting conception. Infertility has become a medical experience as well as a social one. When we speak of infertility, we are often talking about a specific social context in which a presumably monogamous heterosexual couple cannot achieve their desire to create biological offspring. Infertility presents itself on a social stage, where personal desires play out in the realm of social expectations. Infertile couples turn to the world of medicine to help them in their quest for parenthood.

There are numerous possible causes for a couple's inability to conceive, some of which are easier to pinpoint and repair than others. The sterilizing effects of congenitally malformed genitals, hormone imbalances, chromosomal anomalies, cancers, other diseases, and treatments for certain diseases and conditions are often all lumped together into a condition known by one name: "infertility." According to the ASRM and in medical parlance, infertility is "a disease, defined by the failure to achieve a successful pregnancy after 12 months or more of regular unprotected intercourse. Earlier evaluation and treatment may be justified based on medical history and physical findings and is warranted after 6 months for women over age 35 years."[25]

This technical definition, qualified by variables such as age, heterosexual sex, and numbers of attempted cycles, is a construct of recent decades. One medical manual published by the World Health

Organization explains, "The time limit of 12 months is arbitrary, but corresponds with the fact that the majority (approximately 85%) of couples who achieve pregnancy spontaneously will do so within 12 months."[26] There is no research demonstrating declining chances of conception following a year of unprotected sex. In fact, many couples do conceive after years of unprotected sex without medical intervention. The main purpose of the time limit is to alert patients to seek medical help in the race against the woman's biological clock. The arbitrariness of the time limit demonstrates that disease is defined not simply by biological evidence but also by social actors.

The ASRM definition of infertility was arduously debated and painstakingly crafted by medical and mental health practitioners, patients, and patient advocacy groups. Why is infertility called a disease rather than a syndrome, a condition, or a disorder? For some time, medical professionals avoided calling infertility a disease because the term "disease" was presumed to be a stigmatizing label. However, when health insurance providers refused to cover medical services coded for infertility, patient advocacy groups lobbied the ASRM to incorporate the word "disease" into the definition. Resolving an ambiguous condition that in many cases has no known etiology sounds like an expensive and doomed pursuit. A disease, by contrast, demands a call to arms. Diseases deserve research dollars, and patients with diseases are entitled to sophisticated medical interventions. In a footnote to its definition of infertility, the ASRM cites a medical dictionary, which defines "disease" as "any deviation from or interruption of the normal structure or function of any part, organ, or system of the body as manifested by characteristic symptoms and signs; the etiology, pathology, and prognosis may be known or unknown." Infertility fits this description.

Some infertility treatments are designed to resolve the social issues that infertility presents rather than to fix biological problems. Several scholars have noted that IVF does not actually treat the cause of a couple's inability to achieve pregnancy. Instead, it simply circumvents whatever is impeding conception to make pregnancy possible.[27] The first successful attempt at IVF illustrates this point. Louise Brown's mother, Lesley, was diagnosed with blocked fallopian tubes. When her fallopian tubes could not be repaired, doctors manually removed the eggs from her ovaries and returned a fertilized embryo to her uterus, overriding the need for functioning fallopian tubes. The ultimate goal of many medical protocols for infertility is not necessarily to repair or replace broken parts; it is to make a baby and turn people into parents.[28] After the birth of a child conceived through IVF, often all that has changed are a couple's social roles, from nonparents to parents. The biological cause of a couple's infertility may remain unchanged, threatening to obstruct future attempts at conception. The disease has not been cured. It has merely been bypassed.

Historically, the inability to conceive is no respecter of persons. It affects the lives of people of all races, ethnicities, and socioeconomic classes. Infertility is notably a couple's disease. It often indicates that one particular man and one particular woman cannot reproduce *together*. Arguably, either or both partners might be able to achieve pregnancy if they were to attempt to conceive with someone else with better than average fertility. This caveat reminds us that our ideas about infertility are imbued with strong social norms regarding traditional values of heterosexual monogamy. Our culture is sympathetic to heterosexual couples who follow the "natural order" of mating yet cannot reproduce. We certainly do not expect couples to break the marital bonds of fidelity to achieve pregnancy. In fact, elaborate (and lucrative) sperm-banking systems have been created to give women access to healthy sperm without having to resort to extramarital sex.

Social scientists recognize infertility as a physical and social condition that affects women and men psychologically and emotionally. In many cases, infertility is a fixable "betwixt-and-between" condition,[29] the state of "not yet pregnant."[30] Infertility may be defined as a *process* whereby couples come to understand their inability to have children as problematic.[31] Infertility causes grief, though not to the extent that the loss of a loved one might, because many couples find ways to repair their infertility or resolve their childlessness. However, the possibility that couples may overcome infertility at any time makes it a particularly unique and challenging ordeal. Not knowing what the future holds drags out the anticipation and prolongs and intermittently suspends the grieving process. Couples and doctors often believe that any physical impediments to conception can eventually be bypassed, removed, or cured by medical science.[32] This faith in the power of medicine can make medical failures especially devastating. Even when pregnancy is achieved through infertility treatments, couples may grieve the loss of romantic and spontaneous conception. When pregnancy is not achieved, couples grieve the loss of an envisioned biological child.

Infertility is not life-threatening, but it is life-defining. The journey of infertility may incite feelings of personal failure, inadequacy, guilt, depression, powerlessness, and loss of control.[33] Because having biological children is seen as a natural and normal step along the life course, not having children can make couples feel stigmatized as not normal and unnatural or as not having achieved legitimate personhood.[34] Extensive social science research among women shows that infertility threatens women's own gender identity, particularly if the woman sees motherhood as imperative to womanhood and kinship as defined by genetic ties. Infertility destabilizes women's prescribed role and identity and motivates women to invest their bodies, time, emotion, and finances into medical care to avoid the stigma of childlessness.[35]

Throughout history and across cultures, women have been relegated to the domestic sphere to raise children and attend to household needs. Motherhood, particularly in time periods and cultures in which women had no place in the public sphere, has been women's primary identity. For generations, women who have been unable to reproduce have suffered from feelings of personal failure, inadequacy, guilt, and depression. Childless women have historically been stigmatized for failing to live up to their most valuable—and, in some eras, only—social role. Of course, women today do not face the "motherhood mandate"—the social pressure to get married and raise children—to the same extent that previous generations did. At present, over 60 percent of women in the United States participate in the labor force, and women enjoy more promising and lucrative careers than was the case in the past. Women today are more educated than women of previous generations, and colleges now graduate more women than men. American men are more involved in childrearing and housework than at any other time in the past century. Still, women's bodies are physical symbols of fertility. Women alone enjoy the blessings and burdens of pregnancy, labor, delivery, and breastfeeding. When a couple cannot achieve pregnancy, the link between womanhood and reproduction lingers quietly in our subconscious.

When infertility appears in news headlines, we usually hear stories about women. We rarely hear about male infertility in the media and public discourse, and often when we do, the discussions lead

us to believe that male factor infertility is uncommon among infertile couples. Though society is generally sympathetic to women's
struggles with infertility, women are held primarily responsible for a
couple's inability to achieve pregnancy. Why is society so reluctant to
acknowledge male infertility? Even as we recognize its existence intellectually, we find it emotionally, socially, and psychologically difficult
to make room for it in our social world. As Cynthia Daniels points
out, male infertility reminds us that men are as physically vulnerable
to disease as women, a fact that challenges our core beliefs about masculinity.[36] I would add that male infertility reminds us that men are
also emotionally and mentally vulnerable, and that makes us uneasy.
Masculinity is defined by physical prowess, size, and performance;
the inability to impregnate a woman indicates ineffectiveness, incom-
petence, and even impotence and has been found to cause mental and
emotional distress for men.[37] Our collective ability to look the other
way when male infertility is glaring us in the face demonstrates that
we—men and women—are unified in the cause of protecting masculinity. We are all coconspirators in protecting the big gender secret:
Masculinity is fragile. Precisely because masculinity is equated with
power[38] and the achievement of manhood is defined as having power
and being powerful,[39] men and their masculine identities are particularly vulnerable.[40]

Over the past several years I have heard countless anecdotes from
doctors, scientists, patients, colleagues, and acquaintances about couples who thought the wife was infertile, only to learn that their inability to conceive was due to male infertility issues. Perhaps more
compelling are the stories of women who have undergone grueling
infertility treatments in an attempt to overcome their male partner's
infertility. Why are these stories so common? The answers are both
practical and sociological. When a couple cannot conceive, it is nearly
always the woman who seeks medical help first. Sometimes primary
care providers and gynecologists provide quick remedies for the
woman, such as prescription drugs, without ever assessing the man's
fertility status. Even in cases in which male infertility is detected early,
some means for achieving pregnancy focus primarily on the female
partner's body. There are simply more methods available, pharmaceutical and technological, for treating women than men.

From a sociological perspective, one very specific preconceived
notion about gender has determined the direction and practices of

infertility medicine: *Women are responsible for all aspects of repro-duction* from contraception to conception, from fetal health to breast-feeding. When a heterosexual couple cannot achieve pregnancy, the problem is assumed to be *her*. This widespread assumption has re-sulted in a general lack of public awareness of the prevalence of male infertility. It has also channeled the direction of reproductive science and shaped the practices of infertility medicine. If reproduction is believed to be a women's issue, then more doctors are trained and licensed to treat female bodies, and doctors and scientists develop more technologies to treat those bodies. The institutions that evolve over time to administer these technologies become increasingly fo-cused on the treatment of women. Not surprisingly, we now have more institutions and more technologies devoted to the treatment of infertile women than to the treatment of infertile men.

The Heterosexual Paradigm

The director of a large international sperm-banking company, also a prominent male infertility specialist, was asked to speak at a meeting of a gay and lesbian infertility advocacy organization. Since lesbian couples represent the majority of clients at his sperm bank, he gladly accepted the invitation, assuming that the group wanted to hear about family-building options for lesbian couples using donor sperm. How-ever, when he arrived at the meeting, he was surprised to find a room full of gay male couples. Confused, he stumbled through his presen-tation on donor sperm, all the while wondering, "Why am I here?" He had never worked with gay men before. The audience, equally flum-moxed, sat speechless at the end of the presentation. Needless to say, there was no shortage of sperm in the room.

As the sperm bank director explained to me, he believed that he had been invited to speak about his company's products and services. However, the attendees that evening believed that they were going to hear one of the world's leading male infertility experts discuss male infertility. Male infertility specialists treat infertile men, right? The gay men in attendance identified as infertile men. So what went wrong? Assumptions about universal heterosexuality inform and shape our language and social institutions, a phenomenon known in social science shorthand as heteronormativity. Infertility is a disease imbued with heteronormative ideas about family building. The confusion at the meeting stemmed from the fact that in the dominant culture, men are assumed to be heterosexual, so male infertility patients are assumed to be heterosexual men.

In medical parlance, male infertility is synonymous with insufficient healthy sperm, reflecting the heteronormative assumption that when there is only a male infertility issue, eggs are available, healthy, and reliable. Male infertility clinics are designed to address issues such as no sperm, low sperm count, and poor sperm quality. Gay men may perceive their inability to achieve pregnancy through sex as infertility, but chances are that between the two partners they have ample healthy sperm. Before attending the support group meeting, the sperm bank director had congratulated himself on his efforts to promote alternative family-building options. Unfortunately, he had never before considered the ways in which heterosexual norms are built into the language of infertility. He had taken for granted that male infertility medicine is a specialty designed to treat only heterosexual men; he had never considered that the term "male infertility" may be read differently by nonheterosexual men.

In my study of male infertility, all of the research participants were married heterosexuals. Heterosexuality was not a requirement for participation, but I never met an openly gay man or woman during my fieldwork. The bottom line is that male infertility clinics specialize in the treatment of heterosexual couples. Gay men rely on the same resources as infertile women to find an egg donor, a surrogate mother, and the services offered in an IVF clinic to achieve biological parenthood.[41] Because it is statistically improbable that both partners of a gay male couple would be completely sterile and IVF now requires only one sperm, it is improbable that a gay male couple would have any practical reasons for consulting with a male infertility specialist. Similarly, lesbian couples may seek out donor sperm from sperm banks and use the services available in an IVF center, such as intrauterine insemination (IUI) or IVF, but lesbian couples do not seek treatment in male infertility clinics.

The infertility industry was conceived within the heterosexual paradigm and will most likely continue its gestation there. Nonetheless, sperm banks, egg banks, surrogacy programs, and IVF centers welcome gay and lesbian couples. In recent years, patient advocacy groups and mental health professionals have used the term "social infertility" to describe the experiences of gay and lesbian couples who need donor gametes, surrogates, and assisted reproductive technologies (ART) to achieve pregnancy. The term acknowledges that "natural" conception is not an option for same-sex partners and recognizes that same-sex couples often endure the same physical and emotional burdens that heterosexual couples do as they travel the infertility path.

Research Methods

When I first set out to study male infertility, I designed my research study as an ethnography. Ethnographic fieldwork, a popular research method used in the social sciences, entails collecting written data through observation and interviews. As a trained ethnographer, my desire from the beginning was to go where infertile men go, understand infertility in the terms in which they understand it, and observe and learn how infertile men choose to deal with their infertility. My first foray into the world of infertility was to an infertility support group for couples. I introduced myself as a researcher and was invited to attend monthly support group meetings. Over the course of several months, I met dozens of infertile women and their husbands and one infertile man and his wife. On several occasions the token infertile man asked, "Am I the only infertile man here?" The other men present all claimed that they were fertile and were there just to support their wives.

I continued my foolhardy search for infertile men at a full-day conference for infertile couples hosted at a prominent university. The busy seminar schedule offered only one class on male infertility. Though the conference had drawn nearly two hundred people, I was surprised to find just four people in attendance at the male infertility class: two men, another woman, and me. If 10 to 15 percent of couples in the United States struggle with infertility and male infertility is the cause in half of all cases, where were all the infertile men?

Infertility support groups and IVF clinics abound in the United States and serve as great resources for recruiting research participants. However, infertility scholars have had little success in finding and recruiting men in these locales.[42] Rather than studying the infertile (and usually invisible) male partners of women receiving treatment in IVF clinics, I chose to conduct research in male infertility clinics. At the generous invitations of several male infertility specialists, I spent over one hundred hours in five male infertility clinics in the United

States observing clinical encounters between doctors and infertile male patients. I interviewed more than a dozen doctors, nurses, genetic counselors, laboratory technicians, sperm bank staff, and psychologists over the course of my fieldwork. Following my fieldwork I conducted telephone interviews[43] with twenty-four infertile men and their wives (separately) twice over an eighteen-month period.[44] (See Appendix B, "Interview Guide.") The men, representing many walks of life, included a pilot, a carpenter, a schoolteacher, an electrician, and a state trooper. Most men in this study had no children at the time they agreed to participate; a few were raising biological children and stepchildren. All of the men in this study were heterosexual and married or engaged to be married. Marriage was not a requirement for participation, but married couples seem to make up the vast majority of couples seeking infertility treatments. The majority of the research subjects were upper-middle-class and white. Socioeconomic status is a curious variable among infertile households. Some of the men in the study had working-class backgrounds and working-class jobs, but because they had no small children to care for, their wives remained in the workforce. Most infertility studies, therefore, attract many "double-income, no kids," or DINK, couples.

Participation in the study was open to people of all races and ethnicities. The overrepresentation of whites in the research subject pool reflects the patient populations at the medical clinics I visited, even in geographic areas that have large racial and ethnic minority populations. What prevents minority men from seeking out infertility treatment? Are treatments cost prohibitive, are minorities less trusting of infertility medical practices, or is the private experience of not being able to achieve pregnancy interpreted differently by minority men? Are minorities more likely to deny their infertility or need for medical care? Is seeking out medical assistance more emasculating or embarrassing for minorities than for whites? Unfortunately, this study cannot answer any of these questions. The whiteness of the subject pool for this study creates quite a tidy picture of how the most privileged members of society—white, married, heterosexual, middle and upper-middle-class men—who presumably have the most access to financial and medical resources, deal with a blow to their masculinity. If masculinity is defined by power, then this book effectively looks at what happens to the most powerful members of a society when they learn that they are not as powerful as they envisioned themselves to be. This study provides the backdrop for future investigation into the social meaning of male infertility among single and homosexual men and men of various ethnic and racial groups in the United States and elsewhere.

Book Overview

The purpose of this book is to examine how gender and disease are socially constructed within social institutions and by individuals. At the institutional level of analysis, Chapters 2 and 3 show how gender ideology has shaped the development of male infertility medicine and practice. At the individual level of analysis, Chapters 4 and 5 look at how infertility affects patients' understandings of their own personal gender identities. While the first half of the book emphasizes the static and enduring qualities of gender stereotypes, the second half illustrates the fluidity of personal gender identities and the power of individuals to redefine for themselves what it means to be a man and to be masculine.

Chapter 2, "Seminal Work," provides a historical overview of the emergence of male infertility medicine. I argue that the development of male reproductive medicine lagged behind female reproductive medicine, owing to preconceived notions about gender and reproduction, resulting in a system that today is more focused on, and better prepared to treat, women than men. I present unresolved disputes among specialists, clinical errors, and potential health risks as the symptoms of the slow organization of the field and as factors that complicate the decision-making process for patients. Chapter 3, "Doctors Doing Gender," takes a peek behind clinic doors, where semen testing tests patients' masculinity and where doctors employ gendered strategies to connect with male patients. I consider the many ways in which male infertility specialists subscribe to the same traditional gender ideology that they blame for perpetuating the lack of social awareness regarding male infertility, and I discuss the complex role that doctors play in the gender system. Chapter 4, "Just a Medical Condition," delves into the gender work in which infertile men engage to preserve their masculinity. When disease presents a threat to masculinity, individuals create new understandings of disease in order to stabilize their personal gender identities and disconnect fertility status from masculinity. Chapter 5, "Taking Control," describes how and why men embrace medical technologies. Men construct masculine narratives about the lengths to which they would go to make "natural" conception possible and spare their wives from painful and uncomfortable treatments. Chapter 6, "The Politics of Reproduction," reviews the points made throughout the book that demonstrate how masculine domination has influenced and continues to underscore the development, organization, and treatment of male infertility.

This book clarifies one important point: Infertility is not just a women's issue. Some men's bodies refuse to cooperate with society's expectations. Some men do not produce healthy, speedy, potent sperm. This physical inability can be emotionally, mentally, and socially problematic for men. In one of our many candid conversations, Dr. Bradley expressed his chagrin that among infertile couples, men are rarely properly assessed and treated. "It probably doesn't help that your office is hidden in the Women's Health Center," I teased. He looked at me, genuinely confused. "The sign," I said, trying to coax his memory, "on the front of the building." The irony, it seemed, eluded him.

Seminal Work

The fact that heterosexual intercourse makes babies is not a discovery of the modern age. Stories of the shame of barrenness, the blessing of pregnancy, the miracle of birth, and the preciousness of man's seed and posterity resound throughout the Bible. The ancient Roman poet and philosopher Lucretius recorded that men made sacrifices to the gods "in order that they, with copious seed, might render their wives pregnant."[1] Ancient terra cotta, ceramic, and metal votive offerings depicting male genitals and female wombs have been discovered at various sites in Italy, including the oldest sanctuary of Hercules in Rome, where historians believe men engaged in cultic practices to petition the gods for increased fertility.[2] Concerns with both male and female fertility are documented in the writings and artwork of ancient Greece, the medieval Byzantine Empire, and early modern Europe.[3]

After centuries of cultic, superstitious, and religious rites to improve fertility, the discovery of sperm marked a major breakthrough in humankind's understanding of conception. In the late 1660s, Dutch biologist Antonie van Leeuwenhoek handcrafted a microscope. Under its powerful glass lens, he discovered the world of "animalcules," his term for single-cell organisms, including aquatic creatures and bacteria. The world may never know what prompted Leeuwenhoek to place human seminal fluid under the lens, but this inspiration made him the first person in history to observe human sperm.[4] Leeuwenhoek's discovery of microscopic tadpole-like organisms whipping their tails through seminal fluid proved that men play an essential role in human reproduction. Of course, never having seen or imagined a female egg, Leeuwenhoek had a misconception of conception. He theorized that sperm were like plant seeds, containing all the necessary ingredients to grow a person. He figured that a swimming sperm just needed a nourishing home—like a uterus—into which it could burrow and there grow into a fully formed human baby. (It would be another 160 years before German biologist Karl Ernst von Baer would discover mammalian eggs.)[5] Despite his rudimentary understanding of how life begins, Leeuwenhoek's work showed that the human form begins at a microscopic stage, confirming what had been suspected since antiquity: The fate of a man's genetic posterity depends upon his ability to produce healthy seed.

Today, sophisticated microscopes modeled after Leeuwenhoek's first magnifying eye are used to analyze the shape, speed, movement, and number of sperm in semen. Magnifying lenses make microsurgical techniques for restoring fertility possible and allow embryologists to inject eggs with sperm. In this chapter I put infertility medicine under a sociological lens to magnify and illustrate how cultural ideas about gender and the roles of men and women, from the organization of Western medicine in the mid-nineteenth century to the present, have channeled the direction of scientific inquiry and shaped the organization of infertility medical specialties today. The sociological storyline that follows is an ironic one. Men's historically privileged status generally spared them from the scrutiny and highly invasive techniques that were characteristic of early Western medical practices. Meanwhile, women—whose genitals and reproductive systems served as the primary foci of many early medical practitioners—were subjected to all manner of horrors. The result has been the medical system we have today, which is better organized, unified, and mobilized to treat infertile women than to treat infertile men. In other words, male privilege has been a double-edged sword. Although men of the past were fortunate to be overlooked by the medical system, male patients today have a hard time finding answers to their reproductive needs. Early feminist scholars emphasized women's disadvantaged role as "the second sex" in society,[6] but as some reproduction scholars have poignantly quipped, when it comes to reproduction, men are the second sex.[7]

Women, Men, and the Development of Reproductive Medicine

Medical science has organized itself into many specialized fields of study, each devoted to different bodily systems. Of these fields, the study of the reproductive system was the last to be regarded as a legitimate scientific pursuit. Sociologist Adele Clarke argues that knowledge about reproduction was the slowest field to develop into a medical, scientific, and academic discipline because it has been an arena rife with controversy regarding personal and family privacy and sexual and reproductive morality.[8] Within the field of reproduction, the organization of male reproductive medicine has lagged behind that of female reproductive medicine. The American Board of Obstetrics and Gynecology (ABOG) was founded and organized in 1927 to unify the young and burgeoning field of women's reproductive health. In 1947 the ABOG introduced board examinations to certify medical practitioners as specialists of obstetrics and gynecology. By contrast, the American Society for Andrology was not founded until 1975, and no board organization like ABOG has ever been established to certify specialists. Andrology, the study of male reproductive health, failed to coalesce into a certifiable medical specialization as its female-focused counterpart, gynecology, had. But why was this?

One common explanation is that doctors in the past were simply more obsessed with vaginas, uteruses, fallopian tubes, and ovaries than with testicles and penises. Feminist scholarship has long argued that historically, women's bodies have been subjected to more medical scrutiny and interventions than men's bodies, qualitatively and quantitatively. In their book *For Her Own Good: Two Centuries of the Experts' Advice to Women,* Barbara Ehrenreich and Deirdre English show that during the nineteenth century, medical texts framed women's reproductive parts as the source of all manner of maladies.[9] According to their findings, women were subjected to leechings, injections, and cauterization of their sexual organs, as well as clitoridectomy, ovariotomy, and hysterectomy, to cure a variety of ailments, including headaches; sore throats; indigestion; backaches; diseases of the stomach, liver, kidneys, heart, and lungs; tuberculosis; and mental illness. Social historian Ornella Moscucci argues that in nineteenth-century British medical discourse, women and femininity were categorically understood as naturally inferior to men and masculinity and medical writers and practitioners pathologized women's bodies. According to Moscucci, because of the extreme focus on women's bodies, "the growth of gynaecology was not paralleled by the evolution of a complementary 'science of masculinity' or 'andrology.'"[10] Similarly, science studies scholar Nelly Oudshoorn claims that by the beginning of the twentieth century, there were simply more Western medical practitioners oriented toward female reproductive science than toward male reproductive science.[11]

The narrative of women's bodies as more objectified historically by the medical gaze than men's bodies has served as a reliable feminist trope for social science research over the past few decades. However, medical historians have recently argued that the repetition of the "pathologized woman" story in the social sciences has generated a myth that male bodies and male reproduction were not historically medicalized.[12] Some medical texts and records from the nineteenth century indicate that medical practitioners recognized the prevalence of male sterility, employed invasive techniques to try to remedy various male conditions, and labored to understand the correlation between fertility and sperm quality.[13]

Despite evidence that some men may also have been subjected to intense medicalization, the fact remains that from the founding of the American Medical Association (AMA) in 1847 to the late twentieth century, the overwhelming majority of medical practitioners, scientists, and technologists were men during an era when women had few political and economic rights and limited access to education. Women of the nineteenth and early twentieth centuries did not have the social power and few had the scientific education to provide informed consent; as a result, women often served as guinea pigs in medical experimentation. Furthermore, gynecology as a medical specialty served a different function and mapped out a different professional jurisdiction in the late nineteenth century than it does today. Women's reproductive organs were believed to control women's minds and entire bodies.[14] If a woman in the nineteenth century suffered from what we might recognize today as cardiovascular disease, a neurological or autoimmune disorder, a mental illness, or even a common cold, many medical practitioners believed that both the cause and the cure could be found in the reproductive system.[15] Because gynecology operated as the comprehensive female science, the de facto "science of woman," the study of women's reproduction was also the study of female cardiology, neurology, nephrology, urology, psychology, and so on.

Unfortunately, many early gynecological theories and practices perpetuated essentialist and erroneous notions of women as physically driven, irrational, and unpredictable beings with limited intellectual capacity who were in need of men's care, supervision, and control. Throughout the twentieth century, more aspects of women's lives were subsumed under the jurisdiction of medical authorities, and women's bodies were increasingly subjected to new medical technologies. By the latter half of the twentieth century, primary aims of feminist activism were to reverse power relationships between male practitioners and female patients and to empower women to reclaim their right to control their own bodies. The revival of midwifery and projects such as the Boston Women's Health Book Collective[16] in the 1970s raised awareness that women's bodies shared a history as contested sites of power.

Historical documents indicate that some physicians attempted to organize an andrology section of the AMA dedicated to the study of male reproduction as early as 1891, but this new section never materialized.[17] It might be fair to say that a century ago there was no need for a field uniquely devoted to the science of man because every specialty other than gynecology was already studying and treating men. The historical findings on male sterility suggest that andrology originated as a multidisciplinary endeavor. At the turn of the twentieth century in Europe and the United States, neurologists, urologists, gynecologists, endocrinologists, dermatologists, biologists, and zoologists were attempting to treat impotence and male sterility, repair the deleterious effects of venereal disease on male fertility, develop surgical techniques for improving fertility, and perfect the practice of artificial insemination. Dr. Max Huhner's medical tome on sterility in the male and female, reprinted several times between 1927 and 1942, explains how to diagnose male sterility by examining the genitals and analyzing sperm; it also describes a variety of procedures to treat male sterility, including artificial insemination.[18] Though

Huhner made serious work of male sterility medicine in New York City, historians have yet to sort out when, where, or how male sterility medicine was practiced among the general U.S. population during that time.

The scattered science and history of andrology provide a poignant introduction to the gendered politics of infertility medicine. From the 1880s to the 1930s a few medical journal articles indicate that some doctors attempted artificial insemination using donor sperm, but as sociologist Rene Almeling describes, "they did not trumpet the availability of this service" for fear of public reactions and moral and legal concerns regarding its use.[19] Historian Bridget Gurtler's work shows that artificial insemination with donor sperm became a popular treatment in the 1950s for disabled World War II veterans, but its use never entered public discourse. In fact, writes Gurtler, "physicians consciously destroyed records of inseminations and sperm donations."[20] Several scholars note that public discussions of male sterility were taboo in the twentieth century[21] because the condition was presumed to threaten personal masculine identities and incite widespread anxiety regarding race, ethnicity, and nationhood.[22] The entanglement of male reproductive medicine with notions of masculinity—and, more precisely, the association of male sterility with powerlessness—only hindered the science. Meanwhile, women in childless marriages found themselves subjected to an array of crude diagnostic and therapeutic procedures, including postcoital examinations, dilation and curettage, insufflation of the fallopian tubes, electrotherapy of the cervix and uterus, cutting and cauterizing of the cervix and endometrium, artificial inseminations, and hormone therapies as well as dietary prescriptions and restrictions.[23]

As the field of obstetrics and gynecology clipped along throughout the first half of the twentieth century—a period in which the ratio of home births to hospital births reversed from 99:1 to 1:99—andrology foundered as a medical field with no organized mode for establishing best practices or disseminating practical information. By the 1960s, unconnected urologists—mavericks in their field—dabbled in a variety of pharmaceutical and surgical therapies for male sterility, but treatments offered little promise. One pioneer of male infertility medicine recalls working in an infertility clinic in 1970 where the entire diagnostic workup for men included a two-question survey: "Can you sustain an erection? Can you ejaculate?" If a man could answer affirmatively to both questions, he was deemed fertile, and his wife's body was considered the uncooperative one. Not until the 1970s did a handful of urologists begin collaborating to formalize semen analysis procedures, develop parameters for measuring sperm count and quality, and, in 1975, establish the American Society of Andrology. Male infertility clinics, though few and far between at the time, began to attract male patients. Although these clinics were excellent centers for conducting semen analyses and diagnosing male infertility issues, they offered few solutions for repairing male infertility. As had been the case during the nineteenth century and the earlier decades of the twentieth century, when a couple could not conceive, it was most often the wife who bore the blame of barrenness, the stigma of childlessness, and the brunt of medical treatment.

The Feminization of Infertility Medicine

Women trying to conceive often find themselves under the advisement of a gynecologist who may employ female-focused treatments to overcome female and/or male infertility issues. As a simple example, in the 1960s the hormone drug clomiphene citrate was developed and approved by the Food and Drug Administration (FDA) in the United States to induce ovulation in women with irregular menses who were trying to conceive. Clomiphene has also commonly been prescribed to increase ovulation in women with normal fertility whose male partners have poor fertility. The idea is that as more eggs are produced more often, a man with few sperm has more chances to fertilize an egg. Often, this treatment works.

A peculiarity of clomiphene is that this hormone drug has also been found to increase sperm production, but the FDA has never approved its use in men. The male infertility pioneer I quoted earlier reported that over three decades ago, he contacted the pharmaceutical makers of Clomid (the brand name for clomiphene citrate) and offered to lead clinical trials on its use in men, but the company wanted to market the drug solely to women. The patent on the drug has now expired, and because the drug is available in generic brands, it does not generate the same revenue it once did to its original maker. At this point, no pharmaceutical companies are interested in investing in clinical trials for FDA approval for the use of clomiphene for male infertility because it is not seen as an investment that can be easily recouped. Thirty years ago, powerful assumptions about gender ideas limited the use of clomiphene to women; capitalist market interests today have sustained clomiphene's use in women only. Some male infertility specialists use clomiphene aggressively in men, but in today's highly litigious society, many specialists hesitate to prescribe clomiphene for an off-label use such as male infertility. In some cases, women take the drug that could be prescribed to their male partners, and they do so to overcome *his* infertility. Some experts argue that clomiphene is not reliably effective in men, but by exercising a little sociological imagination, we can envision how research to understand the effect of clomiphene on various male infertility conditions at various doses could have taken place, had it not been thwarted thirty years ago. The process of perfecting the use of clomiphene in men is now decades behind research dedicated to perfecting its use in women.

Up until the end of the 1970s, hormone therapies for women and artificial insemination were the top-of-the-line treatments available to infertile couples to remedy male or female infertility. Injecting semen into a woman's uterus improves the chances that a spermatozoon will find and fertilize an egg. Today, artificial insemination involves collecting a semen sample, separating the healthy sperm from the seminal fluid via centrifugation (a process known as "sperm washing"), and then combining the healthy sperm with a prepared solution and inserting the solution into the uterus vaginally using a long syringe. In preparation for the technique, the woman is often prescribed hormones to stimulate ovulation. IUI is considered a first line of treatment for women with irregular menstrual cycles or unpredictable ovulation,[24] but it is also an effective method for improving the chances of conception when the male partner has a low sperm count. When the male partner has no live sperm, the woman undergoes the same procedures, but donor sperm is used.

In vitro fertilization (IVF), which was introduced for human use in the late 1970s, is a process whereby women are administered hormones to stimulate the production of multiple eggs in the ovaries. Mature eggs are harvested (vacuumed out) using a tool inserted vaginally. Semen is collected from the male partner and washed. Eggs and sperm are united in vitro, which is Latin for "in glass," as in a petri dish or test tube where fertilization takes place—hence the appellation "test tube baby." After a few days, the developed embryo is placed into the uterus, where, ideally, it will implant and begin normal fetal gestation. From the time of its inception IVF was used to treat infertile women. However, it has also proved to be helpful in cases in which men have low sperm counts, as it ensures the contact of sperm with egg more systematically than occurs with intercourse or the simpler IUI technology.

In the 1980s, immediately after the introduction of IVF, infertility medicine exploded across Europe and the United States. The infertility clinic developed as a female-centric concept. Infertility clinics and IVF centers treat women. (Infertile men must locate a "male reproductive health center" or "male infertility clinic" for male-focused medical treatments. The non-gender-specific term "infertility clinic" for women once again reflects social assumptions about infertility as a women's problem.) In infertility clinics, women and couples meet with specialists who are board-certified obstetrician/gynecologists (OB/GYNs) who have additional fellowship training and specialized certification in reproductive endocrinology. Women's reproductive systems have been the primary focus of these physicians' education and training. Hence, when women go to an infertility clinic, their bodies often serve as the practical site for all treatments.[25]

The assumption that women's bodies are the proper locus for infertility treatments reflects a certain reverence for the sacred nature of men's bodies on the part of the medical profession. In art and literature, men and masculinity are aligned with the mind, the intellect, the sacred and godly, and the public sphere; women and femininity are equated with the body and blood, nature, earth, and the private sphere.[26] While men in many societies throughout history have enjoyed exclusive access to institutions of higher learning, state governance, business, and worship, women's unclean, irrational, and unruly bodies have been relegated to the home and family life. The dichotomy between male/culture/mind/public and female/nature/body/private has ancient origins but was reanimated in the American collective conscience when the roles of men and women as breadwinners and homemakers, respectively, became more pronounced during the Industrial Revolution, an era that coincided with the rise of Western biomedicine. Though feminist scholars have labored for decades to debunk and deconstruct the timeworn man-woman dualism,[27] this specious, yet resilient, cultural paradigm helps explain the differential treatments of men and women in reproductive medicine. As medical practitioners have sliced into women's reproductive parts, administered hormone therapies, artificially inseminated wombs, removed eggs, and inserted embryos, men's bodies have been left relatively untouched. Even in cases of male infertility, instead of physically manipulating male bodies, doctors often request that the man provide sperm or arrange for a proxy for the man in the form of a sperm donor. Essentially, male infertility gets repaired in female bodies, and many male infertility treatments require women's willingness to undergo medical interventions,[28] reinforcing the association of women with body and blood and protecting the sacred male form.

The success of female-focused treatments in overcoming male infertility issues raises the question *Is it even necessary to have a medical specialty devoted to men and male infertility?* The practical and economic logic of this question is hard to argue, but the question itself reveals some of our strong cultural ideas about gender and the roles of men and women in reproduction, how we define infertility, and how we measure success in overcoming it. Arguably, this question has slowed the development of male infertility science and medicine. After all, why attempt to understand the mysteries of spermatogenesis or invent new technologies and procedures to help infertile men when male infertility can so easily be addressed at the site of the female body?

"Empower the Men"

In 1991 a young Italian obstetrician pursuing graduate work in microbiology at the Free University of Brussels had an idea. While working in the laboratory of the university's infertility clinic, he noticed under the microscope how some sperm and eggs, when put together, fertilized quite nicely, while others failed to connect and form a viable embryo. What if those sperm just needed a little help? How hard could it be to hand-select one microscopic sperm with a pipette and shoot it through the jelly coat of a harvested egg, penetrate the membrane, and fertilize it? In an interview, Dr. Gianpiero Palermo recalled that he had heard of other scientists around the world attempting similar techniques, but none had been successful. "But I'm Italian," explained Palermo. "I don't take 'no' for an answer. So when my boss told me, 'Don't do it,' I thought [the single-sperm injection technique] was very cool because it's cool to bring the ratio [to] one sperm, one egg. One to one, I think, is so powerful."

Apparently, Dr. Palermo had the magic touch. Despite others' failed attempts at the procedure and his boss's resistance, by 1992 Palermo had refined and perfected the manual egg fertilization technique, referred to as intracytoplasmic sperm injection, or ICSI (pronounced "icksy"). IVF-ICSI was a major breakthrough in the treatment of male infertility. Conception through sexual intercourse generally requires that men have a sperm count that meets the World Health Organization's "gold standard" of at least 15 million sperm per ejaculate.[29] Men with lower sperm counts could turn to IUI and IVF to achieve pregnancy, but even those treatments required several million sperm for success. The marvel of IVF with ICSI was that conception became a reality with only a single healthy sperm. As Palermo explained, the purpose of ICSI is to "empower the men" and that is its beauty. The most remarkable aspect of this technology was developed in the next few years as researchers found that they could fertilize an egg using not only ejaculated sperm but also premature sperm cells taken from the testicles or epididymides. Two decades ago, men who were diagnosed with azoospermia, or zero sperm count, were told that they would never have biological children. Today, thanks to biopsy techniques that are used to retrieve sperm from the testicles and epididymides, in combination with IVF-ICSI, azoospermic men regularly father children.

One of the earliest concerns and criticisms of the use of the less-developed testicular sperm was that offspring would be more likely to have birth defects or developmental disorders than would children conceived from fully developed sperm. Some data show that IVF children are twice as likely to have birth and developmental anomalies as are non-IVF children.[30] However, the research comparing IVF children with IVF-ICSI children has been less conclusive and much more controversial. Some studies show a slight increase in developmental anomalies in IVF-ICSI children, particularly children of fathers with chromosomal defects, but no findings have been dramatic enough to discourage the use of IVF-ICSI.[31]

IVF alone is a process that requires sperm, but in clinical practice, men play a minor, sometimes invisible, role. IVF-ICSI using testicular and epididymal sperm cells has drawn men out of the shadows and thrust men's bodies under the medical gaze with its bright lights, needles, scalpels, and microscopic lenses. The extraction of sperm from the testicles and epididymides has required male infertility specialists to add a new specialized skill set to their repertoires and has attracted a new patient population—azoospermic men—to male infertility clinics. ICSI using surgically extracted sperm requires the physical participation of men in the treatment process and has revolution-ized how couples experience male infertility. While infertile men of the past could slip into and out of laboratories practically unnoticed, more infertile men today have the option to engage with medical technologies. Notably, advances in ART with ejaculated sperm and IVF-ICSI using extracted sperm have nearly eradicated the need for donor sperm among heterosexual couples.

The male infertility subspecialty of urology as practiced today, which took root in the second half of the twentieth century,[32] has grown significantly in numbers of practices, practitioners, and pa-tients with each new technological innovation. Male infertility clin-ics often have on-site laboratories where highly trained technicians conduct semen analyses and operating rooms where doctors perform varicocelectomies and testicular sperm extraction procedures. Male infertility clinics may be privately operated, relying on referrals from outside physicians, or they may be part of larger medical systems, af-filiated with IVF clinics within the same system.

Reproductive Endocrinology and Urology: The Male Body in a Tug-of-War

In the age of evidence-based medicine, diagnosing infertility issues and selecting the appropriate treatment plan should be pretty straight-forward, right? Unfortunately, when a male factor is impeding con-ception, reproductive endocrinologists (REs) and male infertility specialists do not always agree on the best course of action. REs treat infertility, but their training focuses on women's bodies and female-centered treatments. General urologists treat male urinary and repro-ductive disorders, but treating male infertility requires sharper skills than their basic training provides. The infertile male body is the Wild West of the medical world. While medical specialties such as cardiol-ogy, neurology, immunology, and dermatology have carefully carved out their territories, delineating the boundaries between body parts and bodily systems, male infertility lies in the borderland between two medical specialties. Both REs and urologists stake their claim on the infertile male body, declaring that they are prepared to help infertile couples overcome male factor problems and achieve pregnancy. But these two types of specialists have different training backgrounds and see male factor infertility from different vantage points. Not surprisingly, they propose different solutions.

Female infertility specialists are board-certified gynecologists who subspecialize in reproductive endocrinology. In preparation for their reproductive endocrinologist/infertility specialist (RE/I) board examinations, fellows are advised that they "should be able to evaluate a woman for infertility and be able to develop and carry out an appropriate plan for management of the infertile woman."[33] On the subject of male infertility, fellows are expected to "be able to evaluate the male partner and diagnose subfertility and absolute infertility and evaluate and discuss patients with these problems."[34] The main focus of treatment for REs is the infertile female partner, for whom they develop a management plan. Though REs may "evaluate" men, management of the male patient is not specified within their scope of expertise. REs are qualified to conduct a physical examination of male patients, but they typically do not.[35] Often, all that REs need to conduct their work is sperm, a product of the male body.

In contrast, male infertility specialists are medical doctors board certified within the specialty of urology, all of whom study and receive some basic training in male infertility during their residencies.[36] As certified by the American Board of Urology, urologists are qualified to assess, palpate, incise, and splay open the male body and its parts. No additional board certification is available for the subspecialties of andrology, male reproductive medicine, and male infertility. Male infertility practitioners most often receive highly specialized training during a fellowship following their urology residency. Some long-time practitioners of general urology may opt to train for a few weeks or months with a male infertility specialist to learn the microsurgical skills of the trade. Other urologists may attend workshops or continuing education courses to learn about the latest innovations and brush up on techniques in male infertility medicine.

Why is male infertility not a board-certified subspecialty? Doctors I interviewed describe their field and urology generally as a disorganized specialty of medicine. On occasion, groups of doctors within the American Urological Association (AUA) have attempted to organize male infertility into a certifiable subspecialty, but there has always been enough resistance from other urologists to stall organizational efforts. Most urologists who treat male infertility appreciate the lack of bureaucratic involvement from organizations such as the American Board of Urology, valuing the autonomy that they enjoy in their practices. To the detriment of both specialists and patients, the lack of an organized subspecialty has resulted in poor patient awareness of the medical help that is available to infertile men. Furthermore, the inadequate training of some urologists who attempt to practice infertility medicine has resulted in ineffective and even harmful treatment of male patients.

Couples who are trying to achieve pregnancy most likely begin by undergoing a battery of diagnostic tests with their primary care provider, the wife's OB/GYN, or an RE/I at an IVF clinic. The female partner often initiates and leads this process.[37] Male infertility specialists strongly recommend that the male partner in all infertile heterosexual couples receive a full fertility assessment, including a semen analysis and a physical examination. However, male infertility specialists speculate that most men never receive the physical examination[38] and that men with poor semen analysis results are rarely referred to a male infertility clinic. This claim is nearly impossible to test and measure, but there is ample anecdotal evidence to support the theory. Male infertility specialists estimate that of the small fraction of men with poor semen parameters who do find their way to a male infertility clinic, roughly half are referred by the female partner's OB/GYN, just under a quarter by RE/Is, another quarter by their primary care physicians, and the remainder by other general urologists.[39] In some cases, men who are found to have insufficient semen quality may receive an immediate referral to a male infertility specialist. In other cases, REs will recommend that the couple use some form of assisted reproductive technology (IUI, IVF, IVF-ICSI with ejaculated sperm), bypassing the need for any additional assessments or medical opinions for the man. Though male infertility specialists accuse REs of being greedy for not referring their male patients to male infertility clinics, the fact is that the ratio of IVF clinics to male infertility clinics is overwhelmingly lopsided. There are many major cities and even some entire states that do not have a single practicing male infertility specialist.[40] For every practicing male infertility specialist in the country, there are approximately five REs practicing infertility medicine.[41] Understandably, the sheer lack of male infertility clinics in some areas discourages doctors from referring infertile male patients to specialists.

Practically speaking, many couples are unaware of the prevalence of male infertility and the existence of male infertility clinics, so they are not likely to seek out specialized services for the male partner if an RE offers to treat them. If a male partner can produce even one sperm through masturbation, the RE can offer IVF-ICSI without surgery to the couple as a solution. If all goes well, the couple will conceive within two or three months and welcome a new baby within a year from their initial consultation. If a couple's dream is to have a healthy baby and an RE can make that dream a reality even when male infertility may be a factor, why seek help from a male infertility specialist?

Involving a male infertility specialist often means marked delays along the path toward parenthood. However, male infertility specialists persuasively argue that male treatments are less expensive than IUI and IVF, as well as less invasive and risky, and enable couples to achieve pregnancy "the old-fashioned way." Following an initial consultation with a male infertility specialist, a male patient can expect to receive treatment within a month and see improved semen parameters within six months; his partner may be pregnant within the year, and together they may have as many babies in the future "naturally" as they could ever hope for. Unfortunately, infertility practice is "more of an art than a science," as a few doctors explained to me. Artificial insemination and IVF treatments often fail, and even when they work, mothers and infants may suffer health complications as a result of the technologies that are employed. Similarly, male infertility treatments do not always deliver what they promise—improved semen parameters—and some male patients discover that their painful surgical procedures were for naught.

In cases of azoospermia that warrant IVF-ICSI using testicular or epididymal sperm, the roles of the male infertility specialist and the RE are fairly straightforward. The male infertility specialist is responsible for extracting the sperm, freezing it, and transporting it to the laboratory for fertilization. The RE oversees the egg harvest, the fertilization process in the laboratory, and the transfer of the embryo or embryos into the uterus. But what are the roles of the two specialists in routine cases of IUI and IVF? What happens when the male infertility specialist gathers information during an examination that sheds more light on the diagnosis, opening up new possibilities for treatment options? In lieu of IUI or IVF, a male infertility specialist may recommend surgery to clear an obstructed duct or remove a varicocele that is believed to be inhibiting sperm production, offering hope that the couple will have their natural fertility restored. In such situations, the roles of the RE and male infertility specialist are less clear, and the two specialists may vie for control over management of the couple's infertility.

Male infertility specialists argue that they are uniquely qualified to "upgrade" the fertility status of the male patient by identifying and treating the underlying cause of the infertility, something that REs and the technologies they employ do not do. If a male patient's fertility status is upgraded, the couple may be able to opt for IUI rather than IVF or for IVF rather than IVF-ICSI. Each step down the "technology hierarchy" saves patients time and money and may reduce health risks to the mother or baby. Depending upon the underlying cause of the infertility, in some cases, male infertility specialists claim that they can move patients entirely away from technology and help them achieve pregnancy through "IBF," a term coined by one doctor I interviewed to refer to "in bed fertilization," or spontaneous conception through sexual intercourse—a method that most heterosexual couples favor over IVF. Ultimately, as a doctor explained to me, the proper assessment of the infertile male patient is about "putting a question to rest." Men should not be left to wonder why they have a low sperm count for the rest of their lives, a situation that may happen when couples opt for high-tech reproductive solutions without discovering the specific etiologies of poor semen parameters.

Male infertility specialists struggle to claim their territory when working with REs but also promote a cooperative team approach to treating infertility in which male infertility specialists and REs work together. I found that this was possible only when the urologist spent clinical hours working inside an IVF clinic, as was the case in two university hospitals I visited. Of course, even in cooperative team arrangements, specialists do not always agree on treatment protocols, but they manage to form compatible working relationships. In private practices, IVF centers and male infertility practices are usually separate entities. When there is big money on the line (and big professional egos), competition for business can turn nasty. Some male infertility specialists I interviewed spoke venomously of REs who refuse to work with male infertility specialists. When asked why some REs do not refer male patients to male specialists, doctors gave flippant responses such as "Greed" or "The RE has a mortgage to pay." One male infertility specialist reported that after seeing a male patient with an extremely low sperm count and recommending surgery instead of IVF-ICSI, he received an irate phone call from the referring RE, who informed him, "I wanted you to extract his sperm. I didn't ask for your *opinion!*"

Some male infertility specialists complained that REs are not held accountable for their actions. As one doctor explained to me, REs just help their female patients get pregnant and then pass them off to OB/GYNs for regular prenatal care and delivery. REs do not have to address the complications that arise from ART, including multiples, premature births, and a variety of birth defects. "What other type of specialist can get away with performing procedures and not following up?" asked one doctor rhetorically. If an orthopedic surgeon performs surgery on a patient's shoulder, he argued, and complications follow, then the orthopedist is responsible for fixing it. The fix-your-own-mistakes philosophy of medicine applies clearly when the practitioner's ultimate goal is to correct problems and cure diseases. But as many scholars have pointed out, infertility medicine as practiced by REs is not about fixing fertility issues. The goal is to circumvent the obstacles to conception and achieve pregnancy technologically. Therefore, there is little incentive for REs to restrict the number of embryos they transfer, for example.[42] If the result of ART is quadruplets, premature infants, or birth defects, neonatology specialists are often called in to follow up with the complications caused by reproductive technologies. By contrast, male infertility specialists, who identify themselves as surgeons first and foremost, regularly follow up with their own patients.

Male infertility specialists frequently described female infertility treatments to me as excessively and needlessly invasive and potentially more harmful than the "simpler" and "less invasive" male treatments. Of course, medical professionals, who live in the world of needles, catheters, naked bodies, and bodily fluids, have a different sense of normal and a more tolerant definition of what is invasive than those of the average layperson. For squeamish nonmedical types, pumping women full of hormones followed by sticking foreign objects up their nether regions and slicing into men's genitals sound equally disturbing.

In early medical consultations, patients receive conflicting information from different specialists about how to improve their chances for conception. For example, OB/GYNs and REs routinely advise couples to abstain from sex for three days prior to the woman's fertile peak, the 24-hour period during the menstrual cycle when women ovulate. By charting basal body temperature, noting changes in cervical mucus, and using over-the-counter ovulation test kits, women can gauge their fertile period with relative accuracy. The conventional wisdom, repeated in popular books and on countless websites, has always been that if a man avoids ejaculation (from intercourse or masturbation), he can strategically "save up" his sperm for his big chance during intercourse at ovulation. In contrast, however, some male infertility specialists advise couples to have "as much sex as possible" in the week leading up to ovulation. They explain that the sheer number of sperm emitted from multiple ejaculations is more important than the concentration in one ejaculation, that sperm can live up to five days, and that sperm "saved up" may weaken or become malformed in the testicles, while sperm freshly produced in the testicles are believed to be the most potent. With no clear consensus or definitive science to provide guidance, couples have to decide on their own which specialists' advice they will follow.

Receiving conflicting advice and information from different specialists heightens couples' awareness of the tension that may exist between the RE who is treating the wife and the male infertility specialist who is treating the husband. How do couples, feeling caught in the middle of a strained rivalry between specialists, move forward and make plans for treatment? They can compare specialists' success rates for their respective treatments, costs for treatment, and the potential health risks associated with some treatments. Some couples may shop around, considering what different infertility clinics offer and what they charge for various services. Choosing services and service providers requires a taxing amount of legwork and research, not to mention a fairly sophisticated understanding of mathematics and statistics.

Calculating Cost, Risk, and Success

In the infertility industry, complicated pricing schemes, incomplete information about insurance coverage, insufficient and conflicting information about treatment success rates, and conflicting research findings regarding the health risks and effects of different treatment options make it challenging for couples to make informed decisions about treatment. A basic price comparison of ART services with male infertility treatments seems relatively simple. According to the Society for Assisted Reproductive Technologies (SART), as of 2013 the average cost of an IVF cycle in the United States was $12,400. IUI ranged in price from several hundred dollars to roughly $6,000 depending on the clinic and on the type of pharmaceutical drugs used to induce ovulation. A male infertility procedure, such as repairing a varicocele or obstruction, ran between $5,000 and $15,000. Assuming that a couple were to base their decision solely on price, IUI would likely be the first choice; their second choice would be surgical repair for the man, and the third choice would be IVF. But what if insurance will cover some treatments but not others? What if insurance covers some steps of some treatments but not entire treatment processes? What if the couple hope to have multiples, such as twins or triplets, which are common after IUI and IVF, or are adamant about avoiding multiples? What if the couple hope to have more children in the future? What if the couple have ethical concerns about discarding extra embryos? Each of these questions complicates the calculations. Furthermore, there may be a female factor adding costs to some steps of treatment or complicating success rates. Advanced maternal age may push the couple toward the quickest treatments. Comparing costs of basic services is not easy, as many factors, including insurance coverage, success rates, chances of multiples, plans for future siblings, religious restrictions, ethical issues, female factors, and maternal age are all weighed in the decision.

Many REs recommend that patients plan and prepare for a few cycles of IUI or IVF, since success rates are relatively low. Conducting a price comparison of IVF services among IVF clinics is difficult when services are packaged differently. Some centers may charge per egg harvest, promising up to three transfers; other centers charge per transfer. More private practices now offer a cost-sharing plan, which charges patients more for IVF upfront but promises a money-back guarantee after so many rounds of failed IVF. In some states, health insurance companies are required by law to cover infertility. Other states require some insurance coverage, but patients may discover high deductibles or low caps on coverage or may find that only certain aspects of the infertility workup and treatment plan are covered.

In other states, infertility treatments are considered elective, and patients have to pay for these services entirely out of pocket.

Predicting insurance coverage for male infertility treatments is nearly impossible.[43] While the insurance codes for "infertility," per se, are sometimes not covered by basic insurance plans, if the doctor codes for etiologies such as hormonal issues, pain, anatomical problems, or anything found to be damaging to quality of life, sexual pleasure,[44] or ability to work, treatments may be covered. As several male infertility specialists explained, some insurance companies seem unaware that certain services for men are actually infertility related. If the doctors choose insurance codes carefully, everything will be covered. Obviously, it is difficult for couples to estimate costs as they begin the treatment process, since different doctors code services differently and insurance coverage varies. If insurance claims are denied, couples may be ill prepared for the medical bills they have incurred.

Unfortunately, many couples spend thousands—even tens of thousands—of dollars on treatments, drain their savings, rack up debt, take time off work, and still never realize their dreams of parenthood. In 2011 the CDC reported that only 47,818 live births resulted from the 163,039 attempted cycles of IVF;[45] the CDC collects no data on IUI success rates. Similarly, only about 33 percent of couples in which the male partner undergoes varicocelectomy achieve pregnancy.[46] These less than stellar success rates complicate couples' decision to pursue female- or male-focused treatment plans. The decision-making process feels less like a careful calculation and more like a game show in which contestants have to choose between door number one and door number two. Many patients endure painful and uncomfortable procedures, risking their personal health. Women undergoing treatments are particularly vulnerable to minor discomforts such as hot flashes, nausea, mood swings, and bruising from daily hormonal injections, as well as more severe life-threatening issues such as ovarian hyperstimulation syndrome and complications during pregnancy due to carrying multiples.[47] Women with whom I spoke also worried that the high level of consumption of synthetic hormones would put them at greater risk for other conditions, such as hormonal irregularities, early menopause, or cancer. Doctors reassure men that the outpatient surgeries they undergo are not particularly invasive or risky and that they can expect to be fully recovered and back at work within 48 hours. In my interviews with patients, however, men reported tremendous pain during and following procedures, extreme swelling and bruising of the genitals, and many days required for full recuperation. Patients are warned that because of the trauma of surgery, improvements in semen parameters will not be evident for at least three to six months; some men never see improvements. Perhaps the most disturbing risks to health that the latest research shows are the risks associated with preterm labor. Because many IUI and IVF treatments result in multiples and because multiples are at higher risk for prematurity than singletons, children conceived through IUI and IVF are more likely than other children to have physical and mental developmental problems.[48] The potential risks to mother, father, and future children associated with various treatments influence couples' decision making.

Variations in the Practice of Male Infertility

Not only do reproductive endocrinologists and male infertility specialists differ in their treatment of male infertility, but among male infertility specialists there are variations in approach. During my fieldwork I observed many inconsistencies in the information that was given to patients at the various sites, particularly in regard to the personal habits that affect fertility. For example, it is widely accepted that heat inhibits sperm production. This explains why—evolutionarily speaking—the male genitals hang in the scrotum away from the torso: to keep the testicles (sperm factories) cooler than normal body temperature. Contemporary theories connecting excessive heat and decreased sperm production abound, including ideas that hot tubs, laptop computers, and restrictive underwear (tight briefs rather than boxer shorts) inhibit sperm production. The scientific research on these theories is scant, but a small study on public awareness found that restrictive underwear and stress were believed to be the two most common causes of male infertility among patients,[49] a belief that may amuse male infertility specialists in light of the myriad etiologies for male factor infertility.

We might expect male infertility specialists to set the record straight on such issues, but they cannot seem to agree. One doctor I shadowed had recently been interviewed by the media about the negative effects of hot tub use on sperm counts. He advised all of his patients to avoid such warm environments, along with restrictive underwear, and he exhorted patients to keep their laptop computers off their laps. Another doctor scoffed at patients who mentioned that they were trying to avoid hot tubs, laptops, and restrictive underwear, saying that such theories were unsubstantiated and the heat generated by these sources was not high enough to affect patients' semen parameters. Another theory hypothesizes that the radiofrequency electromagnetic waves emitted by cell phones damage male fertility. Though findings from several scientific studies support the theory,[50] these findings have been largely ignored (and occasionally mocked) by medical professionals in the United States.

Male infertility specialists also do not agree on the effectiveness of nutraceuticals, vitamins, and antioxidant supplements derived from natural foods that are believed to have medicinal benefits. Nutraceuticals (a term that covers a variety of dietary supplements, herbal products, and functional foods such as oats and bran) are available without a prescription in pill, capsule, powder, or shake form. Some scientists and doctors theorize that antioxidants such as vitamin E help with sperm development and motility. In continuing education courses sponsored by the AUA, urologists are encouraged to recommend antioxidants to patients. Nutraceutical products such as Proxeed claim to improve sperm count, motility, and concentration. When patients inquired about the effectiveness of antioxidants or Proxeed about which they had learned on the Internet, some doctors I observed were very encouraging, while most shrugged, and expressed little confidence in their effectiveness. The lack of consensus again reflects the general lack of unity among practitioners.

The Management of Information

Male infertility specialists carefully manage information, choosing what information to share and how it will be shared with patients. The health risks to offspring associated with advanced parental age and ART is dispensed in modest portions along with a hearty dose of gender ideology. Doctors are quick to share the dangers of advanced maternal age but often ignore and do not share with patients the risks of advanced paternal age. The broad consensus among medical professionals is that women's fertility status declines sharply at age thirty-five and advanced maternal age increases the likelihood of complications, such as miscarriage, hypertension, or incompetent cervix, and negative pregnancy outcomes, such as Down syndrome and Edwards syndrome.[51] This information is fairly common knowledge among the lay public, particularly among women who are socialized in routine medical examinations to be conscientious about their reproductive health. Research conducted on paternal age suggests that male fertility also declines with age, but the facts surrounding the male biological clock are less widely known. Though fertility (ability to achieve pregnancy) might not drop as drastically for men, as they advance into their forties and older, sperm quality diminishes, and the risks for pregnancy loss, birth defects, neurological disorders, clinical syndromes, and genetic diseases increase. These risks are even more pronounced in cases of ART.[52]

In nearly every appointment that I observed, the woman's age was a major point of discussion. Women in their twenties and early thirties were congratulated for pursuing motherhood while they were still young. Women in their late thirties were advised not to procrastinate in pursuing treatment and to take into consideration the time length of the various treatment protocols as they selected treatment options. Women over thirty-nine were gravely informed that because of their advanced age, the likelihood of achieving pregnancy with any treatments was low. By comparison, I never heard a male patient's age discussed during an appointment. The oldest male patients were usually men in their fifties and sixties, often in second marriages, who were seeking vasectomy reversals to restore fertility and enable their younger wives to get pregnant.[53] These were generally considered high-revenue patients for clinics, and even in these cases, the risks of paternal age were never discussed. The fact that paternal age is so easily overlooked while women's biological clock is repeatedly emphasized illustrates how easily popular notions about gender and aging—that men are ever-virile and women are attractive in youth—sustain the gender system, enabling authorities to withhold scientific information.

At one university hospital I had the opportunity to attend a case management meeting, which included a few REs, the male infertility specialist I was shadowing, his nurse, a genetic counselor, a psychologist, and the laboratory technicians. One case on the agenda involved a patient in his seventies and his wife, who was fifty years his junior. The patient was suffering from erectile dysfunction and anejaculation, both attributed to his age. A diagnostic work-up showed that his wife was healthy and fertile. The plan was to put the husband under general anesthesia, acquire sperm through a process known as electroejaculation, and, depending on the quality of the sperm, proceed with IUI or IVF. One member of the group expressed unease with the situation. The foreign-born patient had returned to his native village just a couple of years earlier and married the daughter of an old friend. The non-English-speaking wife had no vocation or employment, and her husband's advanced age put her at high risk of becoming a young widow. It was unclear whether she had been forced into the marriage and the move to the United States. However, the rest of the staff believed that the husband and wife made a very "cute" couple. A few people mentioned that the wife's youth and fertility would boost the clinic's success rate. Another person saw no reason to dissuade the couple from pursuing treatment, including a veiled suggestion that to do so would be disrespecting their lifestyle and privacy. At no point were the risks associated with the gentleman's elderly age discussed and no plans were made to inform the couple of the possible risks due to paternal age. Instead, electroejaculation and IVF for the couple were added to the monthly schedule.

This case illustrates well what happens when traditional gender roles come head to head with sound science. While scientific research would suggest that the offspring of an elderly man are at high risk for birth anomalies, the husband had a reputable career and was a reliable breadwinner. His young wife was eager to have a baby. Together, they presented a picture of perfect heterosexual family life, each fulfilling his or her socially prescribed roles. What was surprising about the situation was not that the clinic helped them—they wanted a baby, after all—but that the clinic did not, to my knowledge, make plans to disclose the potential risks.

Another demonstration of how practitioners manage information is the example of the phenotypic time bomb theory. Like all traits, infertility may be hereditary, but in its severest forms, it is not passed on genetically because people who cannot reproduce cannot pass on any traits, including their infertility. (Simply put, if your parents were severely infertile, you would not exist.) One specialist described the increasing usage of IVF-ICSI as a "phenotypic time bomb,"[54] a term that critics of IVF-ICSI coined to describe how assisted reproductive technologies are now circumventing natural selection. Enabling infertile people to reproduce runs contrary to the evolutionary purposes of natural selection and facilitates the passing on of infertility-related conditions. If men with poor fertility status use technology to reproduce, their sons will likely inherit poor fertility.[55] Increasing use of technology over generations could result in a growing population of infertile men who cannot achieve pregnancy through regular sexual intercourse.[56] When the metaphorical time bomb explodes, we will, in theory, live in a world where all men must rely on technology to reproduce.

In interviews, several specialists relayed some variation of the phenotypic time bomb theory to me, but not surprisingly, evolutionary theories about infertility and survival of the fittest were never shared with patients during clinical encounters. In one clinical interaction that I observed, a very discouraged couple who had been contemplating treatment options for some time asked the doctor whether a male child would inherit his father's infertility issues. The doctor diplomatically explained that not much data are yet available regarding the offspring that were conceived through new infertility treatments, since the children are still young, but that it is indeed conceivable that male offspring could inherit infertility issues. The doctor encouraged the couple to pursue some promising treatment options that would put an end to their emotional suffering and pointed out that whatever technologies they relied on now would still be available to any sons of theirs in the future, and who knows—maybe they would have a daughter! The couple explained that after giving the matter considerable thought, they had decided that they could not knowingly risk passing on the father's infertility issues to posterity. They knew firsthand the anguish of infertility and could not bear the prospect of watching a child of theirs relive their experience. Quite resolved on the matter, they pledged to live child-free or adopt. The doctor's attitude soured, and the dialogue grew tense as he reiterated that he could relieve their suffering and the couple would not be swayed. Once the couple left, the doctor sharply criticized their decision.

Incidents like these, in which doctors try to downplay the possible risks of the treatments they offer, illustrate one of the great conundrums of infertility medicine. Human life is priceless. Becoming a biological parent is an awesome and extraordinary experience. How does one weigh the risks associated with creating human life via technological means against the benefits of desired parenthood? Couples who do overcome infertility are often so elated by their new roles as parents that they easily overlook the imperfections of their beautiful new babies. In the incident above, the doctor saw the couple's heartache and believed that he could cure it, likely assuming that once the couple conceived, the threat of having a less than perfect child would seem trivial in comparison to the love the couple would feel for that child. Infertility specialists choose to practice infertility medicine because they find it to be very rewarding and thrilling work. The couple's preference to live child-free rather than risk cursing future generations with infertility smacked of moral superiority and probably felt to the doctor like an insult to his life work and chosen profession.

Discrepancies regarding best practices for extracting the sperm cells needed for IVF-ICSI also illustrate how tightly practitioners manage information. A variety of medical techniques are used for retrieving sperm cells from the scrotum. The least invasive methods include basic biopsy of testicular tissue, known TESE (testicular sperm extraction), and a more invasive procedure known as Micro-TESE (microscopic testicular sperm extraction), which may be done under local anesthesia. More intensive procedures known as PESA (percutaneous epididymal sperm aspiration) and MESA (microscopic epididymal sperm aspiration) remove tissue from the epididymis and are performed under general anesthesia. TESE treatments generally cost less than $1,000 dollars and may be conducted in a private office setting, whereas the more sophisticated PESA and MESA techniques are performed in fully equipped operating rooms, can cost more than ten thousand dollars, and require longer recovery times.

In one clinic where I conducted fieldwork, azoospermic patients were advised to move directly to MESA and were required to pay in cash before the procedure. A specialist at another clinic commented that he could not understand why some practitioners skip TESE and move all of their patients directly to MESA without ever offering TESE as an option. He claimed that he finds sperm quickly using the much simpler TESE techniques in his office in at least half of his azoospermic patients. Only when TESE is not fruitful does he recommend the more invasive MESA technique. In their own defense, regular MESA practitioners argue that the simpler technologies do not provide as many sperm, but this argument does not make sense when IVF-ICSI requires only one sperm cell per harvested egg. MESA practitioners also point out that MESA is successful more often and that

TESE techniques have higher complication rates due to risks such as puncturing sensitive tissue. These arguments sound logical, but the huge difference in treatment costs raises eyebrows. Are patients who are desperate for a baby being needlessly upsold on services? People who want a baby have a hard time putting a price tag on that desire, and many will expend any and all resources to which they have access on infertility services.[57] Furthermore, the scarcity of male-focused services, support groups, patient literature, and online resources makes it difficult for patients to get a second opinion from another male infertility specialist or to discuss options with other male patients. Aside from the high revenue it generates, MESA may be used as a first line of treatment as a way for specialists to set boundaries of expertise between general urologists and those with specialized training in male infertility. General urologists are often not trained in the microsurgical techniques that MESA requires, though they might feel comfortable attempting simpler techniques such as TESE in their offices. Doctors who have completed fellowships in male infertility may advocate MESA as the ideal sperm procurement method as a way to stake out their turf, demonstrating to patients their more skilled expertise and discouraging general urologists from attempting to treat male infertility.

Urology Gone Wrong

Male infertility specialists most often cited REs as the doctors who bungle treatment of infertile men. However, it became clear during my clinical observations that general urologists without specialized knowledge of infertility were causing the most harm to infertile male patients. For example, male infertility specialists know well that anabolic steroids such as testosterone disrupt the natural relay of hormones and arrest sperm production, so they avoid prescribing testosterone. Yet I observed a few cases in the clinic in which infertile male patients had previously been prescribed testosterone by general urologists who had mistakenly assumed that the drug would boost sperm production. When the patients' sperm counts dropped to extremely low levels or sperm production was arrested altogether, the general urologists hastily referred the patients to male infertility specialists to undo the damage caused by the testosterone. In interviews, male infertility specialists blamed primary care physicians and REs for irresponsibly prescribing testosterone to infertile men. However, in every case I witnessed in the clinic, it was a general urologist who had made the error.

The treatment of varicoceles was another situation in which general urologists engaged in questionable practices. Varicoceles are varicose veins that run along the testicles and are believed to raise the temperature inside the scrotum, inhibiting sperm production. A male infertility specialist who detects a varicocele will recommend a varicocelectomy to cut off the blood running near the testicles that is believed to be causing the low sperm count. There are four grades or levels of varicoceles, based on the size or distention of the veins. The most severe type is grade III, less severe is grade II, next is grade I, and the least severe form is "subclinical," which is detectable only with Doppler ultrasonography. Grades I, II, and III are detectable during palpation by a well-trained specialist. Multiple studies show that repairing subclinical varicoceles does not improve sperm production because they are likely too small and insignificant to affect sperm count.[58]

Several of the male infertility specialists I interviewed reported seeing patients who had undergone varicocelectomies performed by general urologists for subclinical varicoceles. When the sperm count showed no improvement, the urologists referred the patients to the more highly trained specialists. Why would a urologist attempt to correct infertility by removing subclinical varicoceles? General urologists understand varicocelectomy as a treatment option for low sperm, but not all are knowledgeable about the medical literature advising against it for subclinical varicoceles. Also, many general urologists do not have the same level of expertise to palpate the testicles to detect varicoceles. Not trusting his or her own ability to palpate a varicocele, a urologist might decide to check again with a Doppler ultrasound device. If the Doppler reveals a blood-pumping varicocele, the urologist might second-guess his or her initial evaluation, presume the vein to be larger than it actually is, and move forward with surgery. In some cases, it is possible that doctors simply want to offer patients hope by trying something—anything—in an attempt to improve fertility. These doctors maintain a "nothing to lose" attitude going into surgery.

In one clinic I observed an appointment with a couple who were being treated for the husband's nonobstructive azoospermia.[59] He had previously undergone a varicocelectomy with a general urologist. When a postoperative semen analysis revealed that the patient still had a zero sperm count, the urologist informed the couple that no more options were available to treat the husband's infertility. On their own, the couple aggressively researched more options and traveled across several states to meet with a male infertility specialist for a second opinion. The appointment that I observed was their first meeting with a fellowship-trained male infertility specialist, who assured them that more treatment options were available. The husband's varicocele was large enough to consider surgery, but varicocelectomy is found to be ineffective in cases of nonobstructive azoospermia and is not recommended. After the appointment, out of earshot of the couple, I asked the doctor why the previous urologist had performed surgery on an azoospermic patient. He explained that the first doctor believed the procedure would optimize sperm production but conceded it was a "silly" approach: "Shame on [that doctor] who attends these meetings, *should* read the literature, *should* be knowledgeable about what is possible—to not know what the results are of potential treatment. . . . It's unfortunate. It's disappointing."

Though urologists specializing in male infertility are quick to criticize the medical system for not referring infertile men through the proper channels, they do not always recognize that the mistakes that are most harmful to patients occur within their own field of urology. General urologists are highly proficient medical professionals who adroitly treat a vast array of issues ranging from urinary incontinence to life-threatening diseases. They are the unsung heroes who restore dignity in people challenged by serious pelvic trauma, spinal cord injuries, cancer, HIV/AIDS and neurological disorders like multiple sclerosis. Because of the intimate and sensitive nature of their work, urologists are called on to double as marriage counselors, grief counselors, sex therapists, lay religious clergy, and moral leaders for their patients. The skills and intentions of general urologists are not in question. The problem is a medical system in which the proper channels and expertise for diagnosing and treating male infertility are not clearly defined.

Conclusion

I am in awe of the work of male infertility specialists, REs, embryologists, and laboratory technicians. Is there anything more breathtaking than the birth of a newborn baby? Is there anything more sacred and precious than human life? That doctors and technicians can gather genetic materials and apply new technologies to turn heartsick couples into bona fide parents is truly astounding. When the end result is darn near a miracle, can we really complain about the system?

Though from a distance the system seems sufficient, a closer look reveals conflict and distrust among practitioners and confusion among patients. Male infertility clinics are few in number, and there are geographic deserts where couples cannot find a trained specialist to help them. As a result, some infertile men are never properly examined or diagnosed, some men undergo unnecessary and even harmful treatments, some perfectly fertile wives bear the brunt of infertility treatments, and some couples never realize their dreams of becoming parents. In interviews, several doctors pinned the problems of the industry on business competition and personality clashes. It would be easy to suggest that when an infertile man enters an IVF center, a male infertility clinic, or a general urology office, the attending doctor will try to secure business regardless of the patient's issues or the doctor's capacity to help. However, the patient-as-walking-dollar-sign explanation is overly simplistic, and economic interests are not the primary motivation behind all doctors' actions. Though I am not blind to the hefty salaries these doctors earn, in my observation doctors are compelled by the intellectual challenge of solving puzzles and an ego-rooted need to fix problems and make conception possible. One doctor told me that there are three things that make his day: "Having a baby named after me. Getting a spinal cord injury patient to have a family. And having the wife come up to you and say thank you. It's awesome." Easing couples' emotional struggles by showing off some impressive handiwork skills using cutting-edge technology to create new life makes for a superheroic and rewarding career. Male infertility specialists, as well as REs and general urologists, attempt to solve male infertility with the knowledge and tools that are available to them. Sometimes treatments work, sometimes they fail, and the evidence that is available for best practices is often conflicting.

From a sociological perspective we can see that many of the problems that arise in the treatment of male infertility are the outcomes of a long cultural legacy. Since the nineteenth century, society has clung to the gendered ideas that women bear the primary responsibility for reproduction, that women's bodies require more medical attention than men's bodies do, that men are not as susceptible to reproductive disorders as women are, and that the most prized of male anatomical parts should be safeguarded from the surgical knife. Unspoken cultural taboos, such as openly recognizing the existence and prevalence of male infertility, hampered the expansion of knowledge and technological innovation of male reproduction. As women's reproductive medicine took root and developed over the past two centuries, male reproductive medicine languished. I do not advocate the equally extreme medicalization of all bodies, nor is it my intention to give primacy to the Western biomedical model of disease. My point is that science and medicine are driven by remarkably *un*scientific ideas about gender and are shaped by the power dynamics between men and women and between doctors and patients. Women's historically subordinate status has, ironically, resulted in a medical discipline that today is organized and designed to effectively help and treat infertile female patients. Though men's bodies were generally spared the tortures of medical manipulation in the past, at present men seem to have less access to medical help than women do and have less medical, social, and emotional understanding of the health issues they face.[60] As evidenced by the history of male reproductive medicine, the pervasive gender system has the potential to suffocate ideas and stifle creativity and collective imaginations, scientific and otherwise. The study of male infertility demonstrates how gender ideology creates a rigid framework with limited space for scientific thought to move and develop. The infertility industry that we have today developed within the confining walls of the gender system.

Doctors Doing Gender

J ust prior to my first visit to a male infertility clinic, the doctor
whom I would be shadowing warned me over the phone, "Men
just don't take care of themselves. They're like wild animals." As
well-compensated and licensed institutional authorities on human
biology, doctors are particularly powerful players in the social construction of gender. During my fieldwork, male infertility specialists
explained to me that long-held cultural beliefs about women, men,
and reproduction influence the way in which infertile couples are
treated today. The widespread but inaccurate assumption that women
are responsible for all aspects of reproduction was discussed as problematic in the medical conferences on male infertility that I attended.
In seminars and personal interviews, male infertility specialists explained that society needs to get past this popular idea so that male
infertility can be properly diagnosed and addressed by qualified
practitioners. During my fieldwork, however, what became more in-
triguing to me was to hear male infertility specialists' hope for society
to move past outdated ideas about gender when I could see in clinical
practices every day the ways in which medical practitioners and staff
themselves buy into very traditional notions of gender.

Nearly four decades ago, sociologists Candace West and Don
Zimmerman developed the theory of "doing gender," positing that
gender norms and ideas are constructed and perpetuated at the site

of interpersonal human interactions.[1] Building on West and Zimmerman's work in her book *Framed by Gender: How Gender Inequality Persists in the Modern World*, Cecilia Ridgeway posits that society shares a certain cultural knowledge, or consensus, about gender. Like a culture's spoken language, gender ideology is ubiquitous and commonly understood. Individuals speak the language of popular gender beliefs with each other every day. Gender is written in our actions and read in the actions of others. Unfortunately, as feminist scholars point out, the gender beliefs that inform our everyday interactions are based on "hegemonic gender beliefs," or "hierarchical presumptions about men's greater status and competence" in comparison to women.[2]

Everyone, including medical practitioners, is a social actor participating in the social construction of gender. As doctors practice medicine, they *do* gender. Doctors draw on common cultural understandings of gender to communicate with and treat patients. Sometimes, doctors construct gender in blatant ways, as in the comment that "men are like wild animals." Often, however, medical professionals' participation in the social construction of gender is more subtle than blanket declarations about the natures of men and women. Through doctors' and staff members' interactions with patients, as they share medical information or manage medical practices, the language of gender is spoken, and traditional ideas about gender get perpetuated and solidified. Medical practitioners and institutions incorporate common ideas about gender into practices because these ideas are easily recognizable for patients and their use accelerates communication and understanding. However, traditional gender ideas, or stereotypes, are not always accurate and can be disadvantageous and even damaging to both men and women. Medical practices based on gender stereotypes sometimes complicate the medical experience for patients. Furthermore, the traditional gender ideas that are built into medical practices stem from the same gender ideology that perpetuates the notion that women are solely responsible for all aspects of reproduction. Hence, as they practice medicine, practitioners adhere to the same gender system that they criticize.

Semen Collection

New technological procedures, such as intracytoplasmic sperm injection using extracted testicular sperm, reveal astounding ingenuity. Simpler technologies, such as the plastic semen collection cup, remind us that male infertility medicine is a field that is still in its adolescence. The juxtaposition of cutting-edge reproductive technologies and the humble cup is emblematic of the tension created by the pull of new medical innovation against old and immovable ideas about gender. The semen collection cup is at once a sperm receptacle and a wellspring of enduring social ideas about masculinity. Feminist scholar Susan Bordo argues that much of popular science leads us to believe that "men are testosterone-driven, promiscuous brutes whom nature won't permit to keep their peckers in their pants."[3] According to Bordo's "hot man" thesis, male sexuality is aggressive, uncontrollable, and animalistic. Anthropologist and masculinities scholar Matthew Gutmann echoes Bordo's assessment of masculine stereotypes, arguing that men have inherited a sexual destiny that entails a rapacious sexual appetite, heterosexual desire, and homophobia and that has no room for love.[4] But this stereotype is not an accurate depiction of most men most of the time. As Gutmann puts it, penises may be conspicuous and erotic sites of sexual pleasure, but "the fact remains that for the vast majority of men's lives, penises and testicles are not in high states of excitation. The erect penis is not the default."[5]

Perhaps at no time are men more acutely aware of this fact than during an infertility workup when they are issued a plastic cup (usually the same type that is used for urine samples) and are instructed to deposit their semen into it. In my final interviews with patients, several men looked back to their earliest encounters with the medical system and recounted semen collection as the most embarrassing part of the entire experience. For some men, having to provide a sample was more distressing than learning that they were infertile. Men in this study were often given exact times and dates for collection, such as "Tuesday morning between 8:00 and 9:00 A.M." Most men had the option to produce the sample at home and then take it to the clinic or laboratory. However, if they lived more than a one-hour drive from the drop-off facility, they had to produce the sample onsite. When semen analysis results are poor (as was the case for all patients in this study), patients are required to complete a second semen analysis. In some cases, patients were asked to leave another sample "on the way out." Being asked to provide a semen sample on a specific day at a specific time, sometimes in a specific location and sometimes without warning, came as a challenge to literally *perform* and prove their masculinity.

Semen collection is a clear example of how assumptions about men and masculinity are built into institutional practices and medical technology. Men are handed a cup with no instructions beyond "Be sure to fasten the lid tightly when you're done." As the following examples of semen collection illustrate, medical institutions assume that (1) men are well experienced when it comes to masturbation, (2) men can masturbate under any conditions, (3) men will enjoy providing the sample, and (4) men will be able to catch the sample in the cup. Medical personnel often remarked to me that infertility workups are difficult for women[6] and "fun" for men. However, the experience was more often confusing and uncomfortable for men.

After providing his first semen sample on-site at a large urban hospital, Joel, a carpenter in his late thirties, received a phone call from his wife's doctor requesting that he repeat the semen analysis test. Joel tried to explain to the doctor that he would prefer to collect the sample at home and drop it off at a local laboratory rather than returning to the hospital. The reasons that he gave his doctor were legitimate concerns: He would have to wait at least two weeks to get an appointment at the hospital, and the drive into the city would cost him at least half a day of work. In our interview, Joel admitted that his biggest objection was that the hospital setting "is kind of awkward." He explained:

> It's no big deal at the point—until the door shuts, and you're in this little room and you're like, "Alright, this is goofy. This is just weird." It wasn't until I went into the cold collection room that I was like, "This is bizarre." The setting—I mean, you're in this little room with a couch, but quite honestly, I mean if you want to be graphic enough, I'm looking at a cup thinking, "How am I going to get this into the cup. In what position do I need to be?"

As Joel told me, men do not normally worry about "where your semen is supposed to go" when masturbating, so providing a semen sample is a new experience for most men. Joel raises some important questions: *Are patients supposed to stand up or lie down? If the erect penis angles upward, how does one hold the cup?* These kinds of questions remain unanswered because no basic instruction is provided, and patients do not dare ask, for fear of being seen as sexually un-knowledgeable and therefore less masculine.

One measurement of the semen analysis test is the actual volume of semen collected. But how can a man catch all of the semen inside the cup with gravity working against him? Clinics take this into account and ask patients to document what percentage of the ejaculate they estimate was captured in the cup. However, as Joel explained, the general lack of comfort inhibits maximal performance. Regarding his own test results he noted, "Not only was the count so low, but the amount in total was—seemed to be a little low. And I definitely think there's a reflection of that in correlation to the setting. I wanted to get the hell out of there. So once I started my process, I'm like, 'Okay, I've got to get out of here. I've just got to finish this thing.'" Clinics have no formal methods for measuring or documenting patient discomfort and its bearing on semen volume or total sperm count, though doctors try to take this into consideration when going over results with patients.

Another patient, Kevin, a commercial pilot in his late twenties, received his first order for a semen analysis from his wife's doctor. Because he lived more than an hour away from the laboratory where the semen analysis was to be conducted, the doctor directed him to masturbate when he arrived at the laboratory. However, on Kevin's arrival, the staff explained that this particular center was not prepared to have patients provide semen samples on-site. Nonetheless, knowing that he was far from home, they offered to find him a private space for providing the sample. Kevin recounted:

> They take me, and this guy comes over and he hands me this cup and he says to follow him. Then he takes me around the corner and down this hallway, and he's just looking around just randomly for something like some open area. And he tries to put me behind a curtain in this—I guess like a recovery room for outpatient surgery, which I was not comfortable with sitting behind this curtain. I couldn't even believe it. I said, "Are you serious?" As I told my friend, "People can see my feet under the curtain." I don't know if I'm gonna—what if all of a sudden I was on my toes?

After Kevin protested about the location, he was moved to another room that had no lock on the door. At one point, Kevin recalls, a woman tried to walk into the room. He caught the door with his hand before she saw him and then had to keep one foot planted against the door to prevent it from opening again, adding more challenge to an already awkward situation.

Kevin's experience was somewhat unusual, because the center was not prepared for him to provide a sample on-site. However, clinics that routinely ask men to collect semen on-site are not much better. At one male infertility clinic that I visited, all of the patient rooms had large windows overlooking a major freeway. A couple of patients commented that they felt as though everyone passing on the freeway was watching them. After trying for several minutes to perform, all the while distracted by the traffic below, one man gave up and promised the doctor that he would bring in a sample later in the week.

Some men have no better luck even in more private settings. Because of his diabetes, William suffered erectile dysfunction and found it very difficult to masturbate. Furthermore, he and his wife are devout Catholics, a religion that discourages the "spilling of seed." As a compromise with their faith, they decided that the best way to collect semen would be to engage in intercourse, and William would withdraw just prior to ejaculation. Since the couple lived more than an hour from the male infertility clinic, William and his wife rented a nice hotel room near the clinic the night before he was to bring in his semen sample. William hoped that being away from home and work would allow him to relax and enjoy the experience. Alas, the morning his sample was due (at 9:00 A.M. sharp), William could not perform. Frustrated and embarrassed, the couple packed up and went home.

As these accounts illustrate, the setting or location can present challenges, and as William's story shows, so can the timing. Todd, a radio news director in his late thirties, compared the pressure of having to masturbate with the pressure that he faced at work to meet deadlines. Here, he describes trying to ejaculate at home with his wife's help:

> You got this cute wife rubbing it, and it's like it just doesn't work right, so that's kinda challenging to your masculinity. . . . Come on. You're [his wife] sitting there looking all cute. . . . And it's still a very, you know, like not able to take care of business really on time. . . . But it's like when you're working on a project for work, and they say, it's gotta be done by

11:59 and 59 seconds, so we can get it in for 12:03 news, and the next thing you know, you're trying to read, you know, two and a half minutes of news copies, and you keep stumbling over your words.

As Todd describes, providing a semen sample is particularly challenging when the man is up against the clock and people around him have very specific expectations. Todd's analogy also reveals how masturbating for medical purposes turns a presumably pleasurable experience into a form of work.

The norms around masculinity are tricky to navigate. Men are supposed to be sexually competent, with a healthy sex drive, yet they do not want to be perceived as hypersexual or, as Kevin put it, "some pervert." Both Joel and Kevin worried about what would be a normal amount of time to take to masturbate. Kevin recounts:

Then they put me in this room . . . in the corner of this hallway that has a chair and a stretcher type bed and a clock that is the loudest clock you've ever heard in your life that hums and ticks. And [the technician] says, "Okay, come back down that hallway and make a left and bring me the cup when you're done." I didn't know what to expect. It was . . . miserable. . . . You have you and your imagination, which is running thin on my end. . . . And this clock is just tick, tick, tick. I looked at the clock. It was 8:30 in the morning. So then it became this mind game because then I thought I didn't want to show up at 8:33 and hand him this cup, and it got to where it's 8:50 and I'm still standing in this room.

Similarly, Joel found himself in the collection room, thinking:

"Okay, there's someone behind the wall waiting for me to hand this cup to them." . . . You're like, "How much time is this supposed to take me?" . . . You're thinking, "Okay, if I do this too quick, am I going to get laughed at? If I do this—how long should I—? Or should I just wait around? Should I spend a half hour trying to do this, or ten minutes, or an hour?" . . . No one's going to give you parameters like "Oh. Okay. You come in here and view whatever you want to view as far as movies or whatever. There's printed literature. Do whatever you want to do. Take your time." No one's going to tell you what it usually takes; no one's going to give you any kind of parameters. I wouldn't expect anyone to do that, I guess, because it's such an individual thing. But by the same token, you're just standing there going, "All right, this is kind of gross."

Both Kevin and Joel wanted to prove their masculinity in a respectable way and avoid getting laughed at. Joel's hypothetical description of how the clinic experience might go, with someone who welcomes patients, provides instruction, and tries to put patients at ease, is revealing. Though he sees how that would have made his experience more comfortable, he concedes that he "wouldn't expect anyone to do that." Joel understands that if clinic staff were to try to make the experience better for patients by presenting instructions and extending some sympathy, they would be overlooking and violating important masculine norms regarding sexual prowess and male autonomy.

Kevin reported that once he had collected his semen, he wandered the halls with the cup in his hand, trying to find the man who had issued him the cup. When he found the drop-off desk for the cup, he faced another disconcerting experience: "After, you have to fill a form out with the time that this happened. So you have to kind of watch the clock, and then it says, 'How did you do this? Masturbation or other?' And so I sat there for a while thinking, 'What in the hell is "other"?' I've never had an option. I almost put 'other' just to see what the look on their face—I don't know."

Technically, "other" applies to surgical techniques for procuring fresh sperm, such as electroejaculation, used for patients with spinal cord injuries, for example. However, Kevin's reaction to the question captures some of the pressure men feel to intuitively know and understand all things sexual.

While I was visiting one clinic, the specialist I was shadowing allowed me to visit the newly refurbished semen collection room. He confessed that a few years earlier, a journalist from a men's health magazine had come to tour the clinic and later, in his column, facetiously described the collection room as being as cozy as a public restroom with *Good Housekeeping* magazines. The doctor proudly showed off the new leather loveseat, the coffee table with pornographic magazines, and the television set and DVD player with a collection of adult videos. Despite the upgrades, however, the tiny room with fluorescent lighting was still cold, sparse, and clinical.

During my fieldwork I toured a sperm bank that had three rooms dedicated to semen collection. In stark contrast to the medical facilities that I visited, each of these collection rooms had soft, plush furniture and a high-end entertainment system. The rooms were wallpapered with pornographic images. The overhead fluorescent lights were off, and soft lamps provided a warm atmosphere. The lucrative sperm-banking industry likely has more cash to create and furnish collection rooms than cost-saving medical clinics do. Sperm banks are also more dedicated to creating a comfortable experience for men, one that will encourage donors to return again and again. It is worth noting that during my fieldwork, the only female doctor I shadowed was in the process of designing a new men's health clinic where she would be the director. The intended semen collection room, which I toured while it was still under construction, was the size of a home family room, and no expense had been spared in the interior decorating and furnishing. The concept, as the doctor explained it, was that couples could be in the room together, and wives could help their husbands provide a sample in a homelike setting.

In clinics, semen collections not only are used for diagnostic purposes but also are necessary for some treatment protocols, such as IVF and IUI. While I was shadowing one male infertility specialist, he received a phone call from the medical staff at the IVF clinic located in the same hospital. The IVF team had just completed an egg retrieval on a female patient and needed to move forward with IVF using fresh sperm from the husband. Unfortunately, presumably owing to all of the pressure of the moment, the husband could not perform. The male infertility specialist agreed to extract sperm from the testicles, so the couple were sent over to the male infertility clinic. The specialist described the situation to his office staff so that they could prepare a room for the procedure. When the couple arrived, the all-female staff made weak attempts to muffle their snickers and giggles, which were only exacerbated by the frantic wailing and carrying-on of the patient's wife in the waiting room. From all appearances, the staff was enormously amused by the man's inability to perform and by his wife's angst. At a deeper level, their laughter also revealed the embarrassment, discomfort, and even irritation that people feel when witnessing the violation of strong social norms. What kind of man, after all, would prefer being stabbed in the testicle with a wide needle over the presumed pleasure of masturbation?

After Kevin finished describing his own harrowing experience at the laboratory, he concluded, "These people (clinic personnel) become so callous to it. They don't realize how traumatic it is for the person standing there holding the cup." Submitting to a sperm test is a test of masculinity. The simple technology of the small plastic semen cup reflects this fact. Assumptions about men's inherent, all-knowing sexual abilities to perform anytime, anywhere facilitate the general lack of attention, innovation, and design given to semen collection practices. In an age when we refer to our automobiles and smartphones as "sexy" technologies, men's experiences with semen collection show that the technologies used for sexual purposes are incredibly unsexy and frustrating. The primitive design of the semen collection cup reveals the slow progress of male reproductive medicine and the unqualified acceptance of the hot man thesis in our culture.

I do not advocate electroejaculation for all men or any other form of hypertechnologization, but I do wonder whether we could devise a more user-friendly tool. Why not use a condom[7] or balloon to avoid spillage? Why not provide instructions? At the very least, we might acknowledge that semen collection can be humiliating and degrading for some men. As a simple thought exercise, can we imagine a situation in which a woman would be expected to reach orgasm for medical purposes? The very idea is preposterous, breaching all of our social norms around female sexuality. If for some reason orgasm on command was medically necessary for women, how might institutional practices differ? Would women be given more time, more space, more privacy, more comfort? Would women be expected to find the experience fun? The requisite semen collection and the lack of attention paid to it illustrate that the medical establishment does not just accept the hot man thesis; it relies on it for the system to work. The fact that every day new patients to the system face such expectations to perform only perpetuates the masculine norms of male sexuality.

Medical Metaphors

The semen collection cup is a very tangible object with a strong connection to masculine gender ideologies. Now I turn to the intangible metaphorical objects that have a place in medical language in the interactions between doctors and patients. Anthropologist Emily Martin's very important work *The Woman in the Body: A Cultural Analysis of Reproduction* calls attention to the many systems and objects that have been used to analogize women's bodies and bodily functions in medical discourse over the past 150 years.[8] For example, in the nineteenth century, female reproductive functions were described in terms of capitalist calculations of saving and spending, and the body was described as being like a small business with profits and losses.[9] During the Industrial Revolution, the female body was a microcosmic industrial society. Its systems and organs were compared to telephone, police, and sewer systems; appliances; laboratories; assembly-line factories; and radio transmitters.[10] These metaphors served as simple and efficient ways to describe complicated biological processes in terms that carried the cultural values of the day. For a rising industrial society, the uterus was a productive "machine," and pregnancy, labor, and childbirth were hailed as the prime achievements of the female body.[11]

Consequently, capitalist and industrial metaphors pathologized normal and healthy aspects of women's reproductive lives, such as menstruation and menopause. Menstruation meant failed production, and menopause marked the female body as a failed business, a disused factory, and an idle machine. From a feminist perspective these highly mechanical masculine metaphors, created by and shared among male practitioners and scholars, portrayed any female body that was not actively reproducing as a failure and a waste. Because Martin analyzed medical and biological texts, her work sheds light on how doctors and biologists have used metaphors to communicate with each other regarding all aspects of female reproduction. Here, I examine the metaphors that practitioners use to explain male infertility issues to their patients. Like Martin, I take a feminist approach to understanding the gender ideology embedded in these metaphors. However, in contrast to Martin's work, I find that mechanical metaphors are used to bolster gender identities among male infertility patients.

One of the most common metaphors for male reproduction that I heard in appointments with patients was the factory/bridge metaphor. According to this analogy, the male genitals are composed of factories and bridges. The job of a male infertility specialist, as explained to patients, is to determine whether a patient's poor semen results are due to a problem in the factories or some trouble with the bridges. The testicles are the factories where sperm are produced. Factory production of sperm may be inhibited by diseases, varicoceles, trauma, exposure to heat, drugs, toxins, chemotherapy or radiation, hormone imbalances, or chromosomal disorders. The bridges of the male genitals primarily refer to the vasa deferentia, more popularly known as "the vas" (singular) in lay terminology, the part that gets snipped or cauterized in a vasectomy. Just as most men typically have two testicles, there are two vasa deferentia. These are small tubules that carry sperm from the epididymides, just outside the testicles, to the seminal vesicles during ejaculation. Bridge problems include issues such as anejaculation, retrograde ejaculation, obstructions, or congenital absence of the vas deferens.

In her study of female reproduction, Martin posits that medical experts' use of factory metaphors detaches women from their own bodily experiences in detrimental ways. In her extensive Marxist analysis of childbirth, women as laborers are often alienated from the means of production—their own bodies—as well as the goods that they produce—namely, babies. In the case of male infertility, however, the factory and bridge metaphor is employed to stabilize masculine identities and build trust between doctors and patients. A factory is a highly technologized site for mass production; a bridge is a crowning achievement in architecture and construction. Though trouble in the genitals is never good news, the language of factories and bridges provides easily identifiable masculine metaphors that are used to help men to understand their bodies. Male patients quickly grasp the metaphor and accept their bodies as a system of technologies. Human-made technology, in contrast to organic biology, is calculable, predictable, reliable, and reparable. In Chapter 4, I discuss in greater depth the ways in which infertile men characterize infertility issues as a property of their bodies and the body as somehow different or distanced from the self. While it might seem devastating for patients to learn that their factories or bridges are down or out of commission, I would argue that such metaphors actually allow men to separate their infertility from their personal identities.

Male genitals are complex, and spermatogenesis, the generation and development of sperm, is a complicated process. Medical metaphors use lay terms to simplify complex systems, so the factory/

bridge metaphor is intentionally reductive. In addition to the testicles and vasa deferentia, the pathway of sperm includes the epididymides, seminal vesicles, ejaculatory duct, and urethra, all of which play key roles in fertility but are difficult to categorize as solely a factory or solely a bridge. Issues with close bodily neighbors, such as the prostate and the bladder, can also complicate fertility. The epididymis, as one specific example, is a long passageway or bridge for sperm. It also serves a factory function, because it is where sperm cells undergo maturation processes that enable them to swim and fertilize an egg. Once developed, sperm are stored in the epididymides for up to three months. Though the primary function of the epididymides is to store sperm, no one uses a metaphor of the genitals as a holding tank, a storage closet, a waiting room, or a prison cell. What is masculine about sperm being trapped, waiting to get lucky or die of old age? The metaphor of the factory/bridge works because it celebrates technological achievement. It invokes movement, action, production, and progress, which are masculine and empowering.

One male doctor I shadowed uses mechanical metaphors about cars, planes, and motorcycles to explain diagnoses to patients. For example, he tells patients, "The tests show the engine needs fuel. Fuel is hormones, LH and FSH. I'm trying to figure out if your engine's running and your exhaust is blocked or whether your engine's not running and your exhaust is open. . . . I can fix exhaust, but it's hard to fix engines."

This metaphor depicts the male body as a machine with mechanical parts and an energy source. The doctor thus frames the body as a system of interchangeable technological parts. While engines, or testicles, can be difficult to replace or repair, there are several options for repairing blocked exhaust and allowing the transportation of sperm. This analogy sets up the doctor as a mechanic to service the patient's body. Low sperm counts indicate that there is some function in the testicles. Zero sperm counts are rare, but even in those cases the testicles are often still producing sperm. In other words, completely defunct "engines" are extremely rare, and the doctor will likely be able to help with the blocked exhaust.

As the doctor explained to me, "Guys are car people. . . . I think I come out with metaphors that they can relate to. . . . Then they'll understand and will be more empowered and less weak." Indeed, this metaphor is empowering for most men. In the hierarchy of automobile parts, the motor is more important than any exhaust valves and pipes, so in the car analogy the testicles are more valuable than any other parts of the male genitals. By introducing this metaphor in clinical interactions early in the diagnostic process, the doctor carves out an opportunity to congratulate the patient later when the doctor confirms a smoothly running engine, even if there might be a problem with the exhaust. Of course, the communicative power of the analogy depends entirely upon the patient's having an interest in or understanding of automotives. The analogy is not particularly complicated, but in the clinical encounters that I observed, the doctor rattled off this and other mechanical metaphors very quickly with no time for questions or explanation. This doctor assumes the stereotype that "guys are car people," and by repeating mechanical analogies, he perpetuates this stereotype.

Another doctor I shadowed, an avid baseball fan, uses baseball analogies in his conversations with patients. In the language of "bottom of the ninth" and "runner on second," he describes diagnoses and the goals of treatment options to his patients. The doctor explained to me how sports analogies help him build rapport with his patients, especially since his clinic is located in a demographically working-class area. Doctors are not simply striving to explain biology to patients. In the sociological language of identity, they are simultaneously striving to downplay individual differences, like socioeconomic statuses, and emphasize sameness, like gender. Sports analogies aid in breaking down or neutralizing the class distinction between the doctor and patient and highlight the masculine interests the two share. The doctor added that he can even talk "street slang" with blue-collar patients, though I never had an opportunity to observe this in the clinic.

A third doctor I shadowed warned patients who were prescribed hormone drugs to improve their testosterone production that side effects would include "the urge to hit a ball really hard or drive really fast." The doctor and his patients always shared big grins when he said this as though it made the drug therapy sound more appealing, as though it could actually increase biological masculinity. It was unclear and is probably scientifically debatable whether such claims are literal or metaphorical. Either way, references to sports and cars are intended to make men more comfortable and protect them from a potentially emasculating experience. Doctors draw upon stereotypically masculine objects and processes to help their male patients understand reproduction and infertility.[12] The doctors I observed who use metaphors about cars and sports were all male, suggesting that masculine metaphors serve as catalysts in "male bonding" between doctors and patients. Their usage expedites the development of friendship and trust by establishing "sameness" between doctors and patients. When doctors talk about commonly understood masculine objects and hobbies, they communicate: *We are both men. We are alike. We understand each other. You can trust me.*

The Physical Examination

The research protocol for this study, as approved by the ethics committees that supervised it, required that I not be present during the physical examination portion of patients' consultations with male infertility specialists. At the first clinic I visited, the specialist, a man, reminded me to step out for physical examinations, cautioning me that my presence as a woman might cause a patient to have an erection, which would be embarrassing for everyone in the room. A few months later, I shadowed a male infertility specialist who is a woman. I relayed to her the brief conversation with the first doctor and asked her whether she ever worried that her presence, as well as the physical contact she made with patients, might be sexually arousing for men. The woman doctor assured me that the first doctor was being ridiculous and there was no cause for concern. No matter which doctor was right (and this probably depends on the circumstances), the male doctor's request demonstrates that managing patient comfort is also about managing male sexuality.

The involuntary erection highlights one of the great paradoxes of masculine performance. Masculinity is defined by control and power, but according to the hot man thesis, the male sexual appetite is uncontrollable. To demonstrate their masculinity, men must be able to physically perform on command, but sometimes the body performs on its own, against the wishes of the self. Men live with this constant trade-off of power between the self and the body. If I, as a woman, witnessed an erection that I had triggered, that would put me in the power position, subverting the well-established gendered power dynamic that exists between men and women, particularly between men and women who are practically strangers. My presence could expose male vulnerability and threaten masculinity. Though there may be settings in which it is socially acceptable for women to exert sexual power over men, the doctor's office is not that place. Causing an erection could, in a Freudian interpretation, be my symbolic way of taking the phallus, and as the first doctor pointed out, that could be embarrassing for everyone.

The physical examination conducted by male infertility specialists entails visually examining the size and shape of the testicles and palpating the scrotum manually to make sure all of the organs and tubes are properly connected. Though such examinations are usually not painful, the manhandling and intimacy of contact are assumed to be uncomfortable for patients. One doctor described his method for physical examinations as "businesslike": very fast and no talking. Other doctors carefully narrated their actions throughout the examination to reassure and calm patients. Examinations are very quick, described by one patient as "a couple seconds." I usually waited behind examining room doors for no more than two or three minutes before being invited back in to observe the remainder of the appointment. Just as the first doctor I shadowed worried about my presence as a sexually arousing factor, the speed of the examination likely prevents any homoerotic perceptions of the experience by patients. The majority of male infertility specialists are men, and medicine may be the only sphere in which such physically intimate touching is socially sanctioned between heterosexual men.

Aesthetics of the body are fundamental to our cultural beliefs about masculinity and femininity. In our image-obsessed culture, size matters.[13] In most cases of infertility, the genitals appear properly formed and average in size. However, in some cases, infertility is caused by deformed genitals, or a lack of sperm production results in unusually small testicles. When the genitals do appear normal, doctors are diligent about reassuring patients that everything looks fine. One doctor I interviewed told me, "I tell my patients they have big balls." He claimed that men love to hear this, and it is his way to protect his patients' masculinity. In another clinic, I observed a doctor who regularly told patients, after the physical examination, "Other than your really short penis, everything looks fine!" Then he would smile at the wife, if she was present, and laugh heartily. He told me privately that using this kind of humor helps to diffuse the anxiety of the situation and reassures patients that they are still manly and normal. One patient confided that he could tell that the doctor was joking but his wife was "not amused." Many patients appeared confused by the jab, and it took them a moment to grasp the doctor's humor.

Diagnosis

While masculine metaphors and humor may help doctors to establish rapport with patients, it also obscures the severity of patients' infertility issues. Doctors believe that infertility is devastating to men and are very careful to break bad news gently. Though some doctors seem oblivious to the discomfort and humiliation that semen collection may cause patients, many are extremely conscientious and deliberate about protecting their patients' masculinity in direct clinical interactions. When patients' sperm quality is found to be subpar for achieving conception, practitioners strive to rescue the presumably fractured masculine identities of their patients. Doctors manage how information gleaned from the semen analysis is disseminated to patients so as not to offend, embarrass, or distress them. In their efforts to protect masculinity, doctors are cautious about how they use words such as "infertile" and "infertility" with their patients.

According to the American Society for Reproductive Medicine and the doctors I interviewed, the term "infertility" is clinically defined as no conception after at least 12 months of unprotected intercourse.[14] Doctors refer to themselves as "infertility specialists" in interviews, on websites, in brochures, and on business cards. When discussing patient cases, doctors refer to patients as infertile. Yet in clinical encounters I never heard a doctor tell a patient, "You are infertile" or "You have infertility." The word "infertility" is used in the abstract, as in "Sometimes in infertility patients, we see . . ." or "Infertility may be a result of . . . ." One doctor told me that he preferred to use the term "subfertile" with patients, but when pressed to explain the difference between infertility and subfertility, he confessed that they meant virtually the same thing. "Subfertility" is a term that is sometimes used to describe a low sperm count, while "infertility" refers to the inability to achieve pregnancy after a year of unprotected sex. So technically, a man could be infertile because of his subfertility. The terms do not provide much clarification.

Rather than labeling patients as infertile, doctors deliver diagnoses in terms of semen analysis results. They approach patients with information such as "Your count was 10 million; we want to see 20 million" or "During the exam I felt a grade three varicocele, which could explain your low sperm count." While the information is straightforward, patients usually have no frame of reference for interpreting the significance of results, and they look to the doctors to tell them how serious their situation is. Doctors methodically explain the next step in diagnostic tests or treatment options. For example, a doctor might say, "Looks like you had a zero sperm count on your last semen analysis. Let's try another one. If it's still zero, I won't really know if you're producing sperm until I can get in the testicles and look around a little bit." Or the doctor might say, "Based on your sperm count, we can do a varicocele repair, or you can try IUI or IVF." Instead of hearing recognizably bad news, patients are told what they should anticipate doing next.

The terminologies that doctors use affect how patients' view their inability to conceive, their hope for treatment success, and their likelihood for pursuing treatments. Most patients, as I learned through my interviews, do not define infertility in the clinical way. Instead, many described infertility as the inability ever to have children, even with medical intervention, a point that I explore in greater detail in Chapter 4. Had doctors given patients the diagnosis of "infertile" without explicitly clarifying the clinical definition, patients might have believed that they were out of medical options. When patients hear medical options in lieu of an infertility diagnosis, they maintain hope that pregnancy is still attainable and are likely to proceed with treatments. How language is used—or, in the case of "infertility," not used—demonstrates the frailty of masculinity as understood by practitioners. In interviews, a few doctors told me that a diagnosis of male infertility is emasculating and devastating for men, could ruin marriages, and might even lead men to commit suicide. While some men find infertility devastating, there are no conclusive data regarding its bearing on divorce or suicide rates.[15] Evidence does show that men in general are more likely to commit suicide than are women, and mental health professionals chalk this up to higher levels of perceived social humiliation. Doctors' assumption that infertility drives men to suicide reflects their own personal views about how humiliating infertility must be for their patients. Doctors, who see letting patients down easily as part of their job, believe that they must safeguard men's masculinity in the face of adversity.

As the careful use of masculine metaphors and medical language in the clinic demonstrates, infertility is a socially constructed disease. Infertility is also a field in which other diseases get constructed. In male infertility clinics, the fertility-impeding effects of diseases such as diabetes and cancer are brought into focus. Erectile dysfunction, a disorder that was long considered psychogenic and called impotence, is relegitimized as a biological disease because it not only hinders sexual performance but also prevents reproduction. Accidents that cause spinal cord injuries or trauma to the genitals are recast as infertility problems that hamper patients' abilities to generate sperm, have an erection, or ejaculate.

Klinefelter's syndrome, a disorder that is often first diagnosed in male infertility clinics, is constructed through the interactions of doctors and patients. Men with low or zero sperm counts undergo blood tests to detect genetic or chromosomal anomalies. While women are generally born with two X chromosomes and most men have one X chromosome inherited from their mother and one Y chromosome inherited from their father, individuals with Klinefelter's syndrome are born with two X, or female, chromosomes and one Y chromosome. Only one in five hundred to a thousand men is born with the extra chromosome, and the symptoms of the syndrome usually go unnoticed until after the onset of puberty. Many XXY males are born with normal male genitals, are raised as boys, and identify as men in adulthood. However, a subset of people with Klinefelter's syndrome self-identify as intersex persons or as having a sex development disorder. Like all gender categories, "intersex" is socially constructed.[16] Cases of Klinefelter's syndrome that are discovered in male infertility clinics present a complex intersection where socially constructed gender and disease categories come crashing together.

In one case that I observed in the clinic, a doctor informed a patient that his blood work showed that he had an extra X chromosome, indicative of Klinefelter's syndrome, which would explain the patient's low sperm production. Then the doctor sized up the patient and related that signs of Klinefelter's syndrome might also include being tall and lanky, characteristics of this patient's height and build. Other possible symptoms that the doctor mentioned included extra breast tissue or a waist and hips that were more like those of a woman. At this the patient blushed, and the doctor quickly reassured the patient that he is a man and the extra X chromosome means nothing. From a sociological perspective, what does that extra female chromosome mean?

The patient was a happily married heterosexual man, and his wife was with him at the appointment. He cherished a very hetero-normative family ideal and was seeking infertility treatments so that he and his wife could realize their dream of biological parenthood. Biologically and socially, he had the requisite equipment and lifestyle to pass as a man. The doctor protected the patient's masculinity by respecting his obvious male gender identity and offering hope for pregnancy through reproductive technologies. It's what the doctor did *not* say that illustrates how gender and disease get constructed in the clinic. The doctor did not tell the patient some of the more emas-culating symptoms of Klinefelter's syndrome, which might include low testosterone, smaller than average testicles and penis, weaker muscles and bones, low energy, and a higher risk for disorders that are more common in women, such as breast cancer, autoimmune disorders, and osteoporosis. The doctor did not introduce inter-sexuality into the conversation or invite the patient to reconsider his gender identification. The doctor established that the extra X chromosome means nothing by sharing nothing. By filtering infor-mation for his patient, the doctor was participating in the social con-struction of gender. As this patient's case demonstrates, individuals have the power to live out their own personally selected and socially constructed gender identity despite any ambiguous aspects of their biological sex category.

Wives in the Clinic: The Information Keepers

Male infertility specialists not only participate in the social construc-tion of men and masculinity but also take part in the social construc-tion of women and femininity. Before a patient's first appointment, male infertility specialists request that the patient's wife accompany him to the initial consultation with all of her own medical records in hand. The wife's medical history and infertility workup provide important information for making treatment plans. In cases in which the wife has no infertility issues, the couple may be encouraged to pursue male-focused treatments such as surgery. When female in-fertility issues are also a factor, the couple may be advised to begin with more female-focused treatments, such as IUI or IVF. The wife's medical information is necessary for decision making, but doctors also know that wives provide helpful information regarding their husbands' health status and history that is equally important. At one clinic I visited, a woman on staff, a genetic counselor, assessed the important role that wives play as "the keepers of medical information." She explained that wives are typically responsible for everything from scheduling husbands' appointments to keeping track of their husbands' family medical histories. During appointments, patients are asked an array of questions, such as *How many months have you been trying to get pregnant? What genetic diseases run in your family? What medications are you currently taking?* Patients regularly look to their wives to answer these questions.

In one case that I observed, a patient pointed to his wife when asked about the quality of his ejaculate. With careful thought and consideration the young wife described the milky-white color and sticky texture of her husband's semen. Grateful for her frankness, the doctor probed further. *Did the ejaculate ever look yellowish? Was it clear or opaque? Thick or watery? How much semen is ejaculated at one time?* Together, the doctor and wife tried to determine whether the ejaculate was discolored in any way, a possible sign of infection, or whether the thickness or low volume of the ejaculate was hampering fertilization. The wife was the authority in the room, equipped with expert knowledge that the doctor needed, while the patient sat quietly on the examining table.

Patients often turn to their wives to ask about their own family and personal health histories, with questions such as *What was that disease my uncle had? How old was my mom when she died? Did I ever have chicken pox, measles, or mumps as a kid?* In a typical case that I observed, a male infertility specialist met with a couple who had previously been treated by a general urologist. In the following conversation, the doctor gathered information about the medical history and health status of the husband, Tom:

Doctor: No sperm seen in semen analysis?
Tom: No.
Doctor: Who suggested you come here?
Wife: We did. Tom's urologist basically said, "You're done."
Doctor (to husband): Based on your—[*turns to wife*] his FSH [hormone level]?

Wife: Yes.

Doctor (to husband): Did you have any genetic testing?

Wife: No.

Doctor: No other medical problems? How much Vitamin E do you take?

Tom: Ask her.

Wife: Whatever is in a multivitamin plus 400 mg.

As this dialogue demonstrates, three can be a crowd, but wives are integral to the system. Sometimes the wife interjected when questions were directed to her husband. Although the doctor attempted to direct questions to the husband, he knew that the wife had the answers. The doctor and husband relied on the wife to provide necessary information. From all appearances the husband did not seem to mind his wife's participation in the appointment. When the patient said, "Ask her," he did not sound resentful or facetious; he seemed to appreciate that his wife had the knowledge. She did not provide information that the husband did not have access to; she simply served as the information keeper.

Serving as information keepers puts women in an awkward position. At least three doctors with whom I worked described their male patients as being "drug in" by their wives, a word choice suggesting that wives are overly domineering. If patients arrive alone, doctors express disappointment or chastise patients for not bringing their wives, because the doctors rely on wives for information. Yet during fieldwork I detected some contempt on the part of doctors toward the wives. As I observed, male infertility specialists try to maintain eye contact with male patients; they occasionally roll their eyes, cringe, sigh, or turn testy when patients' wives interrupt with questions or comments. One doctor told me, "If the wife talks, I tell her to let him talk." In an appointment, I watched another doctor tell an inquisitive wife, "Be quiet! I'll tell you everything you need to know." A few doctors complained that wives are annoyingly impatient, because, as one doctor explained, "they want to get pregnant yesterday." Husbands and doctors count on wives to remember and recount information, but women's role beyond data storage system is unclear.

Gender scholars point out that gender stereotypes entail both positive prescriptions, aspects of gender men and women *should* display, and negative proscriptions, aspects of gender that they *should not* display.[17] Doctors' depictions of women as domineering, meddling, overbearing, impatient, talkative, and inquisitive are all criticisms of women not heeding the proscriptions of their gender type. Women's expert role in the clinic setting throws off some well-established power dynamics. Describing women as domineering or downright annoying is an easy way to belittle women whose knowledge or behavior men perceive to be threatening. According to traditional gender roles, women should play the more subordinate role in the marital power dynamic. And in the world of medicine, doctors are the experts, not the patients or their wives. In their characterizations of women, I heard doctors' efforts to defend masculinity, their own as well as their patients, which may be threatened by women's active involvement in the clinic.

Keeping medical information is maternal work. Within households, women are primarily responsible for keeping track of the medical information for their families (husbands, kids, grandparents), including family histories, records, and appointments. As wives accompany their husbands to medical clinics, sit in on appointments, and answer questions, they can appear motherly, as if they are accompanying a child to a doctor appointment. A few wives in the study, busy with their own careers and medical appointments, had no interest in attending their husbands' appointments, trusting that their husbands could go by themselves and schedule their own appointments. Doctors saw these wives as evasive and unhelpful. The work of keeping information is overlooked and disregarded as expert labor. The situation presents a double bind for women: Those who do the work are expected to downplay their expertise, while those who will not do the work are judged to be slacking in their domestic responsibilities.

At least one doctor I shadowed believed that women were less likely to understand the biological causes of infertility than were their husbands because, as the doctor explained to me, men have greater aptitude for understanding science. In interviews, however, husbands regularly reported that their wives had conducted more research and were much more knowledgeable on the topic of infertility than they were. Scheduling appointments, keeping track of medical histories and records, researching medical conditions and treatments, and contacting health insurance companies requires time, diligence, organization, attentiveness, and background knowledge. These duties constitute another aspect of household management that gets relegated to women as part of what sociologist Arlie Hochschild calls women's "second shift."[18] When the family enjoys good health, this work goes unrecognized, unappreciated, and unrewarded, demonstrating the inequality in the gender division of labor and unequal power relations in marriage.

Nonetheless, when health issues arise, as in cases of infertility, the labor of keeping information entitles women to a very influential role in decision making. Patients and wives arrive at appointments anxious to get a professional opinion and with a healthy dose of deference for and trust in their doctor's advice. When couples return home after appointments, husbands look to their wives for information, feedback, support, and advice. Some male infertility specialists may be distrustful of patients' wives, particularly if the specialists see themselves in competition with the gynecologists and REs whom the wives concurrently consult. Male infertility specialists have only the duration of their appointments with patients (approximately fifteen minutes) to influence the patients' plans for treatment. At one level, wives symbolize and embody the competition between male and female infertility specialists, and male infertility specialists may worry that patients' wives have already been indoctrinated by REs to pursue strictly female-focused treatments. At a deeper level, doctors may see wives as competing authority figures who have already earned the loyalty of their male patients and have the power to dissuade the patients from following the doctors' recommendations. Indeed, men are more likely to follow their wives' wishes than their doctors' orders. What many male infertility specialists do not realize, however, is that wives are often their greatest allies. In private interviews with patients and wives, it became clear that women often encourage their husbands to pursue male-focused treatments before they will subject themselves to more female-focused regimens, a discovery that I explore in Chapter 5.

Earlier in this chapter, I mentioned that the one male infertility specialist I shadowed who is a woman was designing a male health center where wives could join their husbands in the semen collection room. While other male infertility specialists were not quite sure how to deal with patients' wives in the clinic, this particular doctor has a very specific role in mind for wives in the infertility journey. Starting with couples' first introduction to the clinic, she wants wives to see themselves as more than accessories and to feel integral to every step of the process. Men are not the sole participant in the clinic experience, and the roles of men and women meld into a single identity: a patient-couple. While shadowing this doctor, I did not hear penis jokes or sports analogies, and no patient was told that his balls were big or his penis was short. Any overt constructions of stereotypical forms of masculinity were absent from that particular clinic. Any attempts at male bonding might easily fall flat, since the doctor is a woman. Instead, wives serve as the liaisons through which this doctor builds her rapport with patients. By promoting marital unity, she allies herself with both women and men. By conceptualizing male infertility as a *couple*'s issue, the doctor is also able to downplay the threat of male infertility to masculinity and shore up male patients' masculine identities.

Urology: A Masculine Institution

At a medical seminar that I attended, where I was one of half a dozen women in a sea of men, a well-respected pioneer of male infertility medicine began his "How to Treat Male Infertility" PowerPoint presentation with a picture of himself in his much younger days decked out in a military flight suit standing proudly beside an F4 Phantom aircraft. He described how he had launched his medical career as a flight surgeon in the U.S. Air Force and followed up by saying, "It used to be my butt on the line." Advancing to the next slide, a more recent picture of him suited up in scrubs in an operating room, one hand confidently placed on a large and imposing surgical microscope, he quipped, "Now it's *their* balls!" The audience got a good laugh out of his joke, which in one simple line and two images invoked the military, technology, patriotism, duty, sacrifice, heroism, risk, knowledge, and power over others' most masculine body parts. Gender scholars note that like people, institutions take on masculine and feminine qualities.[19] Medicine, the military, and Wall Street are a few establishments that are identified as masculine institutions, because men historically created and dominated these arenas and their organizational cultures are embedded with masculine values like domination, competition, and individual autonomy and achievement. Some medical specialties in which women have made significant inroads, such as pediatrics, have become feminized over time, while other fields, such as urology, are still a man's world.

At another medical seminar the presenting doctor, a man, concluded his presentation by playing a beer commercial depicting a beautiful woman who engages in clandestine sex with her male doctor to overcome her husband's infertility. The short sketch mocked the infertile patient and extolled the hegemonic superiority, sexual prowess, and "get her done" reliability of the doctor. In a spirit of jest, the commercial reaffirmed the heterosexuality, masculinity, competence, and superior status of the medical professionals who were attending the meeting. The jokes shared by male infertility doctors seem to fit suitably in a field where clinical talk of balls, penises, and sex abound, and they serve a distinct purpose. Humor helps to protect professional masculinity as it demonstrates ease in discussing very private, intimate, and embarrassing bathroom functions and sexual issues. In another society, perhaps in another cultural frame, we might perceive the same work of handling genitals as dirty and degrading or even homoerotic. The use of humor allows doctors to emphasize their specialized knowledge and rise above the indignities of their work.

Perhaps not surprisingly, the only two women doctors in attendance at the medical seminar did not crack smiles as the overwhelmingly male audience laughed along with the beer commercial. Fewer than 10 percent of urologists in the United States are women,[20] and the proportion is even lower among male infertility specialists. During my fieldwork I met a newly minted urologist, a young woman, who was completing her residency alongside the specialist I was shadowing. In one candid conversation she acknowledged how unusual it was for her to choose a career in such a male-dominated field, but she explained that she had a unique appreciation for the fraternity and humor that are characteristic of urology, which other women doctors often find off-putting and alienating. The institutional masculinity of urology is preserved by the simple fact that most urologists in the United States, historically and today, are men who meet the requirements of hegemonic masculinity: white, wealthy, and well-educated, from middle- and upper-class backgrounds. One doctor I shadowed expressed his gratitude for a much older male infertility specialist who had been "like a father figure" to him. Doctors described their training backgrounds to me in patrilineal terms, linking their professional genealogy back to one of a handful of well-known doctors, the major branches of the male infertility family tree, and the group of men who pioneered the field in the 1970s. From the cherished patriarchal lineages of inherited expertise to the sexualized humor, urology is a field dripping with testosterone.

Traditional notions of masculinity saturate the world of male infertility medicine. From the jokes that doctors share with each other to the metaphors they use to educate their patients, they subscribe to and perpetuate very traditional ideas about men and women and about masculinity and femininity. Urology is a haven in which stereotypical forms of gender thrive and flourish. Ironically, the gender ideology that doctors invoke in their interactions with each other and with patients is the basis of the gender ideology that they curse for encumbering the progress of male infertility medicine. Male infertility often goes unrecognized and untreated owing to the prevalent social assumption that women are primarily responsible for infertility. These doctors are calling for a major cultural shift in society's gender thinking when they argue for increased assessments and treatment of male infertility conditions. The dilemma for doctors, then, is how to promote public awareness of male reproductive issues, like male infertility, while fulfilling their self-professed role as the protectors of masculinity.

The Gender System

My reason for highlighting the hypermasculine milieu of urology is to shed light on the stability of the gender system. The concept of the gender system, as developed by Cecilia Ridgeway and Shelley Correll and introduced in Chapter 1, is a multi-tiered theoretical apparatus that operates at the macro level of cultural beliefs and the distribution of resources; the interactional level, where institutions and individuals engage; and the individual micro level, where personal selves and identities are formed. Traditional gender ideology, or "hegemonic gender beliefs," is the cement that holds the system together and braces it against sweeping social changes. Ridgeway and Correll raise the question *Why does gender inequality persist despite widespread efforts over the past several decades to eradicate it?* The scholars argue that when change is introduced at any one level of the gender system, the other levels of the system do not budge, making large-scale social changes in gender beliefs practically impossible.[21] And those sticky gender beliefs about how men and women should look, talk, think, and behave are what perpetuate gender inequality.

The case of male infertility illuminates some of the intricacies of the gender system, revealing how and why gender ideas continue to infiltrate institutions. Male infertility specialists, intentionally or inadvertently, serve as the last great defenders of traditional masculine norms, conventional heterosexual partnerships, biological fatherhood, and natural conception. They are the institutional authorities who complain that assisted reproductive technologies have reduced the role of husbands to the insignificant role of "sperm donors" within their own marriages and promote medical solutions that make "IBF" (in bed fertilization) possible in lieu of IVF. When IBF is ruled out as an option, specialists encourage men to undergo surgery before resorting to donor sperm. They reassure men with Klinefelter's syndrome that they are normal heterosexual men, and they cling to ideas that "guys are car people" and men are the more scientifically minded sex. The reason why patients' wives do not fit well in clinical interactions is because the urologist's office is a sacred masculine socializing space, where doctors teach men to rise above being "wild animals" and train men to take care of themselves and live up to their masculine duties. This is not to say that male infertility specialists necessarily oppose the alternative family-building options that single, lesbian, or gay parents pursue. Simply, they are authorities on heterosexual masculinity and the professional advocates of heterosexual men.

Cecilia Ridgeway argues that the more salient gender is to a situation, the greater are its effects on the behavior of the actors involved.[22] Furthermore, as Ridgeway points out, because gender ideology is understood to be so widely shared, actors like doctors are easily tempted to draw upon stereotypes, even when they do not personally agree with the stereotypes that they invoke.[23] Gender is the loudest, most salient, and most conspicuous aspect of male infertility patients' identities in the clinic, so doctors understandably fall into a very traditional language of gender with their patients. The ubiquitous language of gender provides convenient shorthand for doctors to communicate with patients. Masculine metaphors and penis jokes are used as social lubricant, presumed to make patients' clinical experiences more familiar and comfortable. Male infertility specialists rely on a very traditional heteronormative framework of hegemonic masculinity, biological fatherhood, and natural conception in order to be relevant. But for male infertility medical practice to be relevant, society has to get past outdated traditional gender ideology and accept that men share some responsibility in reproduction. The short-term benefits of subscribing to and invoking traditional gender ideology, such as efficiency in medical practice and expediting social relationships between patients and doctors, are not understood by medical practitioners as outweighing the long-term costs, such as the perpetuation of gender stereotypes, including the idea that reproduction is women's work. As they protect manhood and promote paternity, male infertility specialists become thoroughly invested in traditional gender ideology. When specialists invoke traditional notions of masculinity in everyday interactions, they bolster the gender system and foil their own goals of raising public awareness of men's roles in reproduction and encouraging the male partners in infertile couples to seek medical help.

In the following chapters, I describe the personal agency that individuals have in reconstructing and redefining their own ideas about gender, particularly when they face a crisis of masculinity such as male infertility. Individuals share in society's common cultural knowledge about gender but have the freedom to personally adopt some notions of gender and reject others. Do institutions and institutional figures such as doctors have the same liberty to select what pieces of the prevailing gender ideology they will embrace or reject? All institutions take part in the social construction of gender, and many institutions get away with a considerable amount of gender bending. For example, some institutions promote atypical connections between masculinity and fashion or femininity and sports. However, as long as male infertility specialists subscribe to prevailing gender ideology, they have very little leverage in promoting social change on the gender front, because gender ideology is grounded specifically in beliefs about men's and women's roles in reproduction.

Traditional gender ideology derives from an outdated and simplistic gender division of labor, in which men produce and women reproduce. According to this biological determinist model of gender relations, men evolved from the hunters in the wild of yesteryear into the breadwinners of the public sphere today. Meanwhile, women evolved physically and socially to reproduce better. Popular beliefs about men as the instrumentally competent, assertive, and independent sex and women as the emotionally expressive, nurturing, and sensitive sex are naturalized and elaborated from social understandings of sexed bodies, production, and reproduction. These long-held ideas about gender and reproduction continue to influence how male infertility is handled today. Some men avoid going to the doctor as a way to assert their strength and independence, so some men's fertility status is never properly assessed, and some medical practitioners push women toward infertility treatments even when a male factor is behind a couple's inability to conceive.

Male infertility specialists' desire to debunk the notion that women are responsible for all aspects of reproduction and to promote men's important role in reproduction requires unraveling layers of gender ideology, some of which doctors seem intent on maintaining. Male infertility specialists would like to push a new role for men as reproductive laborers, but it is trickier than that. They want society to understand that sometimes men *fail* in this role. Arguably, the lack of knowledge and awareness about male infertility in the broader culture is precisely what protects individual male patients' masculinity throughout their infertility journey. Childless men are less suspect than are childless women. When a couple cannot achieve pregnancy, it is the wife who feels the suspicion of others, the social stigma of childlessness, and the pressure to seek medical help and the wife who is more likely to internalize feelings of failure.[24] As I observed in male infertility clinics, doctors carefully tiptoe around words such as "infertile" and "infertility," congratulate men on their handsome genitals, and make big promises that the path toward natural conception and parenthood will be a short and painless jaunt. Male infertility specialists want to raise awareness of a disease that is defined by failure without the need for anyone to acknowledge that he is failing.

Like most medical doctors, male infertility specialists believe that their first priority is to help patients feel comfortable in the clinic and to educate them. In a crisis of masculinity like male infertility, this translates into preserving, protecting, bolstering, and shoring up male patients' personal sense of masculinity and manliness. As long as doctors' loyalties are to their patients, they remain loyal to— if not indentured by—the traditional gender system. As I discovered in male infertility clinics, rather than boldly breaking down static and traditional ideas of gender, male infertility specialists belong to a medical specialty that is steeped in a highly masculinized culture, which permeates interactions among professionals, is embedded in medical practices, and ultimately sustains the gender system. Doctors are very skilled and successful at escorting individuals through a private and personal crisis of masculinity. However, their consistent devotion to masculine norms makes male infertility specialists their own worst enemy in any broader move that they advocate toward social acceptance and education about men's central role in reproduction and the prevalence of male infertility.

Conclusion

Throughout this book I argue that the social processes of constructing gender and disease are inextricably linked in the case of male infertility. As doctors prescribe medicine, they reinforce cultural prescriptions of gender. As the simple semen collection cup demonstrates, ideas about male sexuality and masculinity are built into the structure, technology, and protocols of medical institutions. In clinical encounters between doctors, patients, and wives, gender norms are less bureaucratically and uniformly established, but these norms become institutionalized and perpetuated through such interactions. Male-oriented analogies are used to stabilize the clinic experience as a masculine one and to forge male bonds between doctors and patients. The male infertility clinic is a socializing space where men learn what they can expect from their bodies and how they should go about achieving their goals. Once they return to the privacy of their homes, men strive within their marriages, in their private thoughts, and amid their day-to-day careers and lives to make sense of their compromised fertility within a culture that prizes male virility, the ability to impregnate one's wife, and fatherhood. Infertility and masculinity continue to be negotiated, revised, and reproduced beyond the male infertility clinic.

Just a Medical Condition

·

"I literally dropped the phone and started crying," recalls Brandon about hearing the results of his mapping procedure. Mapping is one of a few techniques used by male infertility specialists to find undeveloped sperm in a patient's testicles when no sperm appears in his ejaculate. When two semen tests showed no sperm, the twenty-nine-year-old electrician decided to pursue the mapping procedure that his doctor touted as a less invasive alternative to other techniques. After administering some sedation and local anesthetic, doctors pulled the slack of Brandon's scrotum tightly behind his testicles until the two white egg-shaped organs were visible through the skin. Then they sliced through the scrotal skin, peeled back the outer layer of the testicles, and extracted seventeen tissue biopsies from each testicle with a needle. During and after the procedure, the doctors examined the testicular tissue under a microscope, searching for any tiny seeds of life.

A few days after the procedure, Brandon received a call from his wife, Emily, relaying the bad news from the doctor: There was no sign of sperm anywhere. Brandon cried. Then he called his brother and told him the results of the procedure. Next, Brandon made a three-way phone call to his mother and sister so that he could tell them both at the same time. When he heard his mother cry, Brandon began to cry again. Later, he did not hesitate to share the news of his "sterility" with his dirt biking buddies, all of whom he regards as very close, supportive friends. Brandon admitted, though, that over time, he and his wife began to withdraw from some of their friends and relatives who were busy having babies and seemed insensitive to Brandon and Emily's inability to conceive.

Doctors attribute Brandon's infertility to physical trauma incurred four years earlier in an automobile accident that nearly killed him and left him unable to walk for eight months. Brandon, however, attributes his infertility to God:

> For me, I feel like I'm getting punished. That's the way I feel about it. That's the way I look at it is, I'm getting punished. God is punishing me by not being able to have kids of my own because of everything that I've went through in my life. You know what I mean? I've been punished in some way. I've had some kind of accident or injury where all I do is suffer in pain. I hurt literally seven days a week, twenty-four hours a day. It's like another part of the pain. Instead of it being a physical pain, it's an internal pain. It's a hurt pain.[1]

During our conversation, Brandon recounted the emotional and physical pain related to his accident, his failed first marriage, abuse he suffered as a child, and a history of clinical depression and bipolar disorder. In some ways, infertility feels worse to him than the automobile accident after which doctors said he would never walk again. Then, he believed that he could prove his doctors wrong through sheer will power and physical fortitude, which he did. But infertility feels beyond his control. Brandon's struggle with infertility was compounded by financial troubles, family strife, his wife's infertility issues, and several failed IVF attempts using donor sperm. In interviews, Brandon shattered macho stereotypes of men keeping stiff upper lips as he tearfully poured out his feelings. Considering how easily Brandon expressed himself, it was surprising to hear his difficulty in defining infertility. Brandon answered, "Yes," when asked whether he had ever thought of himself as infertile. Yet when asked how he would define infertility, he responded blankly, "Basically, I don't really know."

All of the men interviewed for this book fit the clinical definition of the term "infertile." However, fully two-thirds of them claimed that they had never thought of themselves as infertile. Like Brandon, many of the men were unsure how to define infertility. A few of them recited the clinical definition of infertility: the inability to conceive after a year of trying. Several defined infertility as the inability to achieve pregnancy "naturally" or without medical assistance. Others said that infertility means that even with medical assistance, pregnancy is still not possible. Some descriptions of infertility were more vivid and graphic. Todd, a radio news director in his late thirties, remarked, "You kind of doubt the toughness of your penis or something . . . like the penis doesn't seem as cool as it used to." When Kevin, a pilot in his late twenties, was asked to define infertility, he responded thoughtfully, "If I was on an island with one million girls, we would all be dead within the next one hundred years, and there would be no one left on the island."

How men conceptualize and make sense of their inability to achieve pregnancy provides an instructive picture of how men engage in gender work. For Todd, infertility suggests a downgrade in the status of his body. For Kevin, infertility portends the end of civilization. Many men in this study understood infertility as potentially emasculating but explained that their own diagnosis or situation was somehow unique and therefore less threatening. Sociologists, anthropologists, psychologists, and philosophers have long examined "meaning making," the human propensity to make sense of our experiences, lives, and world.[2] To hear men strive to create and understand the meaning of their infertility experience is to hear them articulate the meanings of manhood and how one navigates a crisis of masculinity. As men redefine, reconceptualize, and reconstruct infertility, they narrate the process of gender work in which they are engaged and take part in the social (re)construction of gender.

Twenty-three-year-old Keith, a radar specialist in the U.S. Air Force and the youngest man I interviewed for this book, summed up his desire for fatherhood by saying, "It's kind of the only purpose of life, to have a child and pass along things to your child." Keith's description of the purpose of life captures the social norms of parenthood, kinship, and family life that are central to contemporary American culture. People should reproduce; moreover, they should want to reproduce.[3] When one is infertile, what are the purposes of heterosexual marriage, sexual intercourse, and even life? In a culture in which virility is synonymous with masculinity and fertility is often conflated with virility,[4] what does it mean to be an infertile man? A life disruption such as infertility exposes all of our own personal taken-for-granted notions about gender, fertility and parenthood and then forces women and men to reformulate how they view their bodily experience, their expectations for family, and their goals for the future.[5] When couples desire parenthood and a male factor impedes conception, men experience role failure. They fail to be reliable husbands and to become fathers. They also fail to prove the functionality of their essentially masculine parts and therefore fail as men. But failure is not an easily accepted explanation for men or an adequate way to make meaning of what might be a very long-term experience. In other words, failure is not an option, and gender work is mandatory.

At varying speeds and levels of intensity, infertility patients traverse a path that includes discovering their infertility issues, learning about available medical treatment options, making decisions with their partners, possibly pursuing medical treatments, and eventually achieving pregnancy or choosing to repeat medical treatments or pursue other options. There is a parallel emotional and cognitive process that accompanies the physical and bodily experience of infertility. Some men confess that poor fertility makes them feel like "less of a man" or an "inadequate husband," and they have to work hard, mentally, to suppress those thoughts or change that interpretation. Nearly all of the men in this study reported feeling surprised when they first heard their semen analysis results, and they expressed a range of emotions from mild disappointment to deep heartache associated with their childlessness. Most of the men in this study reported that they had either planned their whole lives to become fathers one day or had desired fatherhood ever since marriage. For men who envision themselves as loyal, dependable husbands and aspiring fathers, poor semen analysis results render their perceptions of themselves and the future unclear. Infertility can thwart plans, dash dreams, and ignite feelings of shock, anxiety, depression, and fear. Nonetheless, infertility means different things to different people depending upon their diagnosis, age, health history, financial means, personal interactions with medical professionals, life goals, and belief system and the information and treatment options that are available to them. Men and women have the freedom and power to construct their own definition of infertility and to make sense of the situation in their own terms.

Making Sense of Male Infertility

Medicalization is the process whereby aspects of everyday human experience come to be understood as *medical* conditions. In the 1970s, medical sociologists pointed out that pathologizing, problematizing, and medically treating human conditions and behaviors, from reproduction to homosexuality, was a form of social control. Many scholars questioned the intentions of doctors and saw ever-expanding medicalization as an abuse of professional authority.[6] Doctors have been painted as self-seeking, power-hungry disease-mongers, because medicalization generates business for practitioners as well as for the medical technology and pharmaceutical industries.[7] At the same time, scholars recognize that many burdens are made lighter when they are medicalized and labeled as medical disorders. For example, behaviors associated with addictions and mental illnesses that society once viewed as poor reflections on individuals' moral character are now understood as medical diseases stemming from biological, genetic, or organic etiologies. As a result of medicalization, sufferers are less likely to be stigmatized and criminalized. Families and communities are more likely to rally around sufferers to provide support and relief.

Impotence is a particularly curious case study for understanding the liberating effects of medicalization. Throughout the ages, healers in many cultures have treated impotence in men with an array of therapies that had debatable efficacy. In Western medical practice in the United States, however, there were no reliable medical treatments for impotence before the end of the twentieth century. Most doctors considered impotence a psychological problem, and impotent men were advised to participate in psychotherapy to overcome the presumed mental and emotional issues that prevented them from having satisfying erections. Socially, impotence was considered a reflection of one's masculinity and a taboo topic for discussion. Not surprisingly, few men admitted to being impotent. In the 1970s, doctors invented prosthetic penile implants to help severe sufferers of impotence to maintain erections. Still, impotence was believed to be a primarily psychogenic disorder, and few men sought treatment for it. In the 1990s the development, efficacy, and availability of simple pharmaceutical remedies such as Viagra, transformed our social understanding of impotence. "Impotence" became "erectile dysfunction," or "ED," a medical disorder that could be treated by medical professionals in medical clinics.[8] Characterizing erectile dysfunction as an organic disorder rather than a psychogenic one liberated men from some of the emasculating assumptions that had been associated with impotence. Encouraged by enormous advertising campaigns by pharmaceutical companies, some twenty million American men[9] have sought medical help for their erectile dysfunction.

In her cultural analysis of erectile dysfunction, Annie Potts noted that according to the biomedical model for understanding disease, the body is at fault, not the man. Rather than feeling emasculated, impotent men actually feel liberated by the knowledge that they have a treatable medical condition. They let go of guilt because "there is nothing a man can do or think to change the condition."[10] Like beliefs about impotence, popular beliefs about male infertility can be particularly stigmatizing for men, including ideas that infertile men are sexually inferior, do not understand how to have sex properly for conception, or have a sexual disorder.[11] Another assumption is that infertile men have lower testosterone levels and so are somehow less biologically manly. In most cases, these beliefs are simply myths. Most infertile men have very fulfilling sex lives and all the biological markers of maleness. Like the millions of men flocking to doctors' offices for Viagra prescriptions, patients I interviewed found comfort in the medicalness of their infertility.[12] The availability and accessibility of medical treatments allowed patients to redefine infertility as nothing more than a medical issue. Interestingly, there were no interview questions that asked patients whether they perceived or focused on infertility as simply a medical condition. Instead, the idea of infertility as "just a medical condition" was a common theme in answers to questions about masculinity, emotions, marriage, fatherhood, reflections on the self, and the definition of infertility. After I heard the "just a medical condition" mantra averred by subjects repeatedly, it became clear that couching infertility in these terms is an important step in negotiating masculinity. Infertility, as several men explained to me, has no more bearing on one's masculinity than does any other disorder, injury, or illness.

Thirty-one-year-old Patrick, an industrial chemist, was initially plagued by feelings of shock, sadness, anger, and embarrassment when he learned about his extremely low sperm count. When asked whether infertility had ever caused him to question himself as a good husband, Patrick replied:

Yeah. Oh, God. The one time I think that I was probably at my lowest was when I was thinking there wasn't any real need for me, really, 'cause I can't provide. I didn't think I was going to be able to be a father, so I was going to be not much use to Rebecca if she wanted to have a family. So I began to question why she really needed to have me around, you know? It was something that I really felt at the time. Was I really a good husband? Because I can't entertain the thought that maybe I would not be the father of her children.

Patrick's self-perception revealed a new take on the traditional role of men as "providers." Economically, Patrick is a capable provider, thanks to his advanced education and employment. But when it comes to sperm, he acknowledged that he "can't provide" sufficiently, and that made him question his effectiveness as a husband. He worried that his wife would find him useless in her quest to have a family. Patrick also reported feeling depressed for some time after he received his initial diagnosis. He believed that his depression was affecting his marriage and his work, and he admitted that in quiet moments of reflection he shed tears, thinking about his infertility. When asked whether he believed that infertility had affected his sense of masculinity, Patrick responded:

Yeah, it has. I obviously felt like less of a man, and sometimes it still can hit me down again, but I'm trying to come to terms with that. . . . Hopefully, that's not the case—that I just have some sort of medical condition that means I don't produce quite as much as I should have, and it's just something that we're going to have to deal with. I did feel—I did have some problems with it, though.

For Patrick, conceptualizing infertility as just "some sort of medical condition" is an important step toward believing that his poor infertility does not make him "less of a man."

Over a year later, when I interviewed Patrick again, he and his wife were expecting their first child conceived through IVF. When asked whether he had ever felt that infertility reflected anything about him as a person, he replied:

I tried not to go down that route. . . . I felt myself as leaning toward that kind of thoughts, but I quickly stopped that one. I just realized that it's a medical issue. It's just unfortunate that that's the case. Like I said before, there's not an awful lot I can do about it. It doesn't change who I am, it's just a medical issue. I have confidence that it doesn't make me any different.

Patrick saw more than one mental "route" available to him. He could choose to perceive infertility as a poor reflection of himself as a man, but he "stopped" that thought process whenever he caught himself going that direction. Instead, Patrick resolved to conceptualize infertility as a medical issue, which would have no power to change his self-identity.

When I asked Eric, a technical support specialist in his late thirties, whether he felt that his low sperm count reflected anything about him, he replied coolly, "No. You can't control it, no." Control was a common theme in interviews and one that was rife with contradiction. When asked to describe the feelings or emotions that accompany infertility, many men reported feeling a "lack of control," a negative feeling that incites frustration and grief. Yet, as in the studies cited earlier on erectile dysfunction, I also heard several of these same men explain that when something is beyond one's control, one can no longer be held accountable for it, and it is not a reflection of one's self or masculinity. In other words, a lack of control causes a masculinity crisis, but accepting that something is beyond one's control also preserves masculinity.

Eric had very conflicted feelings about his infertility, at the heart of which was the issue of control. When asked whether his experiences with infertility had had any impact on his sense of manliness or masculinity, he opened up:

Yeah, for sure. . . . It's like, if I were heavyweight champ of the world and somebody came up to me and just out of the blue, you know, said, "Hey, you have a low sperm count," I still think I'd feel like, "Whoa! I can't even do the default thing." Do you know what I mean? . . . I know it's not something I can control, but you do feel a little cheated. I'm an achiever. I sort of have an achieving mentality, where you work hard and then you get something. [With infertility] you can't do that . . . but for me it's like I shouldn't have to. I should be [fertile] by default. But then, the reality is that everybody's got something wrong or problems. And if this is the worst of it in my entire life, you know, geez, you just got to look at somebody in a wheelchair and they can't walk or whatever, and it's like, geez, you don't have anything to complain about.   •

As a hypothetical exercise, Eric imagines that even if he had the über-masculine title of heavyweight champion of the world, infertility would still bruise his masculinity. Having sperm and being able to impregnate a woman is the "default" of manliness, something that every man should be able to do. Eric reminds himself, though, that infertility is not something he can control. Though he feels frustrated that he cannot achieve fertility through hard work, that fact brings some relief. No one is dealt a perfect hand. For Eric, infertility is just a medical condition beyond his control, not a condition worth complaining about compared to other, more debilitating conditions.

Roger, a police detective in his late thirties, fathered one son before being diagnosed with a pituitary tumor.[13] After delicate brain surgery and years of hormone therapy, Roger's fertility was compromised. The hormone depletion caused by the tumor necessitated that Roger take testosterone supplements, which, unbeknownst to him, arrested his sperm production. His infertility became evident when he and his wife decided to have a second child and could not conceive. In our initial interview, when asked whether he felt that infertility reflected anything about him as a person, Roger explained, "It doesn't change my personality, or—you have to forgive me because I'm really getting literal. Yes, it says that I'm a[n] . . . infertile person, you know, and it's not good in a kind of way, but as far as changing my personality or anything like that, no." By taking a very "literal" approach to understanding his condition, Roger defended himself, claiming that infertility could not change who he was. In the same interview, Roger answered, "No," when asked whether infertility had ever threatened his sense of masculinity.

Under the direction of both his oncologist and a male infertility specialist, Roger quit taking his medication in order to boost sperm production. The consequent lack of testosterone resulted in erectile dysfunction, making sexual intercourse nearly impossible. Over the course of several months and various medical interventions to restore both his sexual function and his fertility, Roger watched his sperm counts bounce up and down between zero and normal. In our concluding interview, when asked whether this experience had ever affected his own sense of masculinity, Roger confidently answered, "No." He explained, "I look at it as having a broken arm or something like that. It's just a physical limitation . . . like a broken arm or missing finger or something like that." By defining infertility as a basic "physical limitation," Roger disconnected fertility status from his self-identity.

Medical sociologists have shown that any condition or disease that requires men to subject themselves to medical attention, such as heart disease or cancer, may be emasculating.[14] Yet of all of the medical problems that men face, there are few that hit at the heart of masculinity as male infertility does. The determined way in which men repeatedly explained infertility as a simple medical issue, "like a broken arm," struck me as an attempt to negate the unique and complicated relationship between fertility status and masculinity. As research on alcoholism and impotence shows, medicalization has the power to absolve sufferers of blame and guilt.[15] During appointments, I often heard patients ask doctors whether they had done something to cause their poor fertility and felt relieved when doctors assured them that they had not. Several patients emphasized in interviews that because they cannot control their fertility, poor fertility is not their fault. And because it is not their fault, their fertility status is no reflection of them as a person. Whether or not men are responsible for their infertility (a debate that medical science has yet to sort out), resolving guilt and establishing blamelessness make up a crucial step in renegotiating masculinity.

Focusing on Etiologies

When Kevin, a twenty-nine-year-old pilot, first found out that he had a zero sperm count, he kept it a secret from his wife, Wendy. He explained:

> I had no idea how I was going to tell [my wife], because I . . . thought there was . . . really no chance [for her to get pregnant]. . . . I felt awful because I know that she not only wanted

to have a child, but a child that was ours. And I kind of felt like I wasn't holding up my end of the bargain. I was scared also. Who knows? Was it something that I've done? I had no idea. I have been a pretty, pretty straight and narrow guy, but still in growing up and all—experimented with things. And I was just thinking, worst case, "My God, if I've done something to myself that's causing this . . ."

Kevin called his best friend from childhood, now a physician, to help him interpret his semen analysis results. His friend reassured Kevin that, most likely, he had a birth defect that prevented the passage of sperm into the ejaculate. The friend also informed Kevin that he and Wendy could still achieve pregnancy using ART. Finding out that his zero sperm count was caused by a birth defect and was not the result of when he "experimented with things" allayed Kevin's feelings of guilt, and he felt encouraged to tell his wife about his infertility.

Later, his doctor confirmed that Kevin has congenital bilateral absence of the vas deferens (CBAVD), as his friend had suspected. When asked whether infertility had any impact on his sense of masculinity, Kevin explained that when an ultrasound showed that all other parts of his genitals appeared normal, he felt reassured: "I can handle the thought of some tube not being connected. If they'd have come back and said, 'Hey, you've got extremely small testicles,' then I would have questioned my masculinity." Kevin's interpretation of his infertility was arguably a matter of splitting hairs. Yes, he had a zero sperm count, and, sure, he was missing some fairly crucial anatomical parts, but he took comfort in his healthy-looking testicles and other parts of his genitals. He decided that a couple of missing tubes were no reflection of his masculinity.

Kevin's etiology-specific approach to conceptualizing infertility was not uncommon among the men I met. Aaron, a graduate student in his late twenties, took a similar tack when he discovered that he had a zero sperm count. Aaron's infertility journey was a winding path that began with a semen analysis ordered by his general practitioner, followed by trips with his wife to see an RE/I, then to a general urologist, then to a male infertility specialist, and finally to another, more renowned infertility specialist in a neighboring state. By the time I met Aaron, the stress of this journey was taking an emotional toll:

It really has been a real emotional roller coaster. I mean, in addition to all of the stress of everything being so unknown, there are those added pressures. There's the added pressure of financial [concerns], the added pressure of all these doctors' appointments and tests and stuff. Up to this point I've been very healthy. . . . It's been really hard now and especially over the last, maybe, few weeks or so. There have been times where we end up snapping at each other or yelling at each other, getting upset, or being really short. . . . We kind of have to keep reminding each other we're on the same team here. So it's hard.

Aaron could identify the causes of his distress and marital discord, including disappointing test results, numerous doctor visits, and mounting medical bills. But like many infertile men, Aaron had a difficult time pinpointing the feeling that was bothering him:

It's a little bit of sadness; it's a little bit of frustration. It's also a little bit of something else. I mean, I don't know how to describe it. . . . It's sort of a feeling of lack of control, you know, feeling like you're not in charge of your own life in a way. And that's a sort of a very scary feeling. . . . It's sort of been a combination of those three things. I don't know what actual emotions.

Feeling not in control or in charge incites fear, as Aaron expressed, and defines a crisis of masculinity.

By all clinical definitions, Aaron is infertile. After he and his wife had an unsuccessful year trying to conceive, two semen analyses showed no sperm in Aaron's ejaculate. I asked him whether he had ever thought of himself as infertile:

Aaron: I don't know. Well, yes, but, like, not using that term.
LB: So what do you think?
Aaron: Well, I mean, I guess it's really just a matter of semantics. . . . I focus more on the, you know, like, the "zero sperm." So if I focus more on that, that puts a broader label of "fertile."

Recall from Chapter 3 that many doctors never tell patients that they are infertile. Patients are left to figure out for themselves what infertility is and how it relates to their issues and experiences. When asked to define infertility, Aaron responded, "Not able to produce biological children." Luckily, Aaron's specialist had laid out a "methodical, thoughtful" treatment plan that might make it possible for him to produce biological children. By focusing on the "zero sperm" in his ejaculate, Aaron holds out hope that he is not infertile. In the meantime, he can apply a "broader label of 'fertile'" to himself.

Troy, a jewelry wholesaler in his mid-thirties, also had a zero sperm count. During exploratory surgery, Troy's specialist found that his vas deferens appeared—quite mysteriously—to have been snipped apart. After reviewing Troy's medical history, the specialist concluded that the only possible explanation was that the vas deferens had been inadvertently severed during a hernia operation Troy had had as a small child.[16] Troy described how his zero sperm count initially made him question his masculinity:

> I'm a pretty strong, confident guy. Of course, you start thinking to yourself, "Here I am shooting blanks." . . . You kind of question yourself, your masculinity or your manliness, I guess. But after actually thinking about it intelligently for a few days, no, I would say . . . I'm definitely a man. Just because my plumbing got messed up . . . doesn't make me any less of a man, because I had absolutely nothing to do with it, nothing to do with why I'm going through all this.

When Troy learned that his "plumbing got messed up" because of a doctor's error, he no longer questioned his masculinity or felt responsible for his infertility. Troy's story is unique in that he knew the exact event (and person) that rendered him infertile. He surely could not be held accountable for something that had occurred when he was very young at the hands of a physician.

Infertility scholar Arthur Greil found that most infertile women view the body as an emblem of the self.[17] When their bodies fail, women see themselves as failures. In his research study, Greil identified only one woman in his sample of twenty-two who drew a clear distinction between her body and her self, describing herself as "a victim of a lousy package."[18] This seemingly unusual viewpoint among infertile women turns out to be a common strategy for preserving personal worth and masculinity among infertile men, a technique that they use to avoid the sting of personal failure. Roger considered infertility no big deal, like a missing finger, and Kevin claimed that a couple of missing tubes were no reflection of his masculinity.[19] Though men may initially experience feelings of inadequacy and powerlessness, they are eventually liberated by the Western model for understanding illness. The real culprits are missing tubes and messed up plumbing. The body is at fault, while the *self*, the real seat of masculinity, remains intact and blameless.

A Symptom of Something Bigger

Roger, whose infertility was caused by a brain tumor, described his struggle with infertility as "extremely small compared to the tumor issue." Some infertile men had to deal with other, more serious health issues, including cancer, spinal cord injury, diabetes, and cystic fibrosis, in their past or simultaneously with their infertility. They described infertility as simply a symptom of a larger problem, a minor hiccup along the life course after surviving a life-threatening disease or accident.[20] Emphasizing the more serious root cause of their infertility was yet another way to declare infertility "just a medical condition."

Thirty-six-year-old Curtis, a clerk for the city government, battled testicular cancer in early adulthood before he got married, and his infertility is attributed to the chemotherapy and radiation that he underwent during those years. Curtis says that throughout treatments, his only concern was overcoming cancer, and that the possible negative effects of those treatments on his fertility never even crossed his mind. Some days, he feels angry toward the oncologists, who he claims failed to advise him to bank sperm before his chemotherapy treatments, but most of the time he does not feel justified in getting upset with the doctors who saved his life.

During both our first and final interviews, Curtis seemed very conflicted about his feelings regarding infertility. He defined infertility as "Pretty much somebody who can't have kids. Somebody that might have just difficulty having kids because of something in their body or system or it's not working the proper way." Curiously, however, Curtis claimed that because he is helping to raise a stepson right now, he does not consider himself infertile. Still, Curtis felt turmoil with regard to his inability to provide better financially for his family or afford some of the more expensive infertility treatments. He admitted, "At points, I feel like, you know, like I'm not fully there, as a man." Yet when asked whether infertility had ever caused him to question himself as a good husband, Curtis replied, "No. Not really. Because I just put all the blame on cancer. . . . I know that that's the reason this is all happening, and that's the reason the sperm's not going the way it's supposed to, and I just say, hey, you know, it's cancer's fault." Curtis had developed a coping strategy that enabled him to categorize infertility with the more serious life-threatening medical issue of cancer, which had victimized him at a young age. He avoided guilt and strove to maintain a positive self-perception by blaming cancer for his infertility.

William, a thirty-nine-year-old business owner, was diagnosed with diabetes in adulthood. The diabetes resulted in erectile dysfunction, which often made it difficult for him to have intercourse or even provide semen samples for analysis. William also had poor semen parameters and identified himself as "almost" infertile. He admitted that ED and infertility were both challenging to his sense of masculinity at times, but he found ED more difficult to deal with because it would affect him for the rest of his life, whereas infertility could be solved with medical intervention or adoption. When I asked William whether infertility had been an emotional struggle for him, he responded, "Not really. It can get you down from time to time, but for me, it's just a medical disease. . . . It's just like me getting all depressed with my diabetes. I just haven't. I have a cross I was given to bear, you know?" Like other patients, William regarded infertility as "just a medical disease." William pointed out that diabetes has not made him depressed, suggesting that there is no reason why infertility should be an emotional struggle for him either.

Thirty-eight-year-old Howard, a self-described househusband, incurred a spinal cord injury at age nineteen that had left him paralyzed from the waist down. Howard's semen analysis showed a high sperm count but with poor motility, most likely indicating that his testicles continue to produce sperm but that the sperm weaken and die before ejaculation. Howard uses an injectable medication to create erections and a vibrating device to stimulate ejaculation. Before they married, Howard was very forthcoming with Miriam, his wife-to-be, about the fact that having children would require medical intervention because of his paralysis.

During my first interview with Howard, I asked whether he had ever thought of himself as infertile. He replied, "No." When probed, Howard clarified: "Being a paraplegic myself is a little different. It wasn't so much the fact of being infertile, but the method of trying to ejaculate is a lot different than your average person. So the fertility is definitely there. [The doctor] perceives no problems with us getting pregnant." When Howard said that "the fertility is definitely there," he presumably meant that he has sperm, highlighting the importance of the presence of sperm in sparing a man the label of "infertile." Even though Howard and Miriam can conceive only by means of ART, Howard reports "no problems" with conception.

Howard stressed that dealing with infertility cannot compare to the accident that caused internal injuries, broken bones, and paralysis and left him in the hospital for three months. "This [infertility treatment] doesn't really seem much different than an ordinary doctor's appointment, honestly," said Howard, describing meetings with his infertility specialist. Howard's infertility issues are dwarfed by the life-threatening health issues he faced decades ago. By our final interview, Howard and Miriam had gone through two failed rounds of IVF and were preparing for another round. Again, I asked Howard whether he had ever thought of himself as infertile. "No, I don't," he answered, "I think it's just due to . . . the circumstances that have happened medically."

Marcus, a forty-year-old business consultant, had suffered from cystic fibrosis his entire life, which had necessitated many doctors' appointments in childhood and a lifelong dependency on medications. Several decades ago, when Marcus was first diagnosed, most men with cystic fibrosis did not live past their twenties. At age seventeen Marcus was told that he would never father a biological child because of CBAVD, a condition that is common in boys and men with cystic fibrosis. Thanks to medical advances in the treatment of cystic fibrosis and his own good health, Marcus realized that he would live a longer-than-expected life and believed that he would one day have children through adoption or using a sperm donor. Marcus's first wife did not want children, so they did not discuss these options. After his first marriage ended, Marcus learned that new technological innovations were helping men with cystic fibrosis to father children. I first met Marcus and his wife-to-be, Rita, at a male infertility clinic where they were seeking information about available treatment options.

In our first interview, Marcus claimed that because he learned of his infertility at such a young age, it had never caused him sadness, grief, anger, guilt, or embarrassment. He explained:

> I thought all my life, since seventeen, I could never have a bio-logical child. About five years ago I was told by a doctor that actually now it was possible. That was a giant, exciting, totally new development for me. . . . Now Rita and I are together and, you know, having this possibility, even watching how the science, what it's done, making this possible. It all does seem somewhat miraculous to me. So I guess I'm on that side of grateful for the process.

Technological innovation instilled in Marcus new hope and a new sense of longing to be a biological father. After they married, Marcus and Rita chose to try IVF-ICSI with sperm extracted from Marcus's testicles. Only a couple of days before our scheduled final interview, Marcus and Rita learned that their third IVF attempt had failed. Their male and female fertility specialists, working in concert, attributed the failures to Rita's age, forty. In our final interview, Marcus admitted that for the first time, he was dealing with feelings of disappointment and sadness associated with infertility. He sincerely hoped that Rita would try one more round of IVF, but he knew that this would require some coaxing, since she detested the hormone shots and procedures that IVF entailed and had qualms about the physical toll that pregnancy would take on her body. Rita was ready to move on to adoption, and Marcus was willing to support that pursuit. After spending over $30,000 on treatments, their journey ended right where it had begun. Marcus still thought of himself as "functionally sterile," as he called it, but he now thought of Rita as infertile too.

For Curtis, William, Howard, and Marcus, life had dealt them some serious challenges. Infertility was only one of many medical issues they faced. William found his untreatable erectile dysfunction more distressing than his infertility. Curtis, Howard, and Marcus were just grateful to be alive. In many ways, their previous experiences with the medical system had already socialized them as patients.[21] As Howard described it, infertility felt like any "ordinary doctor's appointment." All four of these men had doctors with whom they met on a regular basis. They were familiar with the medical system and had likely already mentally processed some aspects of the medical experience that other patients in this study found emasculating. Neither Curtis nor Howard thought of himself as infertile; these men believed that if they could reverse their other health issues, at their core was a fertile man.

Denying Infertility's Impact on Masculinity

Conceptualizing infertility as just a medical condition, as a simple case of poor sperm, or as a symptom of a larger issue carved out an escape route for some men—an escape from a crisis of masculinity. If infertility is not one's fault, then it cannot affect one's masculinity. Troy, quoted earlier, argued that because his plumbing got messed up and he "had absolutely nothing to do with it," he was "no less of a man." Howard also believed that the infertility caused by his spinal cord injury did not say anything about him as a person and had no impact on his masculinity. When I asked Paul, a twenty-nine-year-old salesman, whether his low sperm count had had any impact on his masculinity, he replied, "Probably not, because . . . there's other people who have had that problem, and there's nothing you can do about it."[22] Greg, a technology developer in his early thirties, responded similarly:

> Not really. . . . I think of it all . . . as medical. I mean, clearly, I don't like to know that my sperm quality is not where it needs to be. . . . Years ago, that would have determined that I would not have been a father, and that makes me at times sort of question, and be like, is that the way it's meant to be? . . . On the other side, I feel so strongly that [having a baby is] something I want, and that it's something I'm meant to do, and something that [my wife] and I are meant to do together, that I sort of live on the other half of just feeling lucky that we have some options.

Again, the characterization of Greg's infertility issues as medical and the hope that medical options provide steeled him against a crisis of masculinity. Like Kevin, Aaron, and Troy, Greg focused on the etiology of his infertility issues—specifically, his "sperm quality." When asked whether he had ever thought of himself as infertile, Greg explained:

> No, I don't think of myself as infertile. I think of myself as below the averages to make natural pregnancy easy. I don't think it couldn't happen, and I don't think it might not happen over time. I just think the statistics are sort of against us. . . . I'm in a range, as well, which I do have sperm. I do have some that are healthy. I do have some that are normal. So I guess I don't think of myself as infertile. I just think of myself as below average, I guess.

Though Greg admitted that he was "below average," he resisted defining himself as infertile. Instead, he emphasized that he does have some healthy, normal sperm, and he interprets their presence as meaning that he is fertile.

Simply being asked in an interview to describe how a life challenge like infertility has impacted one's masculinity can feel threatening. Pointed questions about masculinity may themselves be taken as a direct affront to one's masculinity, and denying infertility's impact on one's masculinity may, understandably, be a knee-jerk reaction to such questions. Despite all of the evidence stacked against them, including poor test results and persistent childlessness, many of the men in this study altogether deny that they are even infertile. In the parlance of psychology, the men in this study seem to represent classic cases of what the late Sigmund Freud identified more than a century ago as deep-seated denial or abnegation. Among the men who do and do not self-identify as infertile, many deny that their medical issues have any bearing on their personal identity or masculinity. They describe their diagnoses in terms that minimize or hide the severity of their issues. Infertility can be an uncomfortable issue to discuss and a stigmatizing social label. Sammy Lee, an IVF technologist turned male infertility counselor, argues that most infertile men are not aware of their emotional needs and, like the men in this study, do not attend support groups or take advantage of mental health therapy.[23]

Though the discipline of psychology helps to explain the workings of the inner mind, a sociological approach to understanding human behavior focuses more on the relationships and interactions between individuals, institutions, and the broader culture. From a sociological perspective, I would argue that how men understand and conceptualize their infertility is more than a classic case of denial; this is a classic case of sociology, in which institutions, authorities, technologies, and individuals perform a beautiful dance to accommodate the time-honored traditions of masculinity. In Chapter 3, I described how conscientiously doctors strive not to emasculate men in clinical interactions. Doctors often avoid using words such as "infertile" and employ euphemistic language to educate patients. They have great faith in their own surgical skills, and patients buy into the promises of medical technology. To understand their medical issues, patients draw upon the information that they receive from medical authorities and institutions, which, in the case of male infertility, is not much. Male patients have a lot of room to reimagine for themselves what infertility is and what it means. Medicalization brings hope for future fertility and staves off a crisis of masculinity for many infertile men. Greg's case illustrates this point. He recognized that in another time, "years ago," his poor sperm quality would have meant infertility and no chance at biological fatherhood. But in the era of advanced reproductive medicine, it takes only one healthy sperm to be a fertile man and father.

Gender scholars recognize that not all men embody the most powerful, hegemonic form of masculinity, which in the dominant American culture is characterized by whiteness, wealth, education, athleticism, strength, sexual prowess, and heterosexuality.[24] Men who do not fit this categorically racist, classist, and sexist definition of masculinity construct their own alternative forms of masculinity, which emphasize their own personal values.[25] Biological fatherhood is a salient aspect of hegemonic masculinity in which infertile men fall short. To overcome feelings of inadequacy, the men I interviewed defined the relationship between fertility status and masculinity in terms that defended their personal masculine identities. Some men emphasized aspects of their lives that were decidedly masculine or explained how their definition of masculinity differs from broader cultural understandings of masculinity.

Ron, a thirty-nine-year-old special education teacher, described the troubling feelings that had been prompted by his infertility: "I just feel like I'm not holding up my end of the bargain. . . . If she'd married somebody else, she'd probably be pregnant by now and have kids and stuff like that." One taken-for-granted aspect of the marital partnership is that each party brings procreative abilities to the relationship, and men often feel guilty when they default on this assumed aspect of marital commitment.[26] As masculinities scholar Michael Kimmel notes, proving one's masculinity is a process that entails "intense relentless competition" with other men.[27] Ron compared himself to "somebody else," an imagined "other," a man who is fertile and can give his wife children, which left Ron feeling inadequate.

To rectify the situation in his mind, Ron took an age-focused approach to conceptualizing masculinity, contrasting society's ideal with his own idea of masculinity. He explained that within society, "if you're infertile . . . that isn't considered very masculine." But he then clarified, "I'm forty now. I think that if I was twenty, I would definitely feel [less masculine], but now that I'm older, I really don't care what other people say." Ron sees infertility as potentially emasculating and admits that there may have been a time, when he was younger, when infertility might have made him feel less masculine. However, now, at the age of forty, he claims that he feels empowered to deflect social ideas about fertility and masculinity and chooses not to care what other people say about infertility, masculinity, or him. Ron's story illustrates the fluidity of masculinity over the life course. Social norms about masculinity change with age. Ron recognizes this phenomenon and invests in it as insurance against emasculation. He also recognizes that as one ages, it is less important to subscribe to social norms.

The first time I interviewed Scott, a thirty-one-year-old real estate planner, he expressed some feelings of guilt, sadness, and disappointment associated with his infertility issues. He stated that he was "not open at all" about sharing his infertility issues with anyone, including his parents, relatives, and friends. When asked why, he explained, "I think there's a level of embarrassment. I think there's a level of not wanting to have to deal with additional questions or opinions or anyone else getting involved." Infertility is stigmatized in many cultures, including the United States, and people who are dealing with infertility may choose to keep it a secret to evade stigmatization.[28] The desire to avoid embarrassment, as Scott put it, shows that infertility threatens masculinity. However, in the same interview, Scott claimed that infertility had no bearing on his masculinity.

In her book *Gender Differences at Work,* Christine Williams explains that many people have a difficult time defining themselves in terms of masculinity and femininity and explaining their life experiences in the context of gender.[29] This fact was driven home for me in my interview with Brandon, described at the beginning of this chapter. At the end of a very revealing and emotionally raw interview, I asked him directly, "Do you think that this experience has ever made you question your masculinity?" To my surprise, he responded candidly, "Not really." Many of the men I spoke with acknowledged feeling "incomplete," "less of a man," or like an "inadequate husband" in their answers to questions about fatherhood, marriage, emotions, or their self-perception. However, many of these same men responded no when asked directly whether their experiences with infertility had affected their own sense of masculinity or manliness. My job as a researcher is to connect subjects' emotions and insights about infertility and personhood to masculinity, even when the subjects do not see these connections. I would argue that Scott's fear of embarrassment, as well as his fear that others might try to pry or involve themselves in a situation that he would like to control himself, indicates that at some level—perhaps not consciously—Scott recognizes that infertility exposes his vulnerability. His secrecy was a measure to protect his masculinity.

Sociologists theorize masculinity as an index of a man's access to power and resources. While scholars often posit masculinity and personhood for men as being one and the same, men see masculinity as one characteristic of the self that can be conveniently separated from cognitive, emotional, and lived experience. A little over a year after our first interview, I spoke with Scott again. Since we had last spoken, Scott had undergone surgery to improve his fertility, his wife had conceived spontaneously through intercourse, and they were thrilled to be anticipating the birth of their first baby. Scott still claimed that his poor fertility in the past had never had any bearing on his masculinity, but he was able to elaborate on this point more thoughtfully. He talked about a novel he had been reading about a working-class Dominican family living in New Jersey. He described how the male protagonist in the story had to live up to very stereotypical ideals of masculinity: being macho, womanizing, having lots of sex. The book made Scott think about his own social class and culture, and he noted that because of his own cultural background, as a white, educated man, he did not "feel a lot of pressure to be masculine." Scott claimed that for "the upper class there is less masculine requirement," and for that reason, his experiences with infertility had not really affected his own sense of masculinity.[30]

Is there really "less masculine requirement" for "the upper class"? More likely, men in Scott's socioeconomic group already enjoy the privileges of hegemonic masculinity, such as economic power and education. Scott denied that upper-class men have to live up to the ideal of biological fatherhood, yet he and his wife could afford treatment and gladly took advantage of available medical services. Masculinities scholar Michael Kaufman observes that while working-class manhood "stresses physical skill and the ability to physically manipulate one's environment," upper-middle-class manhood "stresses verbal skills and the ability to manipulate one's environment through economic, social, and political means."[31] Middle- and upper-middle-class men with good health insurance and economic resources are able to manipulate their fertility and parental status through economic and technological means. By Kaufman's definition, pursuing expensive medical treatments is actually a way for upper-middle-class men to enact their masculinity.

Marcus, also a white man of means, had a similar take on masculinity. Because of his cystic fibrosis, as a child Marcus had always been physically smaller than other boys his age. He was not athletic and never thought of himself as particularly masculine. When he got to college, he learned that he had strong leadership skills, which he considered to be his most masculine trait. Later, he honed his skills to become a very successful businessman. Marcus says that infertility affects his masculinity only insofar as it means that he cannot do "something other men can do." Infertility does not affect the leadership skills by which Marcus defines his masculinity and that he values most about himself. Marcus's method for negotiating masculinity is to emphasize his nonphysical masculine traits.

Aaron, quoted earlier in this chapter, struggled with feeling out of control and scared about his "zero sperm." He also divulged that when he first learned about his sperm count, he worried that his wife would have regrets about marrying him. Though seemingly mired in a crisis of masculinity, Aaron believed that his zero sperm count had little impact on his sense of masculinity:

Aaron: I think in general society defines masculinity by a lot
of those stereotypical traits, you know—things like sports
and being aggressive in the different fields. . . . I guess that
my definition of that would differ in that I don't see it necessary to be so assertive, so externally aggressive, or like
trying to be macho or things of that nature.

LB: Do you think that this experience with "zero sperm" has
had an impact on your sense of masculinity?

Aaron: Not all that much. I mean, I've never been like a big
macho guy, so no. I don't really feel that it has on that level.

Aaron claimed that a lack of sperm was not threatening to his
masculinity, since he already saw himself and his type of masculinity as being outside the stereotypical norm. Incidentally, when Aaron
shared his insecurities with his wife, she reassured him that she had
no regrets about marrying him and was worried mainly about his
feelings. Wives play an influential role in bolstering masculinity and
empowering men to define masculinity for themselves.

After Nicholas, an engineer in his early forties, learned about his
low sperm count, he made light of it by poking fun at cultural ideas
about manhood and masculinity. Whenever his wife would ask him
to do the heavy lifting or repairs around the house or even to open a
jar of food for her, Nicholas would teasingly say that he was not sure
he was man enough to do the task. Nicholas recognized the cultural
association of fertility status with manhood and machismo but personally found the association silly and unfounded. Nicholas does not
believe that infertility has any impact on masculinity and uses sar-
casm to expose the absurdity of that notion.

George, a musician and coffeehouse waiter in his late thirties, drew
upon biological determinist notions about the natures of men and
women and about masculinity and femininity to explain why infertility does not affect masculinity. George has a zero sperm count with no
sperm production in his testicles, evidenced by their unusually small
size and confirmed by tissue biopsies. Both times I interviewed George,
he sounded exhausted and crushed by his experiences with infertility:

Learning that I was infertile and dealing with the emotions
that come with that, like the fears and the sense of, kind of like

worthlessness and inadequacy that comes with that. And then, dealing with—my wife is suffering so hard. The emotions and feelings of inadequacy that come with that, and then the sadness. Those are my emotions. [My wife's] emotions are more extreme and desperate and more of an absolute kind of a life-and-death struggle. Me, it's me and the suffering, the feeling inadequate and feeling kind of helpless.

George also confessed that he felt "not worthy" to be a husband and, in a "superstitious way," worried that he was not meant to be a father. Despite his struggle, he repeatedly emphasized in our interview that infertility was taking a harder emotional toll on his wife. He explained, "I think it's just more of an emotional issue for [my wife] than it is for me. I mean, it's like the emotions are just like a crisis—reaches crisis level in her heart, so it doesn't really reach that for me except for seeing her suffering like that. I'm not so desperate for a baby inside, where she is."

Though his feelings of helplessness, inadequacy, and unworthiness epitomize a masculinity crisis, when asked whether his experiences with infertility had affected his sense of masculinity, George said that they had but only "to a small degree." As he explained, "I believe that infertility has no impact over masculinity whatsoever, in the fact that I'm infertile. But it can have an impact emotionally because—I don't believe it makes you less of a man—you're that way just because it's like an irrational, emotional kind of response."

For George, masculinity is defined by rationality and protected by rational thinking. While his wife struggles emotionally, reaching "crisis level in her heart," he tries not to succumb to an "irrational, emotional kind of response."

Historically, men have been characterized as the rational sex, while women have been depicted as the more emotional, irrational sex. Feminists have long argued against this dichotomy, which aligns men with the mind (scientific, intellectual, and reasonable) and women with the body (earthy and uncontrollable) and which stems from archaic ideas about reproduction.[32] For ages, reproductive processes such as menstruation, repeat pregnancies, and years of breastfeeding controlled women's lives and dictated their social roles. In the modern day, biological determinist notions of gender derived from the male/female duality are still used—often erroneously—in both scholarly debates and public discourse to substantiate perceived innate differences between the sexes.

George invoked the male-mind/female-body duality to defend his masculinity. As he explained it to me, his wife Tara has a "biological desire" to experience pregnancy. He elaborated, "I think it's partly physiological, but I also think it's chemical. I think she has this chemical thing telling her, driving her." According to George, the need to conceive is "impregnated in her mind." From his perspective, women's emotionality is a bodily experience, biological, beyond reason and control, and the desire to be pregnant can be all-consuming, whereas for men, the desire for a child has no impact on one's levelheadedness or ability to think rationally. While Tara is driven by a primal urge to have a baby growing inside of her, George cannot relate to her physical desire for pregnancy and, intellectually, maintains that infertility has no bearing on masculinity.

George's story returns us to the earlier discussion about the relationship between the self and the body, as it sheds light on the gendered bodily experiences of reproduction. Previous infertility studies found that women felt strongly that their bodily failings reflected something about them as people, while most of the men in those previous studies, as well as this study, easily disconnected their bodily disorders from personhood. Why is there such a gender discrepancy? Though I do not buy into the male-mind-rational/female-body-irrational duality, it can be said that for a woman, pregnancy status is a very physical experience and her not-yet-pregnant body serves as a constant tangible reminder of her (or her spouse's) infertility.[33] Since men likely never imagine themselves carrying a baby for nine months, their bodies do not reflect infertility in the same visible way. Perhaps for this reason, men do not perceive the body to be as intrinsically tied to the self, and men can more easily exculpate themselves from their bodily defects. When I asked George whether he had ever felt that infertility meant something about him as a person, he answered, "No, because it's not something I can control. So, no." Feeling not in control would seem to present a serious crisis of masculinity, but as was discussed earlier, once infertility has been established as beyond a man's control, he is off the hook. It is no longer his fault.

Sex and Marriage

Philip[34] and his wife had had a weak sex life well before they learned about his infertility issues. Philip's wife had little interest in sex, so it was not unusual for several months to pass without any sexual activity between them. In fact, before Philip found out about his infertility issues, he attributed their inability to conceive to lack of sex. Outside the home and unbeknownst to his wife, other women routinely invited Philip to have sex. He considered himself a loyal and loving husband because he always turned down such offers. However, Philip privately confessed that the new revelation of his infertility and the knowledge that there was no risk of pregnancy associated with sex suddenly made extramarital affairs more tempting.

The meanings that we ascribe to marriage and sex are underwritten by social norms regarding the importance of procreation as the purpose of marital unions. When a man's understanding of his own fertility status changes, his ideas about sex and marriage may shift too. Before learning about his infertility, Philip believed that he was fertile and wanted his wife to conceive. Even though they rarely had sex, he did not feel tempted by other women. Considering that birth control is readily available in the United States and extramarital affairs do not have to result in pregnancy, I do not believe that it was the threat of unwanted pregnancy that ensured Philip's faithfulness for so long. More likely, Philip had long considered heterosexual sex the means for achieving biological parenthood, which kept sex reserved for marriage. In our interview, he spoke of the talents and interests that he and his wife share, and he cherished the idea of their having a child together who shared those same gifts. When Philip learned that he was infertile, however, the meaning of sex changed for him. It was no longer the means for conception and shared biological parenthood. Now sex was simply about pleasure. Philip's unsatisfying sex life at home could not bring pregnancy or pleasure, so he felt an increased desire to find meaningful sex elsewhere. Philip's story underscores just how important fertility and conception can be to the meaning of sex.

For men who are trying to conceive with their wives, sex is the biological function that proves their fertility, and biological fatherhood is the desired outcome of that function. Because of the intrinsic biological relationship between sex, fertility status, and fatherhood, attitudes and feelings about sex, marriage, and fatherhood serve as helpful measures or indexes for understanding infertility's impact on masculinity. In interviews, men were asked whether their experiences with infertility had had any impact on their sex lives.[35] One-quarter of the men I interviewed responded that infertility had no impact on their sex lives. These men may have felt uncomfortable discussing their sex lives with me, may have been in denial about infertility's impact on their sex lives, or simply had observed no changes to their sex lives. Male fertility is fairly static relative to women's menstrual cycles, so it does not prompt sexual activity for conception in the same way that women's ovulation does.

The majority of men could see that infertility had affected their sex lives. For some men, such as Philip, infertility added extra strain. Other men believed that infertility had actually improved their sex lives. One-quarter of men said that infertility required them to time sexual intercourse quite conscientiously to coincide with their wives' ovulation. Some of these couples were also trying to abstain from sex a few days before ovulation, and the men were avoiding masturbation. (The guiding theory that men can "save up" their sperm for maximal potency during their wives' ovulation is medically debatable, as was discussed in Chapter 2.) As Ron explained, "You don't want to have sex when three days later it's your peak ovulation time and you know I didn't get a chance to build [sperm] back up again." Although previous research has indicated that "sex on cue" adds stress to marriage,[36] the men with whom I spoke had mixed responses, and some had mixed feelings as to whether timed intercourse was affecting their sex life positively or negatively.

Roger thought that timing intercourse makes sex feel more "scientific," which is "probably not real good." The extreme focus on sex for the sake of reproduction tends to extinguish the romance of intimacy. As William glibly described it:

> You feel like a pair of breeding cows or wolves or something. It's "Okay, next Tuesday, Wednesday, Thursday," you know. You've got to make sure that we have sex. So it's not just a spontaneous love thing. And it's very, very focused on procreation. . . . That's actually why [my wife] quit caring about [her ovulation] earlier in the year. To a certain extent, I think it's a lot easier now. We can just focus on whenever we're both

in the mood, not necessarily when it's gonna help [her get] pregnant.

After more than a year of failed attempts at conception, William and his wife chose to ignore her cycle and just have sex when they were "both in the mood." Other benefits of sex, such as pleasure and affection, became more important to their relationship than conceiving a baby.

Todd discovered that timing intercourse has its perks. He liked that his wife was now initiating sex at least once a month when she was ovulating, which was more often than she had initiated sex before they knew about their infertility issues. He also appreciated that they were enjoying more sexual activities other than intercourse to accommodate medical treatments. A handful of men cited increased frequency of sex as a positive and unexpected benefit of infertility. Nicholas's wife was treated with hormone therapy, which he believed increased her libido, resulting in a more robust sex life. As Scott looked back on his experiences with infertility after his wife had become pregnant, he noted that infertility puts "more stress [on sex], but on the other hand, it was a positive thing because there was more sex." And as much as Curtis wanted to get his wife pregnant, he liked what limited fertility might mean for his sex life in the long term. Curtis would like to have one or two biological children with his wife but not more than that. As he explained it, his low fertility means that he and his wife can have lots of sex, not practice birth control, and not have to worry about having too many children. He admitted, though, that his wife might not be as thrilled as he is about the possibility of more sex. These men's attitudes demonstrate that for some men, sex is more central to masculine identities than is fertility.

Marcus learned when he was still a teenager that he was infertile as a result of his cystic fibrosis. He believes that because he was then at a point in his life at which he was interested in having sex, not children, he took the news of his "sterility" much more in his stride than might other infertile men: "It was kind of a nice thing for a long time. . . . I didn't wear condoms for a long time, until AIDS came out. So it was actually—it was kind of nice. You tell women there's nothing to worry about there, and they relaxed, and it was good." Infertility was actually a boon to Marcus's sex life, because he was able to have sex freely without using contraceptives—at least until he became more aware of the risk of AIDS—and with no threat of unwanted pregnancy. His experience illustrates how fertility status and masculinity vary by circumstance and change over the life course. Marcus's appreciation for infertility as a young man, Curtis's gratefulness for limited fertility in marriage, and even Philip's increased interest in extramarital sex all demonstrate that poor fertility can actually sustain some of the norms that are associated with hegemonic masculinity, including promiscuity and an active sex life. Though the cultural standard for masculinity is a man who can impregnate a woman when he so desires, there are many stages and circumstances in men's lives in which paternity is not desired and can present a major interruption to a man's sex life, marriage, or life path.

ART scholar Charis Thompson argues that infertile women invest their time, finances, and emotions into the pursuit of motherhood to legitimize and stabilize their identity as women. By contrast, men find infertility more threatening to their sexuality. Infertile men work to prove their virility and sexual prowess.[37] In this research study, some men struggled to understand and tease out the relationship between fertility and sexuality. As a case in point, Eric explained that when he first learned about his low sperm count, he worried that he was somehow less sexual or masculine. Later, he read in some patient literature that his concerns are common among infertile men, which helped to quell his doubts. Eric describes the thought process that infertile men go through this way:

> "How can I be infertile? I had sex twice a day, and I'm this super stud," or whatever—what they think of themselves as. And [fertility status] doesn't have anything to do with [sexuality]. So once you just find out information, you learn about it, [insecurity] goes away. . . . When you have a low count, the first thing you think of is "What am I? Half a man? What's going on here?"

Eric worried that poor fertility indicated that he was not a "stud" or was only "half a man." Additionally, his poor sperm quality was caused by a varicocele, which he believed was causing pain during sex. His nervous anticipation of pain made sex less desirable to him. Eventually, he underwent surgery to repair the varicocele. After learning more about his infertility and healing from the surgery, he no longer experienced pain during sex and felt that his sex life had returned to normal.

George did not express any diminished interest in sex due to his infertility, but he sensed that his inability to get his wife pregnant had become a turnoff for her. Sex was the symbolic reminder of their inability to conceive, and he noted that "the idea of sex brings the emotions out" in his wife. Her "life-and-death struggle" with infertility made sex undesirable to her, which only exacerbated George's feelings of guilt and might explain his enduring feelings of inadequacy and helplessness.

For some men, the shock that they feel about their infertility puts their sex lives on hold. After Brandon learned about his infertility, he shied away from sex. As he explains, "It was like, it's not even worth it. Why even do it?" In time, Brandon's sex drive caught up with him, and he warmed up to sex again:

> Brandon: I just changed a little bit. It felt like, why not? You know what I mean? I'm in the mood!
> LB: So you quickly forgot?
> Brandon: I'm trying to put [infertility] behind me. A lot of it. Trying to deal with it. Put it behind me and say, okay, this is my life. I got to put up with this for the rest of my life. There's no way of going around it, and so I just move on.

When conception has been the primary goal of sex for an extended period of time (usually a year or more), infertility can make men question their sexual prowess and the purposes of sex. Though sex seemed intimidating or pointless after he learned about his infertility, Brandon soon remembered the pleasure of sex and decided that sex was still valuable and worthwhile.

Initially, Troy's insecurities about infertility translated into discomfort and insecurity in the bedroom:

> Maybe in the first couple weeks—maybe [sex] was a little awkward for me, at least maybe mentally, just a bit. It's always in the back of your head, maybe, "What is she thinking? Does she think maybe I'm less of a man because I'm doing those [surgeries]?" And I've actually had this conversation with her. She was like, "Oh, my God. Don't be ridiculous. It's silly." So

> maybe a couple of weeks at first [infertility had an impact].
> But no, it didn't affect our sex life. If anything, I think it made
> it a little better, maybe a little more passionate, I don't know.

Fortunately, Troy and his wife communicate openly in their marriage. Rather than hiding his fears, which might in time have inhibited his sexual expression, he shared his concerns with his wife. She was easily able to overlook his infertility, she encouraged him to do the same, and they continued to find pleasure in sex.

Troy surmised that infertility had improved his marriage and love life, not in spite of his insecurities but because he had to overcome those insecurities. In most cases, infertility has only a temporary effect on the timing and meaning of sex, but it can have a long-lasting and positive impact on marriages. Recall from earlier in this chapter that Patrick worried that his wife would perceive him as useless to the marriage and Aaron wondered whether his wife would have regrets about marrying him. Similarly, Brandon worried that his wife would want to leave him for another, more fertile man. He shared this fear with his wife. As he describes, "She said that she would never leave me, and I'm like, 'Are you sure?' And she's like, 'Yes. You're my husband.' It means the world to me to have somebody care for me that much." Despite the added strain on sex, heightened emotions, and increased marital spats, most couples agreed that infertility had actually strengthened their marriages and brought them closer to each other.[38] Patrick, Aaron, Brandon, Troy and others were fortunate to have wives who expressed abiding love for them in spite of their infertility, and that knowledge deepened their marital bonds.

Benjamin, a twenty-six-year-old religious scholar, believed that infertility had had a positive impact on his marriage because, as he said, "I was nervous, and we needed to comfort each other." Ron wondered at times whether his wife would have regrets about marrying him but felt that going through infertility with his wife meant, as he described, that "[w]e can get through anything together, and that if we're able to get through this challenge, like we've gotten through others, you know, then that means that we can really get through anything." Greg also maintained that infertility had affected his marriage "in a good way," noting that "[a]s crazy as that sounds, it really forced us to be nice and to just have a goal that we both really shared and to attack it together. So I think, all in all, it just made us stronger than others." Contrary to popular belief—and even to their own surprise—many patients saw the potential for infertility to fortify their marital relationships.

Fatherhood

In her book *Infertility: Medical, Emotional, and Social Considerations,* psychiatrist Miriam Mazor notes that everyone has fears and ambivalence about parenthood but that "the infertile person must struggle harder with them."[39] In this study, I asked patients whether infertility had ever caused them to question their ability to be a good father. George wondered in "a weird, superstitious way" whether his zero sperm count indicated that he was "just not meant to be a father." Curtis worried that he was not a good father to his stepson and did not feel completely confident about his parenting skills. Joel worried that he was "almost" not good enough to be a husband and father. Aside from these few examples, most of the men reported that infertility had not caused them to question their ability to be a good father.

"Father," as a verb, means to sire a child and also to rear a child. Most men with whom I spoke claimed that they did not see any relationship between the ability to impregnate their wives and the ability to raise children. I asked Greg whether infertility had ever caused him to question his ability to be a good father:

> Greg: Never. Never put the two together.
> LB: Why do you think you didn't connect them?
> Greg: I just really don't feel like my ability or my sperm count
>   has anything to do . . . with my ability to be a father.

Greg saw no connection between fertility status and parenting ability. Ron echoed this idea: "Your actions once the child is born make a good father and mother, whether or not you're fertile or infertile." As Todd explained, "You don't have to have any kind of sperm to be a good father. You just have to know how to love, to discipline, and, you know, that kind of stuff. . . . Sperm is totally irrelevant as to whether or not you're a good dad." Despite the intense anguish that infertility brought him, Patrick believed that his infertility experience actually helped him resolve to be a better father: "I think [infertility has] made me realize how much I want to be a father, and if we are successful, it may be that I think I would try that much harder to be a good father, because it's been so difficult to get there."

While ample research indicates that infertile women often internalize their infertility and interpret it to mean that they are not fit for motherhood, my interviews suggest just the opposite for men. Most of the men with whom I spoke claimed to be well prepared for the duties of fatherhood. Again, why is there a gender discrepancy? Earlier research suggests that women's social world is centered on reproduction, pregnancy, and motherhood, which provide constant reminders that the infertile woman is not fulfilling her appropriate social role, while men are better able to "separate infertility and childlessness from their social and working lives and their relationships with other men."[40] In other words, men maintain a stable and socially valued identity that has little to do with reproduction. Furthermore, most responsibilities of fatherhood do not begin until after the baby is born, whereas motherhood begins at the moment of conception.[41] Women are expected to make lifestyle changes during pregnancy to ensure a safe and healthy environment in which the fetus can grow and develop properly. Medical practitioners, public health advocates, and the media encourage women to forgo alcohol and tobacco, engage in light exercise, take prenatal vitamins, watch their diets, get plenty of rest, and meet with medical professionals regularly. Expectant mothers are encouraged to begin prenatal bonding with their babies by singing songs and reading books aloud. The cultural rule is that motherhood requires a cooperative, healthy body to raise healthy, intelligent, happy babies. Pregnancy is part of the process by which women prove their mothering capabilities. When women cannot get pregnant, they perceive their bodies as uncooperative, genderless, and inadequate for motherhood.[42] By contrast, fewer expectations are placed on fathers' bodies and lifestyles during gestation.[43] Arguably, the span of nine months between conception and birth makes it easier for infertile men to mentally disconnect the ability to conceive a child from the ability to rear a child.

Most men I interviewed did not admit to ever having doubts or fears associated with fatherhood. Surely, some of these men must have had qualms or anxiety about fatherhood, as even fertile men do, but as they talked and shared their ideas about what makes a good father, they sounded emboldened. Interviews challenged men to evaluate their ability to be good fathers and articulate their ideals of fatherhood. While infertility was often described as a situation beyond patients' control, how men raise their children is something that they felt was within their control.

Men were asked to briefly describe what makes a good father. Responses commonly emphasized the importance of "spending time" with and "being there" for their children. The following responses typify what many subjects shared:

> A father is somebody that's there to give children a shoulder to cry on, listen to, play with, and be there as much as possible. And even though you got to work and everything, you still have to be there to support. You can't just let the kid raise himself. (Brandon)

> Being there. I think it's a lot of the same qualities of being a good husband: listening, talking, communicating. Not just talking, but listening and communicating back. I think the biggest thing is freeing up some time to spend, because all the time you spend with your child is time that they're not spending doing something they shouldn't be. (Kevin)

Brandon and Kevin emphasized the importance of fathers listening to and communicating with their children. They described the important role that fathers play in supervising and guiding children. A child cannot be left to "raise himself," and children should be prevented from "doing something they shouldn't be" doing. Brandon also acknowledged the traditional role of men as breadwinners, stating that fathers "got to work."

Some men, such as Brandon and Kevin, described good fathering in terms reminiscent of traditional nurturing ideals of motherhood as they explained that fathers should "be there," "listen to" and "love" their children, and provide "a shoulder to cry on." Marcus and Patrick likewise explained that they looked forward to spending time with their children and providing them with opportunities to learn and develop. They also recognized their own fathers as good role models:

> I try to remember how my father was to me, try to remember all the good things he did for me, still does for me. And I'd try to provide just as much as possible for my son so he can do

what he wants to do, he can be what he wants to be, and give him every opportunity that he wants emotionally, financially, whatever, whatever he wants to do or be. The basic thing that I can do is be there for him for what he needs. And I would say that's the heart of what I'm trying, what I would like to be as a father. (Patrick)

Being able to have them know that they're loved. Being able to give them good educational opportunities. Spending time and interacting with them a lot, as did mine, by the way. (Marcus)

Patrick and Marcus emphasized their masculinity by identifying with the most influential male figures in their own lives: their fathers. Fathers serve as reliable examples of masculinity that infertile men can identify with, relate to, and strive to be more like as they construct their own ideas of masculinity.[44] Men listed positive characteristics that they believed they could embody and that served as self-constructed markers for achieving masculinity. In describing the types of fathers they would like to become, men were able to present themselves as capable, worthy, masculine men.

Two of the men I interviewed are stepfathers. Stepfatherhood was a double-edged sword for these men as they dealt with infertility. On the one hand, it provided them with fathering experience, which legitimated them as capable fathers. On the other hand, being a stepfather generated other insecurities. For example, Derek, a thirty-three-year-old state trooper, confidently responded that infertility did not cause him to question his ability to be a good father. Yet when asked whether his infertility experience had ever caused him to question himself as a good husband, he replied, "Yeah, a little bit. . . . I just look at it from a point, you know, [my wife] was never married when she had her first child. Here's this guy that she said she didn't—the way she talks about him isn't the best, and yet they had a child together. I'm just thinking, 'Well, here I am trying to be a good guy and stuff, and I can't even help produce a child.'" Derek could not help but compare himself to his wife's previous boyfriend, the father of his stepdaughter, which left him feeling discouraged and inadequate.

Curtis also felt conflicted by his role as a stepfather. When I asked him whether infertility had ever caused him to question his ability to be a good father, he paused. Then he replied thoughtfully, "That's a good question, because I want to be better than my dad. I want the best for [my stepson], but sometimes I feel like because I haven't fully experienced my wife being pregnant—I haven't fully experienced all of that, I feel that I put a lot of pressure on myself. And that's how sometimes I mess everything up."

Curtis believed that he was a good father to his stepson, and he wanted what was best for his stepson, but he also wanted "to be better" than his own father. He felt a twinge of inadequacy because he had not experienced pregnancy with his wife and worried that his lack of experience with biological fatherhood was somehow translating into poor fathering skills.

Masculinities scholar Michael Kimmel asserts that the "great secret of American manhood" is that men *"are afraid of other men."*[45] This does not mean that men are fearful of each other or cower from others. Rather, Kimmel argues, men are highly attuned to their own inadequacies and failings, and they live with the constant fear that they will be found out by their male peers, who are presumed not to share those shortcomings. Derek and Curtis were not afraid of their stepsons' fathers but were intimidated by what those men represented: fertile—and therefore capable—men. While infertile men may typically compare themselves to a faceless crowd of presumably fertile men and be struck with feelings of inadequacy, stepfatherhood creates a particularly threatening circumstance in which infertile men define their masculinity in relation to specific fertile men, men whom they know by name and whom their female partners had once loved.

Conclusion

In their attempts to conduct research on male infertility, scholars have discovered that infertile men are not easy to find.[46] They are largely absent from clinical settings, particularly in IVF centers, where most treatments are conducted on women's bodies.[47] Often, the only evidence of men's existence is the semen that they leave behind for testing or fertilization procedures.[48] Men are also not likely to respond to recruiting advertisements. Canadian scholars Russell Webb and Judith Daniluk studied men's experiences with infertility in the late 1990s. They reported that the recruitment process leading up to their research study, which entailed advertisements in newsletters and newspapers and invitations through doctors and medical clinics, took several months, required expansion into another major city, and resulted in only six male subjects.[49] Needless to say, men do not line up around the block to sign up for a study of male infertility.

As I approached the research for this book, I knew that I would have to be sensitive and creative in recruiting research participants. Focusing on male infertility clinics rather than IVF clinics helped me to physically locate infertile male bodies. Couples who had "been evaluated for or diagnosed with infertility" or "because [they had] some questions and concerns about [their] fertility"[50] qualified for participation in this research project and were personally invited by their doctors to participate. More than two-thirds of the couples who were invited to take part in this research agreed to be interviewed. Other scholars have presumed that men do not participate in infertility research because the subject matter is too intimate or embarrassing to discuss. On the basis of my findings, I would argue instead that many men do not volunteer for infertility research in part because they do not think of themselves as infertile, and when they do, they quickly find a resolution to the problem.

Recruiting techniques that were used to attract subjects for infertility research in the past have arguably created biased research samples for study. For example, some psychologists and mental health professionals who have written about infertility have drawn heavily on the narratives of their own patients, specifically people who have sought professional help to overcome the psychological and emotional trauma that they attribute to infertility. Other studies have recruited research participants from infertility support groups, resulting in a similar set of research subjects who self-identify as infertile and may be outspoken about their infertility experiences.[51] Most infertility studies recruit "infertile" women and men,[52] which disqualifies infertile individuals who do not self-identify as infertile. In fairness, the men I interviewed represent a self-selected research sample too, because they were all men who were willing to see a doctor to discuss their infertility issues. Yet these men also held a very wide range of attitudes, beliefs, and ideas about what infertility is and how it affects lives.[53] This research study recruited many infertile men who did not self-identify as infertile and some who could not even define infertility.

At the beginning of this book, I raised the question *Where are all the infertile men?* Infertile men do not participate in support groups, in person or online, to the extent to which infertile women do.[54]

Women fill the ranks of infertility advocacy organizations and mobilize for political action, while infertile men are mostly absent. Popular and academic discourse about infertility focuses on the experiences of women.[55] Why are infertile men missing or invisible? For one thing, many infertile men do not see themselves as infertile. Among both those who self-identify as infertile and those who do not, most infertile men intellectually reframe their infertility issues as strictly a medical condition, somehow distinct and separate from their self and their lived experience. This revelation explains in part why men do not participate in infertility research and why there is not more public dialogue on the subject of male infertility. More importantly, my findings show how infertile men grapple with a gender crisis and engage in gender work. Most infertile men do not escape infertility emotionally and mentally unscathed. However, they are active players in the social construction of gender and disease. They reconsider the cultural value of fertility and the social definition of masculinity, and they decide for themselves what it means to be a man, a husband, a lover, and a father. The narratives of infertile men demonstrate that infertility and masculinity may be defined in myriad unique and nuanced ways. But what these stories collectively show is that reconceptualizing infertility and renegotiating masculinity are requisite parts of gender work for infertile men.

Until nearly the end of the twentieth century, few medical options were available to help infertile men overcome their infertility. Coping with male infertility was primarily a psychological grieving process.[56] Today, male factor infertility can be a highly involved medical process accompanied by the mental processes of decision making and gender work. Disease and gender get constructed at the intersection of private lives and medical clinics. Infertile men perceive their "sterility," "zero sperm," "below average sperm," "missing tubes," or "messed up plumbing" as simply a medical condition, beyond their control, not their fault, and in most cases reparable. The promises of medical procedures and technologies often help men to avert crisis and to avoid grief. Patients who consult male infertility specialists are swept into treatment protocols immediately upon diagnosis, and some couples achieve pregnancy soon thereafter. Many men cling to the notion that if you have a problem that can be fixed, you don't have a problem.

Taking Control

Twenty years ago, a doctor took one look at Jack's semen analysis results—zero sperm–and told him that he would never have a biological child. Jack and his wife considered adoption, but their marriage fell apart before they ever pursued it. Fifteen years later, Jack found himself in a new relationship, contemplating marriage again and still longing for children. He and his fiancée, Sarah, were heartened to learn from Jack's primary care physician that significant progress had been made in male reproductive medicine. They were referred to a local general urologist, who ran another sperm count—again zero—along with a battery of diagnostic tests to check chromosomes and hormone levels. Everything appeared normal and healthy, a good sign that Jack's testicles were producing sperm. The urologist referred Jack and Sarah to a large IVF clinic in a neighboring state. There, REs established that Sarah had healthy fertility and referred Jack to another urologist, a specialist in male infertility.

Like many men seeking information about their fertility, Jack felt frustrated that the path to a qualified practitioner was a meandering, time-consuming rigmarole.[1] Considering how many doctors and tests Jack had been through, he was shocked at how easily the male infertility specialist determined the cause of his infertility. After one quick palpation of Jack's scrotum, the specialist explained that an obstruction was blocking sperm from passing from his testicles to the seminal vesicles and into the ejaculate. Needless to say, Jack was thrilled to hear that his testicles were functioning properly. He hastily signed on for surgery to repair the obstruction and search for sperm in his testicles. Jack recalled waking up in the recovery room after surgery and hearing that the doctor had retrieved live sperm from his testicles: "I was ecstatic! It was just incredible that we had been through this whole process and after meeting with [the specialist] once, he determined that surgery was just a logical step, and that's what we had gone through and now we have sperm!"

As Jack contemplated his new chance at biological fatherhood, he wondered whether maybe he had never been meant to have a baby with his first wife. Now that he had found the right woman and was in a good place in his life, God or fate had opened up new, miraculous medical possibilities. After all, Jack loves children and always believed that one day he would be a father. He reflected:

> My brother has four children, and my oldest brother has three, and I can't say that I've ever been resentful, but I'm sure that at some subconscious level there's been some real disappointment, because here I am a schoolteacher of twenty-three kids, I coach twenty girls after school every day on a soccer team, and it's pretty much always been my life that I would have children. . . . I felt more complete that now there's the possibility of me producing a child.

For fifteen years, Jack thought of himself as infertile. Thanks to medical science, Jack "felt more complete," and, as he told me, finally envisioned himself as "a potential father."

I first met Jack during a postoperation checkup with his specialist in which he learned that, thanks to surgery, sperm had successfully migrated into his ejaculate. Though the sperm were few in number and not particularly motile, the discovery was received as a major victory. In light of his happiness and gratitude toward the doctor, I was surprised in our first interview to hear how horrendous his treatment and recovery had been. Jack explained:

> I was just under the assumption that it was going to be like a vasectomy, in that I would be out doing my thing the next day. I could not really move from the living room. I didn't leave the

living room for a couple days, which was really a tough thing, because [Sarah] had to help me pee in a bottle and that was a tough thing, but she was good about it, because she just stayed there the whole time. . . . I'm not big on taking Percocet or anything, but it just came to the point where it's like, I guess I really need to [take the Percocet], because it really hurts considerably. So I did my thing until—four or five days around the house—until I was feeling good enough to walk. It was a long time before I was able to sort of function.

Despite the intensity of his involvement with medical intervention and the painful aftermath, Jack considered surgery the right decision and a tremendous success. He told me earnestly and repeatedly that his plan with Sarah was to conceive "naturally."

In Chapter 4, I explained how steadfastly men conceptualize their infertility as just a medical condition, a finding that sheds light on the relationships between concepts such as the body and the self, masculinity and control, guilt and denial. In this chapter, as I explore how men move through medical decision making and treatment protocols, I flesh out these earlier themes and explore the complicated relationships between concepts such as medical intervention and bodily control, institutional authority and personal masculinity, and technological versus natural solutions. As men shared the discomfort, pain, and hardship associated with fertility treatments, they spun masculine narratives about sacrifice, heroism, and fulfilling their duty as husbands who protect their wives and (future) children. Like Jack, men perceived medicine as a blessing and an answer, the means for regaining control over their lives and fertility and for making "natural" conception possible. Rather than feeling disempowered by medical treatments or vulnerable to their hazards, men accepted medical treatments as logical and normal steps toward parenthood. Medical technologies were perceived as tools for harnessing power and repairing fractured masculine identities. Use of these tools is central to the patients' stories of masculinity.

Of the twenty-four couples I interviewed for this book, fourteen were given the choice to pursue a male treatment (e.g., surgery, electroejaculation, or drug therapy) in lieu of a more female-focused treatment such as IUI or in vitro fertilization (IVF or IVF-ICSI). Thirteen of those fourteen couples opted for a male treatment first; if it failed, they planned to pursue more female-focused treatments. The one couple who did not opt for the male treatment first were advised by both their urologist and their RE to move directly to IVF-ICSI because of the wife's endometriosis. Another three couples were given the option to pursue IVF-ICSI using sperm surgically extracted from the husband's testicles, which they pursued without hesitation. Two couples were advised to go directly to IUI, and another couple were advised to go directly to IVF, which they all did. Of the remaining four couples, one couple wanted to pursue treatment but could not afford it; one couple were still investigating possible medical options to overcome the wife's more complex infertility issues;[2] the youngest couple in the study, newlyweds, decided to postpone treatment until they were a bit older; and one couple chose to apply for adoption after learning that IVF was their only treatment option, a procedure that they oppose on religious grounds.

To summarize this picture, at least twenty of twenty-four couples desired medical treatments, to whatever extent necessary, to overcome their infertility. Couples preferred male treatments over female treatments whenever possible. When male treatments were not an option or when they failed, couples regularly turned to IUI or IVF to achieve pregnancy. In other words, men did not hesitate to pursue male treatments, which they preferred over female treatments and the use of donor sperm. Throughout this book, I have mentioned the social taboo against discussing male infertility and the invisibility of infertile men. Medical doctors and mental health therapists recognize that men have a hard time accepting that they have infertility issues. My research supports this. However, doctors and therapists would be wrong to assume that men with infertility issues avoid treatment. In this research study, among patients who were either referred to or diligently sought out male infertility specialists, men embraced medical treatments. Even though many men had a difficult time accepting or understanding their diagnosis and many did not self-identify as infertile, they still willingly submitted to medical intervention.

Men and Medicalization

Social research on male infertility takes root at the intersection of two subfields of medical sociology scholarship: infertility research, which has focused mainly on women's experiences with childlessness and reproductive technologies, and men's health research, which has explored not only men's health habits and practices but also the relationship between health status, biomedicine, and masculinity. In the early 1980s, a time when there were many health risks associated with the "artificial" reproductive technologies that were still in development, feminist scholars argued that infertile women were pursuing dangerous, even life-threatening treatment regimens under extreme social pressure to fulfill the socially mandated role of mother.[3] Though the intentions behind this research were noble—to liberate women from the physical harm of medical technologies—later scholars argued that early research painted infertile women as victims of "ideological duping"[4] and pressured them to give up their dreams of motherhood in the name of feminist goals.[5] In the past two decades, infertility scholars, more sympathetic to women's desires for biological children, have paid close attention to the nuanced and complicated power relationships between biomedical practices and infertility patients.[6] Arthur Greil argues that infertile women are "neither passive victims of biomedicine nor uncritical consumers . . . Rather, they are problem solvers, operating creatively within a system they do not control."[7] Similarly, Charis Thompson argues that medicalization is not inherently oppressive and that the infertile "woman's objectification involves her active participation and is managed by herself as crucially as by the practitioners, procedures, and instruments."[8]

Like the study of infertility, the study of men's experiences with Western medicine is a fairly young field of social inquiry. Although medical sociology scholarship took off in the 1950s, sociologists Dana Rosenfeld and Christopher A. Faircloth argue that scholars' emphasis on the distribution of disease and access to health care among historically oppressed groups left white men's relationship to and experiences with Western medicine relatively unexplored.[9] Most research on the medicalization of disorders documents who has the power to medicalize social groups and what groups are most vulnerable to medicalization.[10] Much of this work has failed to provide a gendered analysis, and when gender has been taken into consideration, the primary focus has been on women and women's bodies. Men's bodies, men's gendered medical experiences, and the medicalization of masculinity have often been ignored.[11] Meanwhile, epidemiological statistics show that men make fewer visits to the doctor than women do, are less likely to comply with medical direction, and are more likely to engage in high-risk behaviors and maintain unhealthy lifestyles. Men are believed to be more likely than women to suffer from heart disease, obesity, diabetes, and cancer, and men have shorter life spans than do women. Social scholars have interpreted these numbers to show that hegemonic masculinity is defined by strength and independence and that men view sickness and reliance on medical help as emasculating and signs of weakness.[12]

In recent years, social studies of male-specific medical disorders, such as erectile dysfunction, prostate and testicular cancers, and andropause, suggest that men today may be more accepting of medical technologies than were previous generations.[13] Men, it seems, are willing to participate in rigorous medical interventions when masculine aspects of their appearance, health status, bodily functions, and identity are on the line. Although these two fields of scholarship—infertility and men's health—have different historical bases and trajectories, they have arrived at the same point of discovery: Men and women actively engage with medical technologies to restore threatened gender identities. Infertile women who seek medical services are no longer portrayed as victims of medical science; rather, they are portrayed as informed consumers who intelligently submit to medical technologies for personal gain, to achieve normalcy, and to reaffirm their female identity.[14] By the same token, studies of men and medicine conclude that men perceive medical technologies as the means whereby they can "fight back against the perils of an insecured masculinity."[15]

Historically, men have been the designers and producers of various technologies, have enjoyed greater access to technologies, and have occupied the positions of authority as doctors, politicians, and business and military leaders who oversee the administration of technologies. Women are also users of technology, but more often than men, they are subordinated by technologies as recipients (or victims) of technological interventions.[16] For these reasons, feminist scholars of science and technology have focused on the gendered power dynamics rendered by technology—that is, how men use technologies to gain power over women. The gender paradigm in numerous reproductive studies is fairly consistent: The practitioners who control medical technologies are men; patients are women, often rendered powerless by technologies. But what happens when doctors are men and women and patients are men? How do men experience medical technologies?

In his book *The Birth of the Clinic,* the late French philosopher Michel Foucault argued that the "medical gaze"—the subjection of patients to medical authorities and interventions—is both dehumanizing and disciplining.[17] The medical gaze substantiates a distinct power hierarchy between those who have and produce knowledge— namely, doctors—and the patients who provide their own bodies for examination. Earlier in this book, I discussed how humiliating semen analyses can be for men as they subject their bodies and bodily fluids to the medical gaze. In that context the medical gaze is dehumanizing as it alienates men's bodies from their own personal human identities. However, once diagnosed with poor fertility, men do not necessarily see medical treatments as objectifying. Rather, men interpret their disciplined participation in medical treatments as their means for taking control of the situation. Men regard themselves as protectors of their wives and less vulnerable to the risks of technology. Medical technologies can potentially restore fertility, one facet of masculinity, but their use is also a demonstration of masculinity.

Male Treatments: Natural Approaches

A semen analysis for Paul, a thirty-year-old salesperson, showed a low sperm count with poor motility, most likely caused by the large varicocele his specialist had detected inside his scrotum. Meanwhile, a fertility workup for Paul's wife, Laura, indicated that she had reliable fertility. Doctors offered the couple a few medical options to help them conceive. One option was to artificially inseminate Laura with Paul's sperm via IUI, but Paul's sperm count was so low that the chances for success were slim. A more promising option would be to harvest Laura's eggs and inseminate them with Paul's sperm using IVF techniques and return a fertilized embryo to Laura's womb. In lieu of IUI or IVF, however, Paul and Laura opted for varicocelectomy, a surgery to cut off the varicocele that was suspected of impairing Paul's sperm production, in hopes that they might eventually conceive through sexual intercourse.

The first time I ever saw Paul, he was being prepped for surgery by a team of nurses and medical assistants. No introductions were made because he had already slipped into anesthesia-induced sleep. A couple of weeks later, in our first interview, Paul explained, "We chose to do [varicocelectomy] before jumping ahead to the other nonconventional ways, you might say. . . . [We chose to t]ry to have a child the natural way, if at all possible." He expressed real concern that if they opted for "nonconventional ways," such as IVF, his semen sample might get "mixed up" with the wrong woman's eggs. Furthermore, in light of his Christian beliefs, Paul questioned the ethics of conception in vitro. A little over a year after our first conversation, I reconnected with Paul and Laura, who had just welcomed the birth of their first baby, conceived through sexual intercourse shortly after Paul's surgery. With the image of Paul draped in a blue sheet lying comatose on the operating table surrounded by needles, scalpels, microscopes, and bright lights and the scents of iodine antiseptic, bleached linens, and cauterized flesh inscribed in my memory, it sounded quite ironic when Paul announced, "We were hoping we could do it *naturally,* and we did."

Fertility treatments for men epitomize medical technology at its most sophisticated. Varicocelectomy and other exploratory and reconstructive surgeries utilize state-of-the-art instruments for microsurgical techniques and incorporate all of the technologies of fully equipped operating rooms, including computers for monitoring vital signs and for magnifying, recording, and televising procedures. Patients are administered pharmaceutical drugs to regulate hormones and manage pain as well as general anesthesia. Specialists are highly skilled and accompanied by well-trained staff. Surgical procedures for men are invasive and painful and require long recovery periods. Yet patients perceive these cutting-edge medical interventions as "natural" solutions to male infertility, because they have the potential to enable sperm to eventually fertilize an egg within the context of intimate marital relations in the privacy of a couple's own home.

The CDC defines assisted reproductive technology (ART) as all fertility treatments in which both eggs and sperm are handled.[18] This includes a variety of IVF techniques that manipulate eggs and sperm outside of the bodies of the men and women who produce them. More popularly, ART is a broad umbrella term that may also refer to IUI and the entire constellation of technologies that lead up to IUI and IVF, including hormone tests, hormone shots, ultrasound procedures, and laparoscopic surgeries. On the basis of my observations in medical settings as well as academic and popular discourse, male treatments fall outside the category of ART. This omission facilitates the perception among patients that conception that is made possible through male treatments is somehow not technologically assisted.

Once Paul and Laura conceived a baby through good old-fashioned heterosexual intercourse, the medically invasive road to pregnancy seemed natural.

Scholars have long argued that all aspects of modern life, even seemingly natural things such as food, language, and our bodies, are the products of highly technologized processes.[19] Technologies such as the ones developed and employed for conception, gestation, and childbirth are now so commonplace that we accept them as natural and normal facets of everyday life. Sociologists Robbie Davis-Floyd and Joseph Dumit argue that society has "moved so far into the cyborg realm that only those technological transfusions we call 'assisted reproduction'—safe, monitored, controlled—are considered 'natural' in this post-modern world. It has become unnatural to give birth at home, without the body-altering safety net of high technology. Instead, our culture has naturalized technobirth."[20] What is curious about society's shift into the "cyborg realm" is that technology is now so commonplace that it regularly goes unrecognized, and most people still claim to value "natural" experiences. Male infertility specialists, understanding that couples value a natural reproductive experience, market male treatments as the means for conceiving naturally. One doctor cleverly advocated what he called IBF (in-bed fertilization) over IVF, explaining to patients that corrective surgeries or hormone therapies for men make conception in bed possible. The rhetoric of natural conception resonates with the masculine ideal of sexual prowess, which men demonstrate by impregnating women through sex.

As the innovators, designers, inventors, owners, and controllers of technology, men have enjoyed a long-standing relationship with technology. Technology is seen as masculine, and men's identities are wrapped up in technology. As science and technology scholar Judith Wajcman asserts, "Men's affinity with technology is now seen as integral to the constitutions of male gender identity and the culture of technology."[21] The historical masculinization of technology means that men today enjoy an affinity with technology, a seemingly natural connection, which allows infertile men to frame male treatments as natural approaches to conception. Recall from Chapter 4 how easily men separated their selves from their bodies. This philosophical question of the relationship between the body, the mind, and the self has been debated from Plato and Aristotle to René Descartes to Sigmund Freud to contemporary scholars. From a social construction-ist perspective, the relationship between the body and self is flexible, and individual actors have the power to reformulate the meanings of and relationship between self and body. For male infertility patients, the body is the vehicle of the self—a vehicle that occasionally breaks down and needs repair. Because the body is external to the self and reparable, men do not have to internalize bodily failings as poor re-flections on themselves as men. However, while men do not assume personal fault for their bodily failings, they do assume responsibility for making any necessary repairs.

Anthropologist Marcia Inhorn has studied the infertility experi-ences of men and women in the Arab world for more than two de-cades. She identified two main reasons why infertile Middle Eastern men choose to undergo varicocele repair surgeries: "to bolster mar-riage through shared suffering and to bolster masculinity through fertility."[22] Indeed, men in this study readily pursued treatments that demonstrated to their wives their willingness to endure pain and dis-comfort to resolve their childlessness. Furthermore, some men sought treatments that had the potential to protect their wives altogether from the suffering and difficulties of female medical procedures. Like men in the Middle East, men in the United States desire treatments to restore their fertility, which bolsters their masculinity. To this point I would add that male treatments give men the sense that they can re-tain some control over a situation that feels desperately beyond their control. Technology is empowering, and male treatments give men an active role in the infertility journey. Until the end of the twentieth century, infertile men had very few options for medical treatment, and men often felt "left out" of the medical process for overcoming infertility.[23] Participating in treatments helps to assuage any guilt men may feel about their wives' involvement in treatments to over-come male infertility issues.

Eric, a technical support specialist in his late thirties, chose vari-cocelectomy over IUI and IVF to overcome his low sperm count. Like Paul, Eric had moral concerns about IVF and wanted "to go the most *natural* route possible at first," so surgery followed by sex presented the optimal choice. Clinics generally require patients to submit semen samples every couple of months after surgery to monitor changes in sperm count and quality. Unfortunately, Eric's major medical insur-ance policy would not cover the cost of semen analyses, so Eric decided to analyze his own semen. He ordered a home semen analysis kit on the Internet, which included a microscope, slides, and instructions for measuring a variety of factors, such as sperm count, motility, and morphology. Every month or two, Eric would put his own ejaculate under the microscope and check for improvements. In the meantime, Eric's wife, Stacey, monitored her own fertility signs, and they continued to have sex regularly in hopes of conceiving. Eric's do-it-yourself approach to monitoring his fertility was unique among the men I interviewed. Yet his story captures men's attitudes toward technology—namely, that technology is a tool. Technology is implemented and controlled to benefit its users. It does not replace nature but keeps nature moving on course.[24]

Eric's low sperm count was likely caused by a painful varicocele. However, his wife, Stacey, had been married once before and had been unable to get pregnant in her previous marriage, a situation suggesting that she had some infertility issues of her own. A full medical workup did not show any apparent fertility problems for Stacey, and specialists were unable to determine whether she was partially responsible for the couple's inability to achieve pregnancy. In separate interviews, Eric and Stacey expressed that their childlessness generated a greater emotional struggle for Stacey than for Eric. Eric hoped that being able to take advantage of male treatments and having his own technology on hand to monitor his fertility would relieve some of the stress for Stacey:

> Eric: I think it's my issue medically, but it definitely affects her. I mean, I take responsibility. I mean, I carry it around. I know she worries about it, but I don't want her to, you know. I want to take responsibility and do my own semen analysis. I feel like it's my issue. I'd much rather it be this way.
> LB: Okay. "Be this way" than which way?
> Eric: I'd rather have the problem. If one of us is going to have the problem, I'd rather have it.
> LB: Why is that?
> Eric: That's a good question. I feel like I deal with problems pretty well, and I don't want to see anybody else have them. I feel like if anybody can beat it or get around it or whatever, it's me, so I'd rather deal with it.

Eric assumed the very masculine role of autonomous hero, and his story is a reminder that masculinity is demonstrated by taking control of a situation. Earlier infertility research has documented how helpless men feel when their wives are subjected to infertility treatments, yet the availability of male infertility treatments today helps men feel in control. Eric took responsibility for what was likely Stacey's medical issue too, hoping to free her from the additional emotional distress of treatment by taking care of the situation on his own. Eric claimed that if anyone could "beat" a problem, it was him.

While Paul, Eric, and others had reservations about the ethics of IVF, couples generally had no moral or ethical concerns about male fertility treatments such as surgeries and sperm extractions.[25] William and Sue, a Catholic couple whose story appears in Chapter 3, oppose IVF because they believe that it is immoral for conception to occur outside of the body. They also had ethical concerns about what to do with any potentially unused embryos.[26] Since they believe that life begins at the moment an egg is fertilized, they could not justify destroying leftover embryos, but they also felt uneasy about selling or donating the embryos to others or storing them indefinitely. When they first sought out infertility specialists, they hoped that male treatment options for William and possibly hormones or surgery to improve Sue's fertility would allow them to conceive spontaneously through sexual intercourse at home. When they learned that IVF was the only option available to them, they stopped seeing their specialists and contacted Catholic Social Services to pursue adoption.

In Chapter 4, I quoted Roger, the police detective, who compared his infertility issues to a broken arm or missing finger. He wanted to steer away from IVF because he had ethical concerns regarding how to deal with any potentially unused embryos. Furthermore, his wife, Linda, a homemaker in her late thirties, had heard on a news program that the hormone injections that are required for IVF may cause cancer in women. When I asked Linda whether she had any similar concerns about Roger's therapy, which entailed daily hormone shots, it had never occurred to her that he could be susceptible to the same risks. Linda described her husband as a very masculine guy who wears T-shirts and jeans, has a deep voice, watches football, and works as a "rescue hero." Though Linda sees herself as vulnerable to the dangers of pharmaceutical technologies, she evidently assumed that her masculine husband was immune to them.

Linda's assumption that hormone therapy would be risky for her but not for her husband represents two running themes in couples' decision making: (1) Men are less threatened by and vulnerable to the risks of medical technologies than women. (2) Men should seek medical treatment to protect their wives and future offspring. Ironically, these essentialist and sexist notions about gender and gender roles make room for a more egalitarian approach to addressing infertility. Feminist scholar Judith Wajcman notes that early feminist analyses of technology "dismissed technoscience as inherently patriarchal and malignant" and were "pessimistic about the possibilities of redesigning technologies for gender equality."[27] In the treatment of male infertility, however, women do benefit from the close association of masculinity and technology. For example, Scott and his wife, Melanie, opted for varicocele repair surgery first, because they were concerned about the risks to mother and baby associated with IVF. Melanie, a pediatrician, admitted that several of her young patients had been conceived through IVF and displayed no birth defects or problems, but she still needed time to research and consider all of the potential risks to herself and any children. Scott preferred pursuing surgery for himself first to protect his family and so that they could, in his words, "conceive naturally." Neither Scott nor Melanie had any qualms about varicocelectomy or the risks that it entailed. Indeed, men's affinity with technology facilitates the construction of male treatments as natural solutions. It also encourages men's involvement in reproductive technologies, promoting shared responsibility for reproduction among heterosexual couples and, more generally speaking, gender equality.

IVF: A Normal Path to Pregnancy

Jack, whose decision to undergo surgery was described at the beginning of this chapter, expressed great confidence after surgery that Sarah would get pregnant naturally. However, six months after surgery, Jack's sperm count had stagnated at low and immotile, Sarah was still not pregnant, and they were growing increasingly impatient. At the recommendation of their specialists, they decided to pursue IVF, and Sarah got pregnant on their second attempt. From the outset, Jack could have avoided the hassle and pain of exploratory and reconstructive surgery by opting for a simple biopsy in conjunction with IVF-ICSI. Nonetheless, he harbored no regrets about his decision to undergo the invasive surgery. After all, he was able to provide fully developed, freshly ejaculated sperm for the IVF treatment. The last time I spoke with Jack, as he and Sarah were preparing for the birth of their baby, he told me that they had enrolled in a seminar to learn and practice meditation techniques to use during labor and delivery. Women have been going through natural childbirth for centuries, Jack explained, and he and Sarah hoped that these meditation techniques would minimize anxiety and help delivery feel less like a "procedure." Jack reflected, "It's pretty odd because I think of our pregnancy as normal now, and I'm sure not everyone thinks that way, but it just seems like this is the route that we took and we're no different from anyone else."

When male treatments are not an option or they fail, couples usually turn to more female-focused treatments, such as IUI and IVF, to conceive. Treatments that were once considered unnatural are quickly reconceptualized as normal, natural steps on the path toward parenthood. Though Jack preferred to get his wife pregnant naturally, through intercourse, he now thinks of his wife's pregnancy, made possible through IVF, as "normal" and "no different than anyone else['s]." Also, focusing on creating a natural childbirth experience through meditation techniques helped Jack and Sarah to naturalize what had been a very technological process for both of them. IVF is the crowning achievement of biotechnology, yet no parent wants to feel that his or her baby is the artificial product of a science experiment.

In her study of assisted reproductive technology, anthropologist Gay Becker reported that couples initially perceived reproductive technologies as unnatural means to pregnancy. However, if conception occurred through technological intervention, couples "often made a concerted effort to treat the process *as if* it were natural."[28] In the same light, reproductive technologies scholar Sarah Franklin found that women described their bodies and themselves as not normal and going against nature when they were struggling with infertility.[29] Yet after conceiving through IVF, many women described IVF as a "natural process," a "miracle" not unlike natural conception, and as "just doing what nature does anyway." Franklin writes, "This affirmation of the 'naturalness' of IVF is consistent with the infamous plasticity of ideas about 'the natural,' and their ability to be readjusted even to circumstances which patently contradict this claim."[30] British sociologists Karen Throsby and Rosalind Gill studied men's experiences with IVF and found that men, among couples dealing with male or female infertility or both, "repeatedly disavowed that IVF is a technological procedure."[31] However, men seemed to have a very ambivalent relationship with IVF, evidenced by the fact that they defended IVF as "natural" yet simultaneously celebrated IVF as the best option science had to offer.[32] In other words, when men feel that their own masculinity and virility is in question, they downplay the technological intrusion of IVF on the natural biological process of conception. As Throsby and Gill suggest, men try to make sense of their IVF experience through the lens of hegemonic masculinity and gendered scripts. As men strive to defend their own virility, they simultaneously emphasize the value of scientific and technological achievements.

In my research, when IVF was the only option or the second-best option, couples were usually able to overlook any initial reservations and see their IVF experience as natural and normal. Six of the couples I interviewed elected to undergo varicocelectomy surgeries before trying IVF. Three of those couples achieved pregnancy through sexual intercourse within a few months of surgery. Of the three couples who did not immediately conceive, two pursued IVF-ICSI before our final interview, and one couple were making plans for IVF-ICSI with testicular sperm extraction the last time we spoke. None of the six varicocelectomy patients regretted their decisions to have surgery, including those who eventually moved on to IVF. The lack of regret on the part of the three men who had undergone what turned out to be needless surgeries demonstrates men's desire to take part in the regimens of reproductive medicalization.

Greg, a technology developer in his early thirties quoted in Chapter 4, acknowledged that only a few decades ago, his poor sperm quality might have meant that he would never become a biological father. He felt strongly that having children was something that he was meant to do, and he was grateful for medical advances that could help make pregnancy possible for him and his wife. Greg chose to undergo varicocelectomy to improve his semen parameters. Before surgery, Greg's specialist warned him that, initially, the trauma to his testicles caused by the treatment would negatively affect his sperm production. Greg was reassured that in time, as he healed, sperm production would pick up again, and he could expect to see great improvements in his sperm count four to twelve months following surgery. Four months after Greg's surgery, a semen analysis showed no improvements in his sperm count, so he and his wife, Jane, eagerly pursued IVF-ICSI.[33] A few months later, Greg's specialist ordered another semen analysis, which showed that Greg's sperm count had increased beyond presurgery levels to a normal fertile level, indicating that he and his wife could likely conceive spontaneously through intercourse. As luck would have it, Jane had already conceived through IVF-ICSI and was pregnant. Within the span of a few short months, Greg and Jane had participated in the most high-tech, cutting-edge services available for treating male and female infertility. Still, neither Greg nor Jane reported any regrets about choosing both the varicocelectomy and IVF-ICSI, even though either therapy alone would have been sufficient to achieve pregnancy. Greg's improved sperm count and quality bolstered his masculinity, and he looked forward to the possibility of conceiving naturally in the future, should they want to have more children.

For some men, the most difficult part of pursuing IVF over male treatments is accepting that their role in the treatment process has been minimized. Patrick, whose deep heartache about his infertility is described in Chapter 4, was not given any male treatment options. Because of his particular diagnosis, he and his wife were advised to move directly to IVF-ICSI. Patrick openly expressed his willingness to take part in medical interventions and regretfully explained:

> I would have happily taken as much treatment as required . . .
> if it would have helped. So if hormone replacement therapy
> was the option, I would have done it. If surgical extraction was
> the option, I would have done that. But as it turned out, there
> wasn't an awful lot I could do other than supply my sample as
> an option. . . . So unfortunately, most of the procedures were
> left to [my wife].

The heartache caused by Patrick's infertility was amplified by his inability to participate in treatments. He was left to stand by and watch his wife submit to the rigors of treatment on his behalf, which generated feelings of powerlessness.

When Troy learned that he had a zero sperm count due to a severed vas deferens, he and his wife, Lori, were offered two treatment options by their specialists. They could try reconstructive surgery for Troy or IVF-ICSI for Lori using sperm aspirated directly from Troy's testicles. Surgery for Troy would be highly invasive with no guarantees. However, if the surgery were successful, Troy's sperm count could be restored to normal, and Lori could conceive "naturally," so Troy opted for the surgery. When asked whether he would ever decline a treatment because of possible pain or discomfort, Troy replied, "No. I pretty much went in this headstrong. I said, 'Hey, anything they're willing to try or do.' I was just going to tough it out and go for it regardless. To answer your question, no, I didn't decline anything they asked me to try." Troy was game for "anything" his specialist suggested, and choosing to "tough it out" was a way for Troy to demonstrate his masculinity.

After reconstructive surgery, some weak sperm appeared in Troy's ejaculate, but his specialist determined that it would not be sufficient to let the couple conceive through intercourse. Troy and Lori moved to their second choice option, IVF-ICSI using aspirated sperm, and Lori was soon expecting twins. Troy, Jack, and others who endured surgeries and eventually resorted to IVF techniques were thankful for the opportunity to participate in male treatments. Even though these treatments did not improve their sperm counts enough to achieve spontaneous pregnancy within the desired timeframe, the men's appreciation for the improvements suggests the importance of sperm to men's personal sense of masculinity. Sperm makes the man.

Pain and Masculinity

Like Troy, the other men I interviewed were unanimous in saying that they would never decline a treatment because of potential pain or discomfort. I was not surprised to hear men say that they would never avoid treatment to avoid pain, that they would be willing to "tough it out," as Troy put it. Nonetheless, because of my own preconceived ideas about masculinity, I was surprised to hear a few men admit that treatments were painful. At the end of my first interview with Jack, he reiterated:

> It was a long recovery. I was unable to do a lot of things for eight or ten weeks after the surgery. That was a little frustrating. It was in the middle of winter. I had to talk [Sarah]

through using the snow-blower, but it was a little frustrating and it was probably . . . one of the most painful things—if not, *the* most painful thing—I've ever had to endure. I would do it again in a heartbeat, even if we didn't have the same results; there was just a need to know that we have ruled out everything in an attempt to have a biological child.

I often heard doctors tell patients they could expect to be fully recovered within a few short days, but Jack claimed that the pain—perhaps the worst pain of his life—lingered for months. As Jack's story illustrates, pain can be incapacitating. While masculinity is defined by maintaining control, physical pain is often beyond one's control. Pain controls its sufferers. I assumed that men would downplay their pain to demonstrate toughness. However, as I listened to patients' accounts of pain, I realized that these stories were men's way of explaining to me the lengths to which they were willing to go for the sake of their families, showing just how tough they were.

Kevin, a pilot in his late twenties, knows the pain of treatment. Diagnosed with zero sperm due to CBAVD (detailed in Chapter 4), he willingly submitted to testicular sperm extraction for the purposes of IVF-ICSI. Kevin was put under general anesthesia, and his specialist removed healthy chunks of tissue from his testicles, home to many sperm. Kevin had no complaints about pain related to this first procedure. Later, though, he received a telephone call from the doctor's office explaining that the laboratory technicians were not satisfied with the quality of his frozen sperm, and were requesting that live sperm be extracted the day of his wife's egg retrieval to use instead. Kevin was briefly warned that this quick procedure would not take place in the hospital under general anesthesia but would be conducted in the clinic with local anesthetic.[34]

"Wendy and I talked about it," explained Kevin, "and I said, I don't wanna half-ass this. . . . I wanted to do everything I can to make it work." On the day of Wendy's egg retrieval, Kevin arrived at the clinic, where he was administered a five-milligram tablet of Valium, a low-dose tranquilizer, to help him relax. As Kevin recalled, the specialist "literally jogged into the room and the whole thing took twenty minutes total. [The specialist] gave me a local [anesthetic] and immediately cut in, so it wasn't like the local did anything." In a voice strained with agony, Kevin described the experience as "*awwwww-*

ful." During the procedure, he tried to "play tough." He breathed deeply, held still, and fought back tears. When the nurse offered her hand to hold, Kevin retorted, "No!" According to Kevin, after the procedure was over, the nurse told him that he had done amazingly well, especially in comparison to other men, whom she had witnessed screaming and crying during that same type of procedure. It was clear that Kevin took great pride in his threshold for pain. It was important for him to explain to me, a woman, just how excruciating such procedures can be and to emphasize that he was able to bravely muscle through the pain. In terms of masculinity, he was not willing to "half-ass" his role in the treatment process in any way that might compromise its success, and he was pleased to hear that he had outperformed other men in the same circumstances.

At the end of our final interview, I asked Kevin to define masculinity. He responded:

> Not wearing your emotions on your sleeve, willing to risk your life for someone else, not being afraid to defend your family or your country. I don't really see it as much—I don't see the provider thing as much, because so many women now—and it should be—they're the breadwinner. I don't see the guy as having to bring home the bacon. But I still do see it as—for some reason—I still see the perception of, when some crazy guy has road rage and comes toward you or your family, you need to protect your family.

Kevin's display of courage in the clinic matched his personal definition of masculinity. He had refrained from crying, and though he did not exactly risk his life, he was willing to put himself in harm's way for the sake of his family. Kevin's response also reflects some of the complexities of postfeminist masculinity, as he recognizes that women's increasingly visible role as breadwinner displaces men as providers. Kevin happens to be highly trained and well compensated in his profession. However, his wife is also well educated and has a full-time career, which diminishes Kevin's ability to demonstrate his masculinity through providing the economic foundation for their life together. Kevin is also unable to prove his masculinity by providing sperm, which he confessed makes it "hard to feel like a complete, normal man." For Kevin, stepping up to treatment and braving real physical pain provided an opportunity to demonstrate his masculinity to his wife as well as the many family and friends with whom he claims he has been open about sharing his medical experiences.

David Morris, author of *The Culture of Pain*, posits that our experiences of pain are shaped by the culture in which we live and our deepest personal beliefs.[35] Though pain is a real physiological experience, the meanings that we ascribe to pain are socially constructed and, in the case of male infertility, tied up with our other socially constructed ideas about gender, masculinity, disease, and what it means to be infertile. In a study of female infertility, Israeli scholars Orly Benjamin and Hila Ha'elyon found that many women describe the pain associated with IVF treatments as obligatory.[36] One woman said, "Painful or not painful. It does not matter. You do everything for a child." Benjamin and Ha'elyon write, "The term 'for a child' means both 'to conceive a child' and be primarily devoted to one's child. Thus, IVF treatment becomes a motherly duty."[37] In the same vein, Jack, Kevin, and other men I interviewed thought of enduring pain as part of their role responsibility. However, for them, this duty extends beyond the sake of any future child. Men suffer pain as a show of support to their wives and for the sake of their own masculinity. Infertile men's narratives of pain inflect a masculine discourse that translates pain into masculinity. Experiencing pain means knowing that a man gave it his all, that he was willing to do everything in the quest to have a child. Enduring pain fearlessly is a heroic display of masculinity, and if enduring painful treatments means restoring fertility, then personal masculine identities are salvaged on two counts.

Marital Decision Making

In 1993, infertility scholars Judith Lorber and Lakshmi Bandlamudi examined the power dynamics of treatment decision making among couples that had been diagnosed with male infertility.[38] At the time of their study, female-focused treatments such as IUI and IVF were the primary solutions to male infertility. The authors argued that because women bear the social onus of childlessness as well as the burden of medical treatment, women have less bargaining power in decision making. Most women in their study took responsibility for their husbands' infertility by submitting themselves to painful and invasive treatments. Some women felt coerced and pressured by their husbands to undergo IVF to produce a biological heir when the women did not want to, a phenomenon that the researchers attributed to "the constraints of a patriarchal relationship reinforced by the cultural mandates of biological motherhood and technological solutions."[39] It is important to note that Lorber and Bandlamudi based their study on data that had been collected in 1989. Technological and social changes since then have changed the politics of marital bargaining. Today, men can be much more physically involved in the treatment process, thanks to the advent of IVF-ICSI and testicular sperm extraction and the growing popularity of other surgical and hormone treatments. Furthermore, data from my interviews suggest that marriages today are more egalitarian and that women have more control over their bodily experiences.

In individual interviews, I asked husbands and wives to describe how they made decisions for treatment with their spouses. Men and women were also asked whether they believed that each person—husband and wife—had an "equal vote" in the decision-making process. Most couples reported that the decision-making process was simple because they generally agreed on the best course of action. For example, Aaron, a graduate student in his late twenties, explained that he and his wife, Tiffany, discussed all of their options together:

> I feel like most of [the decisions] actually have been fairly even because we both want the same thing. . . . So I feel like most of the choices have been presented in a way where it seems more probable in terms of reaching our goal. So even though we've obviously talked about all these different choices, I feel like for the most part, we come into those discussions already pretty much agreeing.

In a separate interview, Tiffany confirmed that because their "ultimate goal is the same," she and Aaron find that they are "on the same page" when it comes to making treatment decisions.

When husbands and wives find that they agree, it is often because they both agree with the male infertility specialists' recommendations. For example, Jack and Sarah agreed that they should begin with reconstructive surgery for Jack and then move on to IVF-ICSI if necessary:

Jack: We just sort of talked about what we wanted to do, what we felt comfortable with and who we would speak to next. . . . I don't think it was a very difficult conversation or decision that we made. We both . . . had similar goals, and . . . so it was never any anxiety around our discussions. We just sort of went from one appointment to the next, and doctors helped me to where we needed to be.

LB: In the decision-making process, do you think there was one person whose vote counted a little more?

Jack: I'm thinking it was fifty-fifty.

Sarah similarly reported:

I think from the beginning, we were pretty much on the same page, that we knew we wanted a child, and we . . . both knew that this was biologically—that was our first choice. Obviously, we had talked about all the options that were out there, adoption and everything. . . . As far as the surgery was concerned and things like that, he never had a doubt in his mind that he was gonna go through that, and I supported whatever he wanted to do. . . . When it came to the in vitro, and [the doctors] said that's what we needed to do, we both kinda were just in agreement that that's where we were going. Anything that came up that was new, where we didn't know, we just had a discussion, and we seemed to just pretty much agree from the beginning on everything.

When specialists proposed male-focused treatments as an option, men and women reported that they discussed options together and found that they were, as both Tiffany and Sarah described, "on the same page." In these cases, subjects characterized the process as "collaborative," and each spouse's vote in decision making was "equal" or "fifty-fifty."

Sometimes, one or both spouses claimed that the wife had more power in decision making in cases that required more female-focused treatments. Nathan and Louise were diagnosed with both male and female infertility issues. However, because of the severity of Louise's infertility issues, the couple were advised to move directly to IVF. When I asked Nathan, an engineer in his late thirties, whether he believed that either he or his wife had "more vote" in treatment decisions, he responded, "No. I think it's fifty-fifty." In a separate interview, I asked Louise, a medical technologist in her early thirties, the same question. She replied, "I have pretty much more vote." When asked why, she responded, "I don't know, because I'm a woman, and I know better for myself." While Nathan reported an egalitarian, or "fifty-fifty," approach to decision making in their marriage, Louise believed that she had more power in decision making, at least when it came to infertility treatment

While many men in this study liked the idea of democratic decision making in marriage, a few men conceded that perhaps their wives had more power in decision making. I asked Troy to describe how he and Lori made treatment decisions:

> Troy: We really sit down and weigh the pros and cons and our options, and whatever sounds best to us, we do. It's not like she makes the decision. I make the final decision. We really have to come to an agreement, which we pretty much did the whole way through. . . .
>
> LB: Would you say that either of you—maybe your vote counts a little bit more in the decision-making process?
>
> Troy: I mean, to be honest, probably hers. . . . It's her body, and . . . she ultimately would have the final say, "Well, I'm not doing that," [after] which I would have to go back and rethink a few things. But, honestly, that really wasn't the case any part of the way, but if you want a . . . more definite answer, I would say Lori probably had the ultimate decision.

At first, Troy reported that he makes "the final decision," though he and his wife have to come to an agreement. After some reflection, he retracted his answer, admitting that his wife had "the ultimate decision." If masculinity means being in control and assuming the role of the head of the household, it may be difficult for some men to recognize or admit when wives have more power in decision making.

In a separate interview with Lori, a junior vice president at a manufacturing company, I asked how she and her husband made decisions about plans for treatment. She replied without hesitation, "I'd say that the ultimate decision relies on me. . . . Troy is one that . . .

wants to make sure that I'm comfortable with . . . what we're doing, and if I agree, then he kinda like listens to my judgment call. . . . It's just kind of been that way." Like Lori, other wives who were facing the last-resort option of IVF seemed well aware that they were in the control seat. When I asked Brandon's wife, Emily, an administrative assistant in her late twenties, who had more say in decision making, she replied candidly, "I'm more demanding. Probably I do." Thirty-one-year-old Rebecca, a chemist, explained that she and her husband had "equal say" until they reached the decision to pursue IVF. She related, "I think [Patrick] was willing to let me lead. . . . For me, it was a bit hard, the whole process, physically."

The physical investment required in IVF usually afforded women more power in decision making. In a case described in Chapter 4, Marcus and Rita pursued three rounds of IVF. Marcus explained that it was important for them to agree on how many embryos to transfer for each round of IVF, but it was up to Rita to decide how many IVF cycles to pursue. After three rounds, she decided to call it quits. Marcus admitted that he would have liked to have attempted one more round, but Rita's "vote weighed more heavily," because "it's her body." In a separate interview, Rita acknowledged that Marcus "would respect my feelings if I felt like I was tired of the process." The "it's her body" rhetoric articulated by Troy and Marcus suggests that the politics of reproduction that is battled out in nationwide contraception and abortion debates spills over into the private marital decisions that couples face in the journey of infertility. These men are versed in progressive social scripts and understand that women, even within the patriarchal institution of marriage, have the social and political right to control their own bodies.

Two men in this study unabashedly deferred to their wives to lead the decision-making process, because they believed that their wives' professional training better qualified them to make treatment decisions. In private interviews, these two wives corroborated that they indeed had more power in decision making than did their husbands—and rightfully so. Scott and Melanie opted for varicocele repair over IVF because Melanie, a medical doctor by training, needed more time to consider the potential risks to mother and child associated with IVF. Another subject, Todd, was diagnosed with an unexplained low sperm count, and his wife, Teresa, was diagnosed with polycystic ovarian syndrome.[40] Todd supported his wife's decision to pursue IUI first, because he believed that as a biochemist, Teresa could make a more informed decision than he, a radio news director, could. Todd acknowledged that Teresa had more power in decision making but quipped, "I think she probably made all of [the decisions], but she might have, like, made me feel like I was a part of the decisions. . . . You know how women . . . make the husband's feel like they're a part of the decision-making process? They have that way of figuring it out." Todd's remark humorously captures the delicacy of gendered power relations. Teresa believes that she is more knowledgeable and more capable of making treatment decisions, but she understands that in a patriarchal and democratic culture, her husband should have at least an equal vote in the decision-making process. To protect his masculinity, she tried to make him feel that he was contributing to the decision-making process.

In contrast to the study by Lorber and Bandlamudi, no women or men I interviewed reported feeling pressured by their spouse into treatments that they did not want to pursue. Though there were no reports of coercion, husbands and wives did reserve veto power in decision making. Women believed that they had the right to veto female treatments with which they were not comfortable, and a couple of men exercised veto power based on their own personal or moral objections to certain treatments. Linda, mentioned earlier in this chapter, wanted her husband, Roger, to pursue male treatments before she pursued any female treatments. If her husband's treatment failed to help them conceive, she would try IVF. The problem is that Linda and Roger did not agree on the nature of embryos or how to handle any embryos that might be left over after IVF. Linda explained their predicament: "We kind of disagree, because I'm sure that there's a good possibility that there wouldn't be any embryos left, and [if there were,] I would probably donate them to science, I'm guessing. . . . I think that's an option, whereas he feels like it's alive, and he didn't feel comfortable. . . . So that kinda marks IVF out of our decision making." Because Roger believes that embryos are alive, granting them personhood status, he cannot justify donating his own children to scientific research. Linda does not see embryos as living persons but feels morally obligated to respect her husband's beliefs and wishes, so IVF is not an option for this couple.

Similarly, Kevin vetoed sperm donation. He claimed that he had more power in decision making than Wendy did, because he "ruled out donor sperm" from the beginning. Friends of Kevin and Wendy had twins using donor sperm, and Kevin could see the challenge that the situation presented for them:

> The children are almost two years old, and the wife still struggles very much every time someone says, "Oh, you know, she has your eyes, or—" It's a constant battle with them. She's constantly emotional over it. . . . I don't know how I would react. I don't know how [my wife] would react. And I just feel like we're a team. Either we're both in it or we adopt and consider that [we're] both in it.

Kevin worried how he and Wendy "would react" to a baby that was the biological offspring of his wife and another man. Kevin thought that Wendy felt similarly, and the issue was settled, but one evening, Wendy's mother telephoned and encouraged Wendy to reconsider using donor sperm. When Kevin sensed that his role in decision making was being threatened by his mother-in-law, he reasserted his role by vetoing sperm donation. Though Kevin questioned his wife's desires, in a separate interview, Wendy expressed no interest in donor sperm and believed that she and Kevin had a "pretty equal" say in decision making.

For Linda, Roger's moral objections to IVF spared her the physical toll of treatments. In Kevin and Wendy's case, however, to appease her husband, Wendy underwent the more invasive IVF-ICSI procedure instead of the simpler donor sperm insemination. After two failed rounds of IVF, Kevin conceded that although he maintains more decision-making power in the marriage, the ultimate decision to quit IVF would be up to his wife.

Sperm Donation

As Kevin's story illustrates, the use of donor sperm can feel threatening to men. Resorting to donor sperm is acknowledging that, as anthropologist Gay Becker writes, men have failed to "uphold the patriarchal status quo through their biological contribution to the creation of a child."[41] When masculinity is defined by competition and outdoing others, it can be terribly humbling to turn to another man to make up for what one lacks. Laura, whose story is discussed earlier in this chapter, explained that her husband, Paul, would have a tough time with sperm donation and the thought of "raising another man's child." A couple of doctors I interviewed pointed out that the processes associated with assisted reproductive technologies reduce the role of husbands to mere sperm donors. What role would be left for men if they could not even do that much?

In interviews, men and women were asked to describe their thoughts about sperm donation. Many reported that they had never given the possibility of using donor sperm much consideration and had never discussed it with their doctor or spouse. Though they claimed not to oppose the use of donor sperm in principle, they felt uncomfortable with its use for themselves. The majority of couples believed that the question of using donor sperm did not apply to them if the husband had any sperm in his ejaculate or found in his testicles. Even though using donated sperm at home or in conjunction with IUI is a much simpler and less expensive solution to infertility, couples unanimously preferred the more invasive and expensive types of treatment that would make biological paternity possible.[42] Earlier, I argued that many men strive to protect their wives from the dangers of IVF by undergoing male-focused treatments. However, men preferred that their wives undergo IVF or IVF-ICSI using the men's own sperm before resorting to the less invasive treatments associated with donor sperm, and wives agreed. To summarize, men's desire for biological offspring trumps their desire to protect their wives from the risks of treatments. While sparing one's wife pain and discomfort was articulated as a chivalrous display of masculinity, fathering a biological child is a more highly valued aspect of identity and masculinity. Men and women also expressed that having a baby that was biologically the mother's but not the father's was unsettling. Several men and women described adoption as a more equitable option because the child would carry neither parent's genes.

When Todd learned that he had a low sperm count, he suggested to his wife, Teresa, that they consider using donor sperm. Here, he recaps their conversation:

> Yeah, I tossed that idea to her, and she said she didn't want to do that because she works with DNA at work, and she—her biggest hobby is genealogy, and so she's like, "Oh, no, I want to make my own." I'm like, "Even with me?" And she's like, "Of

course, with you." "But, you know, think about if you could
have like Rick Springfield's kid or something like that?" She's
like, "I love you." Oh my gosh. It's weird. I just can't get over
that she loves me, because I'm just kind of goofy.

Todd's story reveals some of the insecurities that men feel about their
poor fertility. Todd wondered whether, given the option, his wife
would prefer the genetics of another man over his. Teresa's response
reflects the social value of having biologically related children and the
ways in which wives seek to protect their husbands' masculinity. Ultimately, the love that his wife expressed for him (and his DNA) allayed
Todd's fears.

Couples generally regarded sperm donation as a last-ditch effort to make pregnancy possible, an option that most couples did
not seriously consider until they had exhausted all other options.
Only two couples I interviewed eventually resorted to using donor
sperm. George and Brandon, whose stories are recounted at length
in Chapter 4, both endured extensive diagnostic procedures to locate sperm in the testicles. After they had spent thousands of dollars
on fruitless treatments, their only remaining choices were sperm
donation, adoption, or child-free living. Both of the husbands explained that not having children was not an option, and though
they had no objections to adoption, sperm donation presented the
most appropriate solution because their wives desired the experience of pregnancy.

The first time I interviewed George, he understood that he had
a zero sperm count and planned to undergo exploratory surgery to
search for sperm. When I asked him about his thoughts regarding
sperm donation, he responded:

I kind of feel in the back of my mind that she wants to have
the experience of . . . giving birth, of having a child and having that happen in her body. . . . I think ideally we both would
want it to be biologically both of ours. But next to that, I think
she would really want that experience of carrying a child and
delivering a child and having it be inside her, and I think she
really wants that, you know. I think physically she pines for it,
so I think that's definitely on the table.

Early on, George told me that a child with biological ties to both him and his wife was their first choice, but he saw the potential for sperm donation to satisfy his wife's desire to experience pregnancy. A year later, George and his wife, Tara, had spent their entire savings on procedures attempting to locate sperm in George's testicles. In our final interview, George claimed that not being able to get pregnant presented a "life-and-death struggle" for Tara, and he said that watching her suffer was worse than dealing with his own emotional suffering. George resolved that utilizing donor sperm would be the only way to relieve his wife's suffering.

Tara believes that she could love an adopted baby just as much as a biological one, but adoption seems like an expensive option, and the stakes are too high. At the time of our interview, one of Tara's friends who had adopted a baby was going through a custody battle with the baby's birth father. Tara explained, "I've known other people who go through the adoption process, and then something goes wrong in the end, and they either lose the rights they thought they had, or they lose the child, or the child was taken away, and I just don't think that I could deal with that." Tara also really wanted to experience pregnancy:

> Just the feeling of having a life growing inside of you, I think is amazing, and I want to go through that. I mean, as a woman, I want to experience that . . . my nurturing of a child inside of my body from my own blood and from my own nourishment, and giving birth and having this . . . connection . . . like I created this being, and, you know, just sort of that connection. I feel like I see pregnant women, and I don't even mind like the big belly thing and stuff like that, and it's something I've always wanted.

Tara's first choice was to have a baby with George's sperm and her egg, but once it was clear that George had no sperm, she realized, "I don't have a problem with the sperm donation, because . . . you have a baby. It becomes yours no matter what. [Sperm donation] never really bothered me."

Using donor sperm challenges the "natural order" and the patriarchal imperative that men biologically father their own children.[43]

Yet once it was clear that George had no sperm, he focused on fulfilling his wife's desire for pregnancy and easing her emotional crisis as the most important way to express his masculinity. Donor sperm became the means to that end. George negotiated the obstacle that his zero sperm count presented by reconstructing the problem as his wife's suffering and reinterpreting donor sperm as a gift to his wife. Moreover, George and Tara decided not to tell most of their family and friends about George's diagnosis or decision to use donor sperm. By selecting a donor who had interests and physical characteristics similar to George's, they hoped to have a child who would appear to be genetically George's. His masculinity would be preserved as long as they kept the sperm donation a secret.

Brandon, too, was devastated by his lack of sperm and had no reservations asking his brother, Justin, to provide donor sperm. Brandon recalls, "I called him and told him I had a zero count and pretty much asked him if he'd do me a favor. And he was like, 'What kind of favor?' And I was like, 'Would you possibly be able to donate for me?' And he was like, 'No question about it.'" Justin's willingness to help out was a great display of brotherhood: supportive, protective, self-sacrificing. Unfortunately, what seemed like a great plan turned into a disaster. Justin had to fly cross-country to the city where Brandon's wife, Emily, was undergoing IVF. While Justin was away from home, his pregnant wife, Amanda, went into preterm labor and, tragically, lost her baby. A few weeks later, Brandon and Emily learned that their IVF attempt had failed. When Brandon and Emily approached Justin to provide a second sperm donation, Justin and his wife "beat around the bush," claiming that Justin could not get the time off work to travel. Emily surmised that Justin's wife was opposed to the idea of Justin fathering Emily's baby when they were experiencing trouble having a child of their own. Brandon and Emily pursued a second round of IVF, using an anonymous sperm donor, which also failed. By the time I spoke with them in our final interview, they had taken in a young foster child and had put infertility treatments on hold for a while. Emily had not completely abandoned the idea of getting pregnant with donor sperm, but they needed time to bond with their foster son, save money, and come up with a treatment plan.

Both Brandon and George grieved their own infertility and were torn by their wives' suffering. While other patients in the study generally did not (or refused to) consider donor sperm as a treatment option, these patients saw sperm donation as a practical solution to infertility. For these two husbands, fulfilling their wives' desires for pregnancy was the best way in which they could perform their roles as husbands and demonstrate their masculinity. These two cases illustrate that when individuals fail to live up to the social ideals of masculinity, men may emphasize other forms of masculinity, such as their desire and ability to ease their wives' suffering.

While previous scholars of infertility have emphasized the use of donor sperm as potentially emasculating for men, it is important to recognize that the sperm-banking industry was created to protect masculinity. The "technosemen market," as sociologists Lisa Jean Moore and Matthew Allen Schmidt call it,[44] ensures the fidelity of women in heterosexual couples. One specialist I shadowed divulged that in his profession, it is not uncommon to "have to dance around the infidelity thing" with patients. He recalled the story of a patient with a zero sperm count whose wife suddenly became pregnant. According to the specialist, the patient "was a pilot, so he was gone days at a time. But [the patient] looked at it as a miracle, and I didn't discourage that outlook." Another patient, the father of four children, was diagnosed with a zero sperm count due to CBAVD. "I think he figured that one out," surmised the doctor. "He didn't come back for any follow-up. . . . He didn't want to have anything to do with [his wife] anymore." It is certainly possible that women in various societies throughout history have resorted to extramarital affairs to solve the problem of male infertility. Extramarital sex is physically and logistically a much simpler process than using donor sperm and is arguably more effective. However, extramarital sex is a major violation of social norms and the marital contract to such an extent that it is never broached as an option for overcoming male infertility. Infidelity is stigmatizing for cheating wives and especially emasculating for the men who have been cheated on. Sperm donation is a more socially acceptable and technologically sophisticated remedy to male infertility.

The sperm-banking industry is an elaborate technological enterprise and bureaucratic apparatus comprising an international network of medical doctors, scientists, technicians, and laboratories. Sales agents and marketers recruit clients and donors, while counselors help match them. The technologies are impressive: large cryopreservation rooms filled with huge gas tanks; thousands of tiny vials of sperm catalogued by race, ethnicity, and nationality; and elaborate computer databases for tracking sperm, matching donors with recipients, and freeze-packing and shipping sperm around the world. Though over half of sperm bank clientele today are lesbian and single women, sperm donation technologies were created decades ago to get the sperm of a fertile man into a heterosexual woman's body without her having to engage in sexual intercourse with a man other than her husband. Using donor sperm essentially circumvents the moral question of extramarital sex and socially legitimizes the use of another man's genetic material for conception. Cultural practices that are intended to preserve female chastity, from chastity belts to clitoridectomy, are, at their root, about controlling reproduction, women, and potential threats to masculinity. Likewise, the advent of donor sperm ensures women's fidelity and concomitantly protects masculinity.

Conclusion

As I argued in earlier chapters, negotiating masculinity is not optional. Over the course of their lives, men—fertile and otherwise—are bombarded by the inescapable challenges of trying to measure up to the most hegemonic ideals of masculinity. To navigate the treacherous terrain of infertility, patients embrace medical technologies and treatments as the means for harnessing control over conception. Male patients often loosely define infertility in terms that make room for medical interventions. Most men in this study defined infertility as a permanent condition: "the inability to conceive" or "the inability to have a biological child." Many of these same men interpreted the causes of their own infertility as temporary medical conditions that could be easily remedied. Hence, men did not self-identify as infertile and could avoid the stigmatizing and distressing label of "infertile" as long as they were willing to comply with medical protocols. Those who did self-identify as infertile also sought medical treatments to overcome their condition. Though medical and epidemiological research studies indicate that men are statistically less likely than women to use medical services and make healthy lifestyle choices, this study shows that when men fall short of physiological and social ideals of masculinity, they willingly traverse the course of medical therapy.

Masculinities scholar Alan M. Klein posits that men develop a "moral hierarchy of norms" to guide their actions.[45] In Klein's research on male bodybuilding, he discovered that men are willing to sacrifice living up to certain masculine norms for the achievement of other norms. For example, some bodybuilders use illicit anabolic steroids, because their desire to be large and muscular outweighs their concern for the numerous adverse health risks associated with steroid abuse. As Klein explains, "One norm is more valued than another, canceling out a violation of the lower norm." Infertility medicine is nothing like anabolic steroid use; infertility treatments are not illegal, and complication rates and health risks are very low by comparison. Still, the "moral hierarchy of norms" devised by Klein provides a helpful framework for understanding how men can turn the potentially humiliating experience of infertility into a carefully constructed display of personal masculinity.

Medical treatments to improve fertility require a man to put his body on the line, subjected to the medical gaze, which can feel morally degrading and physically uncomfortable or painful. However, as the stories presented in this chapter illustrate, when many infertile men weigh the benefits and risks of treatment against the social and emotional cost of infertility, they elect treatment. Consistent with their personal hierarchies of masculine norms and values, they choose fertility at any physical or financial cost over childlessness.

The narratives that I have shared here reveal the specific norms and values of masculinity that motivate infertile men to take advantage of medical treatments. This list includes having sperm, having a biological child, impregnating one's wife through heterosexual intercourse, protecting a wife from physical discomfort or pain, relieving a wife's emotional suffering, protecting future children from possible birth defects, solving problems scientifically, and being willing and able to face danger and endure pain fearlessly. Recall how grateful Jack was for the surgery that restored sperm to his ejaculate, even though his sperm count was not sufficient to impregnate his wife. Jack re-sorted his hierarchy of norms and values to emphasize that a biological baby from IVF is better than childlessness and having some sperm is better than having no sperm. Then there was Paul, who valued conception through sexual intercourse over IVF, childlessness, and even his own freedom from medical intervention. He opted for surgery for himself in lieu of treatment for his wife. Similarly, Eric underwent surgery and monitored his own fertility because he wanted to "take on" and "beat" the problem of infertility on his own to alleviate his wife's emotional and physical suffering. According to Eric's hierarchy of norms, accountability and self-sacrifice are more important than denying one's infertility or refusing medical assistance. Scott and Todd trusted their scientifically minded wives to make educated treatment decisions and supported their wives' plans. They valued science over patriarchal or democratic decision making in marriage. Kevin did not intend to "half-ass" treatment and felt proud that he had a higher threshold for pain than other men. And once George accepted that he would never realize biological paternity, he decided that giving his wife the opportunity to experience pregnancy through the use of donor sperm was a compassionate way to alleviate her anguish. Poor fertility is emasculating, but infertile men are able to reprioritize their personal masculine values to accommodate the demands of treatment protocols. As they do, they rewrite the rules of gender for themselves and reinterpret what it means to be a man: Real men protect their wives. Real men tough it out. Real men take one for the team.

The Politics of Reproduction

When social scientists talk about the politics of reproduction, we are talking about the set of themes, cultural ideas, and power relationships undergirding controversial reproductive issues such as contraception access or abortion rights. What does it mean when a group of white U.S. Congressmen sit down together to make decisions about women's access to contraception and abortion? What does it mean when black women are more encouraged or less encouraged than white women to take advantage of abortion services? What does it mean when families choose to terminate a pregnancy on the basis of the gender of the fetus or the perceived risk of Down syndrome? These questions highlight the power relationships between different social groups and define the politics of reproduction. Many infertility scholars and activists have advocated increased state regulations regarding the safety of infertility services for women, mandatory health insurance coverage for infertility treatments, legal support for gay and lesbian parenthood, or improved compensation for gamete donors and surrogate mothers. Although I have not examined or advocated state regulations of any kind, the story of male infertility elucidates our current understanding of the politics of reproduction. Any research that sheds light on who controls reproductive bodies and technologies, who gets access to reproduction-related services and resources, and who or what shapes popular attitudes toward reproductive issues expands our understanding of the politics of reproduction.

Historically, men were the controllers of reproductive technologies, women's bodies, and reproduction. The sluggish development of male reproductive medicine affirms the strength of the cultural paradigm, which reveres the perfect and sacred nature of the male body while casting women's bodies as unruly and justifying their subjection to excessive medical scrutiny, experimentation, and intervention. The result of greater medical focus, past and present, on women's bodies is a medical system that today is better prepared and better organized to treat women's bodies than to treat men's bodies. Women bear the brunt of infertility treatments, even in cases of male infertility, for a variety of reasons. First, male infertility often goes undiagnosed.[1] Even when it is properly diagnosed, medical doctors can employ female-focused treatments for overcoming a variety of male infertility issues. For example, women can take hormone medications to hyperstimulate egg production and couples can opt for IVF to make conception possible. Because IVF with intracytoplasmic sperm injection (IVF-ICSI) requires only one sperm, it is easy for doctors to "treat" male infertility issues without ever notifying a man of his poor fertility or referring him to a male infertility specialist. Female infertility specialists outnumber male infertility specialists nearly five to one in the United States, and male infertility clinics are located only in large metropolitan areas, thus being inaccessible to most American men. While REs are board certified to treat female infertility, the lack of a board certification for male infertility has resulted in the mismanagement and even harmful treatment of male patients' infertility issues. The current state of infertility medicine reaffirms that among many couples, women continue to bear the brunt of all aspects of reproduction. Even when men want to play a larger role in reproduction, the dearth of available medical institutions and technologies often frustrates men's efforts. The gender story in the infertility industry reaffirms masculine domination as a basis of the politics of reproduction.

Technology, Progress, and Reproductive Control

In 1900, nearly all babies born in the United States were born at home. By 1940, more than half of babies in the United States were born in hospitals, and by 1960, 99 percent of babies were born in hospitals.[2] Society's collective ideas about reproduction shifted dramatically during the twentieth century. Reproduction, once considered a natural process, became a medical issue that requires intervention from medical doctors and technologies. Over the past half century, most aspects of reproduction have become medicalized, from labor and delivery to family planning and contraception. The birth control pill debuted in 1960.[3] By 1982, 76 percent of American women of reproductive age reported having taken the birth control pill.[4] Heterosexual couples essentially went from using no birth control or natural or primitive forms of birth control for centuries to being able to suppress ovulation and avoid conception very effectively. Women quickly embraced their ability to time pregnancies to fit in with the other demands and opportunities of modern life. Parenthood was no longer the default social role of heterosexual adults; it had become a role that men and women could elect on their own timeline. If reproductive control was the goal of the late twentieth century, contraception and assisted reproductive technologies were two sides of the same coin. Pregnancy-on-demand became the new norm, and consequently, society was ripe for a technology such as IVF.

As in any study in which technology plays a starring role, the question of progress generates tension throughout this book. Do scientific pursuits and technological innovations lead to progress? Technologies streamline processes and improve efficiency and convenience, but do they improve quality of life? Does technological progress lead to social progress? Such philosophical questions arise in discussions of the environment, education, entertainment, and agricultural, military, and industrial development. They are complicated by global political issues regarding human rights, democracy, capitalism, citizenship, religious freedom, and access to food, shelter, clean water, and high-quality medical care across populations. While most scholars would agree that digging a well in sub-Saharan Africa illustrates the social good that can come from technology, we are less likely to celebrate the technologies that are employed to deforest poverty-stricken countries to supply wealthy nations with more fast-food hamburgers.

The question of progress haunts much feminist thought and scholarship, particularly in regard to reproductive medicine. In response to the overt and questionable medicalization of reproduction during the nineteenth and twentieth centuries, many vocal feminists of the past thirty years have rightfully argued that Western medical practitioners overstepped their bounds, using technologies to usurp physical and political control over women's bodies.[5] Today, many feminists emphatically call for the end of the extreme technologizing of women's bodies and reproduction. However, when the contractions of childbirth become too excruciating to endure—and I am speaking from personal experience here—we demand an epidural for ourselves and every other woman around the globe. As long as we are on the subject, can we get prenatal care and birth control for all women and high-quality medical care for babies and children everywhere? Indeed, feminists often find themselves caught in a love-hate relationship with medical technologies and with the institutions that control them.

While some technologies have fostered masculine domination over women's bodies, others have liberated women. The progressive value of any given medical technology may be measured by its capacity to grant individuals control over their bodies, their bodily experiences, and ultimately their health and well-being, relationships, time, careers, and life trajectories. In the case of reproduction, progress may be best defined as any movement toward reproductive control. As scholars and activists in the growing field of reproductive justice point out, reproductive control is as much about having children as it is about not having children.[6] Infertile heterosexual men and their partners seek medical treatments that will restore male reproductive control, free women from excessive medicalization, and make biological fatherhood possible.

Early in this book, I argued that male reproductive medicine has lagged behind female reproductive medicine, resulting in fewer specialists today who are properly trained to treat infertile men and fewer effective treatment options for male infertility. Admittedly, the tone of words such as "overlooked" and "lagged behind" suggests that more medical treatment options would mean progress and that is necessarily good. Although I am reticent to say that the increased medicalization and technologization of male reproduction are sure signs of progress, it became clear in interviews that infertile men do equate technology with progress. One infertile man told me that he would rather have erectile dysfunction than male infertility. As he explained it, he just wanted a pill like Viagra to solve his problems. His struggle to get a clear diagnosis and find a qualified doctor with a simple solution left him feeling frustrated and humiliated. From a feminist perspective, men's increased participation in reproductive medicine not only addresses men's desires but also has the potential to relieve some of the burdens of reproduction that women bear and thus could contribute to gender equality and social progress.

Anthropologist Marcia Inhorn has written extensively and poignantly about Arab men's experiences with infertility in the Middle East.[7] On the basis of her observations, Inhorn categorizes some male infertility treatments along with circumcision and vasectomy as examples of male genital cutting.[8] She expresses suspicion of some surgeries for male infertility because, as she points out, treatments often do not improve fertility, making them nothing more than exercises in proving one's masculinity by enduring pain. Are male infertility treatments sophisticated technologies or medically unnecessary torture techniques? I would argue that well-trained male infertility specialists in the United States are quite judicious about recommending surgery as an appropriate option for improving fertility. Postsurgery pregnancy rates are higher in the United States, and I did not detect the "buyer's remorse" among the men I interviewed that Inhorn found among the Middle Eastern patients of male infertility treatments. While I am wary of medical technologies that are more harmful than helpful, I am also sympathetic to patients' demands for more attention, more intervention, and ultimately more control over their reproductive lives. The truth of the matter is that in most medical fields, treatments begin as experiments, and only the adventurous, desperate, or dying are willing to be the guinea pigs. When practitioners hone their skills and experimental treatments develop into beneficial solutions, everyone wants in on the action. Thus, the relationship between technology, progress, and reproductive control is an ever-evolving one.

Embodied Politics

In their book *Missing Bodies: The Politics of Visibility,* Monica J. Casper and Lisa Jean Moore argue that the bodies of people who are oppressed, in need, or in peril are regularly hidden from public view, which most often includes the bodies of women, children, and minorities.[9] Sometimes, these bodies are exploited to the point of hypervisibility when it serves the purposes of the state, the media, or capitalist interests. Throughout this book, I have grappled with the ironies of the politics of visibility as it relates to men's bodies and reproductive experiences. Feminist scholars have criticized much of Western thought (history, philosophy, science) for being phallocentric—that is, for taking a male-centered view of the world and rendering women's lives and work invisible.[10] The constant visibility of men and their lives and work perpetuates the privileged status of men and masculine domination in a broad social context. However, as the case of male infertility demonstrates, sometimes invisibility protects men, masculinity, and male power. While female infertility support groups, websites, blogs, news programs, and literature abound, male infertility is hidden from public view and absent from public dialogue. IVF clinics proliferate, but men are generally absent from these settings. When a heterosexual couple experience childlessness, it is the woman's body that is visibly and conspicuously not pregnant, stigmatizing *her* as infertile. Infertile men enjoy a good amount of invisibility.

The sociohistorical association of women with the body and the private sphere and men with the intellect and the public sphere has excused men from many aspects of reproductive labor. The male-mind-public/female-body-private dichotomy determined the gendered division of labor, which influenced the development and organization of female and male reproductive medical disciplines and continues to affect how infertile men and infertile women experience infertility today. Historically, women's bodies were the focus of medical exploration and experimentation, the targets of men's intellectual pursuits. Other scholars of infertility have shown that infertile women today often perceive their inability to conceive as a bodily failure and a poor reflection of themselves as worthy women, mothers, and people.[11] These findings suggest that women have internalized the long-standing female-body association and regard the body as the seat of the self. Emily Martin's work has shown that the technological metaphors that are used to describe female reproductive processes and the reproductive technologies that are used on women's bodies actually alienate women from their own bodies.[12] In light of women's understanding of the body and the self as intrinsically tied together, technological alienation is potentially traumatic for women.

In contrast to infertile women's experiences, my research shows that infertile men more often conceptualize bodily problems as no reflection of personhood. The male-mind association enables men to dissociate broken plumbing and poor sperm production from personal masculinity. If the body and the self are distinctly separate and the self is the seat of masculinity, then infertility is no reflection of one's masculinity or personal worth. In clinical interactions, technological metaphors celebrate the power of the male body and facilitate bonding between male doctors and male patients. Men's historical affinity with technology and the strong association between masculinity and technology helps infertile male patients to embrace technological solutions comfortably. The result of the historical division of labor is an infertility industry today that caters primarily to women, but the masculine association of men and technology makes men prime candidates for infertility treatments.

Crisis Interrupted

The journey of infertility often entails profound feelings of grief and loss.[13] Patients feel a loss of normalcy and loss of a gendered identity, and they grieve the absence of the baby that was intended to be part of their lives and family. Forty years ago, Elizabeth Kübler-Ross, a prominent psychiatrist, introduced a model for understanding the grieving process that included five stages of grief: denial, anger, bargaining, depression, and acceptance.[14] Kübler-Ross's work has been critiqued and modified by various scholars, but by and large, her model has transformed practices for clinical psychologists, and is widely accepted by scholars and clinicians as the definitive model for understanding how individuals experience loss. If the fact that many infertile men do not self-identify as infertile represents denial, I would argue that it is the hope offered by doctors and the promises of medical technologies that allow men to redefine their medical condition and suspend them in the first stage of the grieving process.

In 1999, Russell Webb and Judith Daniluk published a study of men's experiences with male infertility. The men in the study had been interviewed several years after their initial diagnosis and admitted that they had experienced a period of denial immediately after their diagnosis, followed later by other stages of grief.[15] In the 1980s and 1990s, few medical treatment options were available to infertile men, and infertility was a lifelong experience. In this millennium, in male infertility clinics, many infertile male patients experience a quick and seamless move from diagnostic consultations to therapeutic treatments, which delays the subsequent stages of grief. If the treatments work and the couple achieve pregnancy, the grieving process ends. Recall the story of Joel, who said that he "almost" reached a point at which he thought he might be an inadequate husband and father. Once his wife became pregnant, he was able to put infertility and all of the anxiety it generated behind him. When the void in their family was filled with the anticipation of a new baby, Joel stopped grieving and looked forward to fatherhood. Very few patients in this study ever had to consider how sperm donation, adoption, or unrealized parenthood would affect their lives. Utilizing medical technologies alleviated despair and was perceived as a natural and normal step toward parenthood.

Contrast Joel's experience with the infertility journeys of Brandon and George, who endured the most medical treatments of any men I interviewed, had no sperm or chance at biological paternity, and were the most distraught men I met during my research. They were certainly not in denial and openly shared their feelings of anger and depression. In most cases, patients were inundated with medical information and decisions before they had time to consider all of the social implications of their infertility. It was only when treatments failed to work for couples that infertile men moved through the stages of grief.

Conceiving Masculinity

Hegemonic masculinity, as a theoretical tool, has been criticized for its underlying universal assumption that masculinity is always and only defined by power, for relying on overly simplistic categories of identity, for essentializing masculinity as a biological identity applicable only to men, and for failing to address the multiplicity of masculine forms and the complex power relationships between those forms.[16] As stated at the beginning of this book, masculinity is slippery, because ideals of masculinity vary across time and space, and among and between social groups and individuals. But as illustrated throughout this book, masculinity is also sticky, because in all its incarnations, masculinity is irrevocably equated with power and demonstrated by exercising control over circumstances, things, people, and selves. Because of its sticky quality, masculinity serves as the glue that cements the colossal, multi-tiered gender system apparatus together. Until masculinity and femininity are redefined as something other than power and powerlessness, respectively, there is little leeway for reimagining the gender system.

Ubiquitous gender beliefs incessantly and unforgivingly remind men that they do not measure up, that they must improve or change themselves to live up to the dominant ideals of manhood.[17] Men are keenly aware that poor fertility status should, in theory, reflect poorly on their masculinity in the eyes of society. When men experience infertility, they do not forfeit their masculinity or resign from manhood. Rather, they engage in the physical, mental, and emotional labor of gender work to renew, reconceptualize, and restore their masculinity. The men in this study demonstrate that individuals can rewrite the rules of gender for themselves. They reconstruct masculinity in their own terms, on the basis of their own personal experiences, beliefs, age, race, social class, and conceptualization of infertility. The fact that the men I interviewed refused to accept their poor fertility status as a reflection of their personal masculine identity demonstrates the slippery, flexible, and even flimsy quality of the concept of masculinity. Nonetheless, these men carefully controlled and manipulated their bodies through medical regimens and managed how their fertility issues were understood by others in order to meet society's ideals of manhood. Men may construct narratives of masculinity in unlimited ways, but masculine narratives repeatedly highlight themes of power, control, strength, bravery, and triumph. These recurring themes demonstrate the stickiness of masculinity: though power can be creatively construed in a variety of ways, masculinity is inevitably defined as some enactment of power, be it physical, mental, emotional, or economic.

Although infertility indiscriminately touches the lives of men of all races, ethnicities, and social classes, only those with access to financial and medical resources—and a good amount of luck—will succeed in overcoming it. What about the many infertile men in America who do not have the time or resources to solve their infertility issues or choose not to? Do they have the social power to subscribe to a kinder, gentler, less macho masculinity, as many men in this study claimed to do? The homogeneity among the sample of research participants in this book invites more research on the experiences of male infertility among nonwhite men, working-class men, or gay couples. Further research can compare social constructions of male infertility across socioeconomic classes, ethnicities, religions, cultures, and subcultures. Women's experiences with male reproductive medicine and women's role in men's reproductive health are also relatively unexplored fields of social inquiry. Within marriage, women are highly influential in their husbands' medical treatment decisions and reserve the right to control their own bodies. These findings suggest that although masculine domination persists in the medical sphere, the institution of marriage is progressing toward a more egalitarian power relationship. More research can be done to explore how women conceptualize male infertility, relate to their male spouses, and define masculinity. The findings and ideas in this book can open doors to research on all aspects of male reproductive health beyond infertility, including circumcision, sexually transmitted infections, vasectomy, vasectomy reversals, testicular and prostate cancers, paternal age, disability, postwar reproductive health in veterans, and more.

As research delves into the variety of men's reproductive health experiences, our social understanding of gender is elaborated and refined, because the social constructing processes of disease and gender are so tightly intertwined. Personal masculinity, defined by power and control, is tested when men's physical health is compromised, particularly in the case of reproductive health, because procreative power and sexual potency are so central to masculine identities. The case of male infertility illuminates some of the intricacies of the gender system and the durability of gender ideology. At the institutional level of the gender system, preconceived notions about masculinity inform and shape medical practices, and traditional hegemonic gender norms are invoked in doctor-patient interactions. However, as the patients in this study demonstrate, individuals understand gender norms and have the power to redefine masculinity and its relationship to fertility status for themselves. As patients engage with medical technologies, they draw on popular masculinist discourse to describe their experiences and, in the process, reconstruct a new social understanding of male infertility.

Appendix A:
Research Participant List

NAME	AGE*	OCCUPATION	DIAGNOSIS	RACE	WIFE†	AGE*	RACE
Clinic 1							
Howard	38	Househusband‡	Spinal cord injury	White	Miriam	28	White
Patrick	31	Scientist	Oligospermia§	White	Rebecca	31	White
Jack	42	Teacher	Azoospermia‖ due to blockage	White	Sarah	30	White
William	39	Businessman	Erectile dysfunction and oligospermia due to diabetes	White	Sue	36	White
Greg	31	Technology developer	Varicocele	White	Jane	32	White
Keith	23	Airman	Oligospermia	White	Regina	26	White
Scott	31	Real estate planner	Varicocele	White	Melanie	31	White
Clinic 2							
Kevin	28	Pilot	Azoospermia due to CBAVD	White	Wendy	27	White
Roger	38	Police detective	Pituitary tumor	White	Linda	38	White
Eric	37	Tech support specialist	Varicocele	White	Stacey	35	White
Paul	29	Salesperson	Varicocele	White	Laura	34	White
Clinic 3							
Derek	33	Police officer	Varicocele	White	Jill	30	White
Todd	37	Radio news director	Oligospermia	White	Teresa	39	White
Nathan	38	Engineer	Oligospermia	White	Louise	32	Asian
Troy	35	Jewelry wholesaler	Oligospermia due to severed vas deferens	White	Lori	33	White
Marcus	40	Business consultant	Cystic fibrosis	White	Rita	39	White
Ron	39	Teacher	Oligospermia	White	Kathleen	32	White
Clinic 4							
Aaron	29	Student	Azoospermia	White	Tiffany	29	White
Benjamin	26	Student	Anejaculation	White	Clara	21	White
Joel	38	Carpenter	Varicocele	White	Heather	37	White
Clinic 5							
Brandon	29	Electrician	Testicular trauma	White	Emily	28	White
George	38	Musician	Azoospermia	White	Tara	28	White
Curtis	36	City clerk	Azoospermia due to chemotherapy	Hispanic	Jasmine	25	White
Nicholas	42	Engineer	Varicocele	White	Margaret	39	Asian

*Age columns represent age at time of first interview.
† Wives' occupations have been omitted to protect the couples' anonymity.
‡ Howard's self-described occupation is "househusband."
§ Oligospermia = low sperm count.
‖ Azoospermia = zero sperm count.

Appendix B:
Interview Guide

General Information

1. Name:
2. Age:
3. Highest level of education:
4. Occupation:
5. Marital status:
6. Are you currently living with your spouse/partner?
7. Do you have any children together?
8. Do either you or your spouse/partner have any other children, not from this relationship?
9. How long have you been married/living together?

The Medical Encounter: Diagnostic Process and Treatments

10. How long had you been trying to get pregnant—not practicing birth control—before you sought medical intervention?
11. Did you or your spouse/partner initiate contact with the doctor regarding your inability to get pregnant?
12. Why did you choose to seek medical intervention?
13. What is the diagnosis/cause of your infertility?
14. What steps (tests, procedures, examinations, technologies) were taken to determine your diagnosis?
15. What medical professionals did you meet with before you had a diagnosis?
16. Has your diagnosis ever changed?

17. Do you trust this diagnosis?
18. Do you trust the medical doctors and staff you have met with?
19. What type of doctor is best qualified to treat infertility? Male infertility?
20. Who is the most competent doctor you've seen so far, and why?
21. Who was the least competent doctor you've seen, and why?
22. What treatments have you pursued so far?
23. How much have you spent on infertility treatments? What percent of the total has been covered by health insurance?
24. How much do you anticipate infertility treatments will cost you?
25. Have any of the treatments been physically painful or uncomfortable?
26. Have you ever set limits regarding the amount of time or finances you will invest in infertility treatment before seriously considering other alternatives?
27. Have you ever considered other alternatives because of physical exhaustion or pain due to treatments?
28. How influential is your doctor in helping you decide what will be the next step in the treatment process?
29. Have you ever questioned your doctor's advice?
30. Looking back on the treatments you've been through so far, would you do anything differently if you had it to do over again?

The Collective Experience: Decision Making and the Emotional Aspect

31. What role did your spouse/partner have in your decision to seek help from a physician?
32. Did you or your spouse/partner locate infertility specialists?
33. Who schedules appointments?
34. Who makes decisions regarding plans for treatment? Is each partner's "vote" equal in decision making?
35. In your view, whose problem is this (man, woman, couple's)?
36. Who is responsible for getting this treated?
37. Explain why you would like to have a biological child.
38. Have you considered sperm donation or adoption as possibilities for parenthood? Which would you consider first—a sperm donor or adoption? Why?
39. What are your thoughts or concerns about sperm donation?
40. What are your thoughts or concerns about adoption?
41. Some patients report feeling depressed and devastated by infertility. Others go through the grieving process, which includes feelings of shock, denial, anger, guilt, and fear. Could you please describe the emotions that have accompanied infertility?
42. Could you please describe the emotions experiences by your spouse/partner?
43. Has your spouse/partner experienced grief?

44. Do you think infertility presents a greater emotional struggle for men or women?
45. Have you had to take care of your spouse/partner's emotional well-being? How?
46. Has your spouse/partner taken care of you? In what ways?
47. What impact has infertility had on your marriage/relationship?
48. Have you seen counselors or therapists to talk about the emotional, financial, physical issues that have accompanied infertility? Has that been helpful?
49. Have you attended a support group? Is the support group for men, women or couples? 50. Does it provide emotional support? Is it a place for gaining scientific knowledge about infertility?
50. Do you spend time researching the scientific aspects of infertility? Less or more than your spouse/partner?
51. How open have you been about your diagnosis with friends, family and acquaintances? Do you share your experiences regarding the diagnosis and treatments with others? With whom?
52. Do you ever try to hide what your infertility experiences from others? From whom?
53. Has infertility affected your relationships with others? How? With whom, i.e. men, women, co-workers, friends, relatives?
54. How do you think others perceive your experience/diagnosis?
55. (For infertility not due to ED . . .) Which do you think would be a greater psychological or emotional struggle—dealing with infertility or erectile dysfunction? Why?

Lifestyle, Health, Sex, Fatherhood: A Look at Masculinity and Femininity

56. How has seeking medical treatment changed your lifestyle or routine? For example, do you have to take time off work for appointments or treatment? Have you had to sacrifice vacation or leisure time for treatment?
57. Have you had to change your personal habits, i.e. eating, exercise, working, sleeping, drinking, smoking?
58. Has the knowledge that you are infertile affected your sense of sexuality or sex life? Do you see yourself as a sexy and sexual person? Has your sexual self-perception changed since your diagnosis?
59. How have infertility treatments, i.e. medication, surgery, examinations, affected your sex life? How have treatments affected your sense of sexuality?
60. How do you think your spouse/partner would answer questions 45–48?
61. Have you ever had a medical condition or diagnosis in the past that has required as much or more attention than infertility? If so, how does your past experience compare or contrast with this one?
62. Have the financial demands of infertility treatment put a strain on your household finances?

63. Have you or your partner assumed most of the financial responsibility for treatment?
64. Have you always envisioned that you would someday become a father/mother? If not, when did you first realize that you wanted to become a father/mother someday?
65. How long has your spouse/partner wanted to be a father/mother?
66. How would you feel about your life if you didn't become a father/mother?
67. Has infertility ever caused you to question your ability to be a good father/mother?
68. Has infertility ever caused you to question yourself as a good husband/wife?
69. Have you ever felt that infertility reflects something about you? Does infertility ever seem to represent a personal failure?
70. How might your spouse/partner answer questions 53–58?
71. Have you ever thought of yourself as infertile?
72. How would you define infertility?

Masculinity

73. Do you think society has a standard view or consensus about how men should think and act?
74. Do you think society has a standard view or definition of masculinity?
75. Can you define or describe masculinity? What attributes would you ascribe to a masculine person?
76. Do you believe infertility has affected your (or your spouse/partner's) masculinity or sense of "manliness"? If so, how?
77. (For women . . .) Do you ever take steps to protect your husband/partner's masculinity? How?

Closing Questions

78. Are there any questions you wish I would have asked you?
79. Are there any other thoughts you would like to share regarding your experiences?
80. Were there questions that you chose not to answer or restrained from sharing some information, but would be willing to answer completely on an anonymous written survey?
81. May I contact you in the future to get an update on your fertility treatment?

Notes

Chapter 1

1. Rowe et al, 2000; ASRM website, available at http://www.reproductivefacts.org/detail.aspx?id=2322.

2. Greil 1991.

3. van der Ploeg 1995.

4. http://www.reproductivefacts.org/detail.aspx?id=2322.

5. Mosher and Pratt 1990. In 1955 and 1960, investigators at the University of Michigan and the Scripps Foundation for Research in Population Problems launched the Growth of American Families Surveys. These surveys were succeeded by the National Fertility Study in 1965 and 1970 and were followed by the National Survey for Family Growth (NSFG) in 1973. The NSFG is a multi-wave longitudinal study, which did not include male respondents until 2002.

6. Martinez, Daniels, and Chandra 2012.

7. Spar 2006.

8. Chachamovich et al. 2010; Culley, Hudson, and Lohan 2013; Fisher and Hammarberg 2012.

9. Moore 2007, 148.

10. Carlsen et al. 1992.

11. Daniels 2006.

12. Ibid., 59–60.

13. Ibid., 54–55.

14. Ridgeway and Correll 2004.

15. Ibid., 523.

16. West and Zimmerman 2002.

17. Wajcman 2000, 454.

18. Connell 1995, 35.

19. Connell 1995; Goffman 1959; Kaufman 1994; Kimmel 1994.

20. Kimmel 1994, 135–136.

21. Ibid., 129–130.

22. A. Clarke 1998.

23. Becker 2000; Thompson 2005.

24. The term "infertility" replaced "sterility" in the scientific community around the late 1960s and slowly grew in popularity among the general public. As Sandelowski and de Lacey (2002) note, the media hype surrounding the birth of Louise Brown popularized the term "infertility" and solidified it as part of the public lexicon.

25. Practice Committee of the American Society for Reproductive Medicine 2008a.

26. Rowe et al. 2000, 5.

27. Franklin 1997; Sandelowski and de Lacey 2002.

28. Thompson 2005.

29. Sandelowski and de Lacey 2002.

30. Greil 1991.

31. Greil, Leitko, and Porter 1988.

32. Becker 2000; Franklin 1997; Inhorn and van Balen 2002; Sandelowski and de Lacey 2002; Thompson 2005.

33. Franklin 1997; Whiteford and Gonzalez 1994, 1999.

34. Becker 2000, 33–34; Franklin 1997, 134–137; Riessman 2000, 11; Thompson 2005, 121; Whiteford and Gonzalez 1994, 30.

35. Becker 2000; Franklin 1997; Riessman 2000; Thompson 2005.

36. Daniels 2006, 68.

37. Culley, Hudson, and Lohan 2013; Dooley, Nolan, and Sarma 2011; Epstein and Rosenberg 2005; Fisher and Hammarberg 2012; Inhorn 2012; Moore 2007; Smith et al. 2009; Thompson 2005.

38. Kaufman 1994, 146.

39. Kimmel 1994, 125.

40. Connell 1995, 54; Kaufman 1994; Kimmel 1994.

41. Though social categories such as gender and sexuality are highly fluid and allow space for creativity, there is a biological reality to reproduction that limits the services that infertility clinics can offer. Since 2000, scientists in Japan and Australia have successfully created mouse embryos using eggs from two female mice and no sperm. In the United States a team of researchers actually created sperm from embryonic stem cell material, which was then used to fertilize a mouse egg. Such scientific experimentation is considered a bold step toward lesbian parenthood because it proposes the achievement of conception without male sperm. However, many scientists and the lay public are skeptical about whether such attempts at fertilization would ever work

for human conception. Arguably, strong heteronormative cultural values have slowed the development of scientific pursuits that are most beneficial to homosexual couples. Currently, human conception requires exactly one egg and one sperm, and the laboratories for combining these two gametes are always connected to IVF centers, not male infertility clinics. If one day technology can create life from just two sperm or just two eggs (or any random number of gametes), these treatment options will probably be made available at IVF centers. (For a more thorough explanation of the jurisdictions and capabilities of IVF centers and male infertility clinics, see Chapter 2.) Expanding male infertility clinics to include gay couples would most likely require that male infertility specialists greatly expand both their knowledge and their training, which would overlap with the work of reproductive endocrinologists. Practitioners might well find this expansion redundant and inefficient, undermining the point of specialization.

42. Anthropologist Helene Goldberg set off for Israel in 2002 to conduct research on infertility. She began her ethnographic work in IVF clinics that claimed to specialize in male infertility. She writes, "As I entered Israeli clinics, I found that men had not only been missing from writing and debates about infertility, but that they were often also missing in the clinics. When they were present, they often seemed to be in the background, and I had difficulties locating men to interview. . . . I had come with the desire to learn about men's experiences but very often found that all that was left of the men in the clinic was their sperm. Sperm as an iconic signifier became central to my research, and rather than exploring the male experience, my study became one of analyzing the social construction of male infertility and the image of sperm" (2009, 205). Goldberg's experience explains in part my decision to limit this research study to male infertility clinics, places where I was guaranteed to find men. As Charis Thompson explains in her book *Making Parents,* men "elude the ethnographic gaze because of this treatment asymmetry: men just aren't around as much because they aren't required for most of the procedures" (2005, 120).

43. The decision to interview by telephone was a practical one. The research subjects are scattered from coast to coast in eight different states. Although telephone interviews prevented me from reading the subjects' body language and facial expressions, they granted respondents a degree of anonymity that may have encouraged them to discuss their experiences more openly.

44. During the course of my fieldwork, doctors met with twenty-nine male patients who fulfilled the criteria for participation in the study, twenty-four of whom became participants. Two men declined to participate before I met them. Three couples agreed to allow me to observe during their appointments and provided me with contact information. However, when I later tried to line up interviews, two of the couples were unreachable, and one couple declined to be interviewed.

Chapter 2

1. Thanks to historian Angela Hug for drawing my attention to this passage, Lucretius 4.1237–38. See Brown (1987).

2. I am grateful to historians Rebecca Fleming and Marion Bolder-Boos for educating me on votive practices, and I credit Bolder-Boos for her current research on Hercules worship in the sanctuary of Praeneste.

3. This is an admittedly abbreviated and Eurocentric history of infertility practices. Fertility desires and rites are also recorded in the histories of many societies across Asia and Africa. I limit my focus on Europe, because Western biomedicine in the United States emerged from the Hippocratic ideas originating in Greece and were later developed in the Age of Enlightenment in the Western world.

4. Leeuwenhoek observed "the spermatozoa of thirty different animal types over a forty-six-year period of time" (Payne 1970, 101). Leeuwenhoek's microscope was likely based on an invention by Robert Hooke. Though the two scientists' claims of seeing microscopic organisms seemed very far-fetched in their day and nearly cost them their membership in the Royal Society, today Hooke and Leeuwenhoek are credited as the inventors of the microscope and the fathers of modern microbiology.

5. German biologist Karl Ernst von Baer published his discovery of mammal eggs in his *Epistola de Ovo Mammamalium et Hominis Genesi* in 1827.

6. de Beauvoir 1951; Firestone 1970; Friedan 1963.

7. Inhorn et al. 2009a.

8. A. Clarke 1998.

9. Ehrenreich and English 2005.

10. Moscucci 1990, 2.

11. Oudshoorn 2003, 26.

12. Benninghaus 2012; Kampf 2013.

13. Benninghaus 2012; Mondat 1844.

14. E. Clarke 1873.

15. Ehrenreich and English 2005.

16. Boston Women's Health Book Collective 1973.

17. Niemi 1987.

18. Huhner 1942.

19. Almeling 2011, 26. Artificial insemination using donor sperm was considered ethically questionable until the 1960s. The 1978 Parentage Act finally legitimized the practice in the same decade when sperm banking became a popular enterprise.

20. Gurtler 2013.

21. Christina Benninghaus's (2012) history of male sterility medicine in Germany from 1860 through 1900 shows that doctors and male patients often kept a man's infertility a secret from his wife.

22. Daniels 2006; Gurtler 2013; Kampf 2013.

23. Huhner 1942.

24. When single or lesbian women with healthy fertility and predictable ovulation cycles use donor sperm, they may forgo the ovulation-stimulating drugs and insert the sperm themselves (vaginally, depositing sperm near the cervix) in the privacy of their own homes, using syringes (or "basters") provided by sperm banks.

25. Technology scholar Irma van der Ploeg labels couples diagnosed with male infertility "hermaphrodite patients." On the basis of her analysis of medical texts on IVF, she points out that even when the man's body is the cause of a couple's infertility, the woman's body remains the object of intervention. Thus, male infertility becomes a property of the female body, and the male body is rendered invisible in treatments. See van der Ploeg (1995).

26. Wilshire 1990.

27. Haraway 1991; van der Ploeg 2004.

28. van der Ploeg 1995.

29. As a reference point, average sperm counts in the United States are 20–40 million sperm per ejaculate; some men may have as many as 100 million or 200 million sperm per ejaculate.

30. Data vary by study, but most studies conclude that birth defects are found in about 3 percent of IVF infants compared with under 2 percent in the general population. The following medical studies support these findings: Chen et al. 2007; El-Chaar et al. 2009; Goel et al. 2009; Olivennes 2005; Olson et al. 2005; Schieve, Rasmussen, and Reefhuis 2005.

31. Alukal and Lamb 2008; Christianson et al. 2009; Hawkins et al. 1999; Squires, Carter, and Kaplan 2001.

32. The first urology fellowships to focus on male reproduction began in the late 1960s under Dr. Frank Hinman at the University of California at San Francisco.

33. American Board of Obstetrics and Gynecology 2004.

34. According to both the American Board of Obstetrics and Gynecology (ABOG) and the American Board of Urology, there are no "official documents" that state specifically what an RE or urologist is actually qualified to treat upon completion of board certification. As a representative of the ABOG explained to me, any medical doctor can practice infertility medicine without board certification and would have no reason to fear legal recourse from patients for doing so. The main purposes of board certification is to supply doctors with credentials to show that they have attained a certain level of expertise within a specific field and to make doctors more marketable to clinics, particularly in the highly specialized urban medical job market.

35. None of the male patients in this study was physically examined by a reproductive endocrinologist at any time. When patients come to male infertility clinics, it is presumed that they have never received a physical examination for infertility.

36. Board examinations test the expertise of urologists in the following categories: "ethics, professionalism, epidemiology, andrology (including infer-

tility), calculous disease (including endourology and shock-wave lithotripsy), congenital anomalies, pediatric urology, urologic disorders of females, infectious diseases, neurourology and urodynamics, obstructive diseases, renovascular hypertension and renal transplantation, sexuality and impotence, adrenal diseases and endocrinology, trauma, urologic pathology, urologic imaging and interventional radiology, urologic oncology, and geriatric oncology" (American Urological Association 2009, 13).

37. Becker 2000; Greil 2002; Thompson 2005.

38. In this study, all of the male patients had provided a semen sample to another doctor (most often the wife's OB/GYN) for testing before being referred to a urologist or male infertility specialist. None had been physically examined before seeing a male infertility specialist.

39. These figures were reported to me by one doctor whom I shadowed and are specific to his clinic; they are consistent with the findings of Rosenberg and Honig (2007).

40. Nangia, Likosky, and Wang 2007.

41. Because male infertility is not a board-certified practice, it is difficult to calculate the exact ratio of female infertility practitioners to male infertility practitioners. Numbers of female infertility practitioners (REs) are kept by the ABOG and the AMA; no figures are kept for urologists who have fellowship-trained in male infertility. Membership figures provided by the American Society for Reproductive Medicine shed some light on the numbers. Of the 5,087 active physician members, 2,479 are REs, compared with only 538 urologists (Eleanor Nicholl, Public Affairs Manager at ASRM, personal communication).

42. Since my interviews with doctors were conducted, Dr. Michael Kamrava, a reproductive endocrinologist, made big headlines after he transferred twelve embryos into his patient, Nadya Suleman. Suleman, more popularly known as "Octo-Mom," subsequently gave birth to octuplets in 2009. Dr. Kamrava made history with his attempt, but he was expelled from the American Society for Reproductive Medicine and had his medical license revoked by the Medical Board of California for his "extreme" practice. Though guidelines for number of embryos to transfer have been well established for over a decade, doctors ultimately make the decisions. Dr. Kamrava's fate serves as a cautionary tale to reproductive endocrinologists to use wisdom in making transfers.

43. In this study, patients' predictions of cost, including out-of-pocket expenses and health insurance coverage, were inaccurate. Some patients spent much more out of pocket than they had anticipated, while others were happily surprised by unexpected insurance coverage.

44. The universal coverage of pharmaceutical drugs for erectile dysfunction for men compared with less than suitable coverage of birth control for women by many health insurance companies is evidence enough that the world of medicine is shaped by strong gender norms. Apparently, sexual pleasure is

an inalienable right for American men, and women should be forced to carry men's offspring, but that is a story for another book. In the case of male infertility, if a male patient stated that the cause of his infertility was impeding sexual pleasure (not necessarily related to erectile dysfunction), doctors claimed that they could get treatments covered.

45. http://www.cdc.gov/art/index.htm.

46. Practice Committee of the American Society for Reproductive Medicine 2008b.

47. Elster 2000; Gera et al. 2006; Wang et al. 2003.

48. Elster 2000; Wang et al. 2003.

49. Rosenberg and Honig 2007.

50. Agarwal et al. 2008; Agarwal et al. 2009; Erogul et al. 2006.

51. De La Rochebrochard and Thonneau 2002; Luke and Brown 2007; Nicolaidis and Petersen 1998.

52. De La Rochebrochard et al. 2006; Kidd, Eskanazi, and Wyrobek 2001; Sloter et al. 2007; Snajderova et al. 2009; Williams et al. 2004.

53. I had the opportunity to sit in on several vasectomy reversal appointments but chose not to include in the research sample men who had "elected" infertility.

54. Phenotypes are the observable characteristics of a species based on genotypes or genes.

55. Couples with a male factor due to genetic conditions such as cystic fibrosis, for which infertility is common, are referred to genetic counselors to determine whether or not the wife is a carrier. Precautions are taken to ensure that the disease is not passed on to male offspring.

56. Hawkins et al. 1999.

57. Spar 2006.

58. Practice Committee of the American Society for Reproductive Medicine 2008b.

59. I was able to observe this couple's appointment, but they declined to be interviewed.

60. See Inhorn et al. 2009b.

Chapter 3

1. West and Zimmerman 2002.

2. Ridgeway and Correll 2004, 517.

3. Bordo 1999, 229.

4. Gutmann 2009.

5. Ibid., 28.

6. Most women are required to provide blood samples. Depending on the clinic and the circumstances, some women also submit to an ultrasound, Clomid challenge, hysterosalpingogram or laparoscopic procedures.

7. Before the mid-twentieth century, masturbation was considered morally

repulsive and psychologically and physically damaging to men. According to Huhner's medical text (1942), men were instructed to have sex using a condom and then bring the condom to the doctor for sperm analysis. Doctors told me that they avoided using condoms because they are lined with spermicide. However, biotechnology manufacturers could create condoms without spermicide to use for masturbation in lieu of the cup.

8. Martin 1987.

9. Ibid., 34–35.

10. Ibid., 36–37.

11. Ibid., 59.

12. Throughout my own personal medical experiences as a woman, including gynecological examinations, infertility workups and treatments, prenatal care, labor, delivery, breastfeeding, breast cancer screening, and birth control, no doctor has ever explained my body or body parts to me as a factory, bridge, car, plane, motorcycle, or sport. I cannot recall any metaphors used to describe my body.

13. Bordo 1999.

14. Practice Committee of the American Society for Reproductive Medicine 2008a.

15. Gaylene Becker (2000) argues that divorce rates are low among infertile couples, but there are no statistics to support this observation. One doctor claimed that published data show that Hispanic men are highly likely to commit suicide if they are diagnosed infertile. He could not cite the source, and my own searches for such a reference were fruitless.

16. As the Intersex Society of North America acknowledges on its website, "Intersex is a socially constructed category that reflects real biological variation. . . . So nature doesn't decide where the category of 'male' ends and the category of 'intersex' begins, or where the category of 'intersex' ends and the category of 'female' begins" (http://www.isna.org/faq/what_is_intersex). For the most thorough research and discussion on the social construction of intersex in American culture, I recommend Suzanne J. Kessler's (1998) *Lessons from the Intersexed.*

17. Prentice and Carranza 2002.

18. Hochschild 1989.

19. Acker 1992; Bowles and Klein 1983; Connell 1995, 73; Kimmel 2008.

20. No organizations keep exact figures on the male to female ratio in urology. As a helpful point of reference, however, we know that of the 18,505 M.D.s who belonged to the American Urological Association in 2011, only 1,618 were female.

21. Ridgeway 2011; Ridgeway and Correll 2004, 528.

22. Ridgeway 2011, 71–73.

23. Ibid., 163.

24. Greil 1991.

Chapter 4

1. I omitted overused filler words—including "well," "like," "you know," and "I mean"—from subjects' quotations in Chapters 4 and 5.

2. Dewey 1933; Frankl 1963; Krauss 2005.

3. Whiteford and Gonzalez 1994.

4. Loe 2004; Potts 2000; Thompson 2005.

5. Becker 2000.

6. Conrad 1992; Zola 1972.

7. Moynihan, Heath, and Henry 2002.

8. Loe 2004, 39–40; Nicholas 2000.

9. www.viagra.com.

10. Potts 2000, 93.

11. Goldberg 2009, 215; Tjørnhøj-Thomsen 2009.

12. Of course, men have not turned out in droves for infertility treatments, as they have for ED.

13. Most likely, he fathered the first son before the tumor developed.

14. Courtenay 2000; Emslie and Hunt 2009; Nicholas 2000.

15. Conrad and Schneider 1980; Potts 2000.

16. The specialist reported that as soon as he saw the ruptured vas deferens, he knew that it had been severed by surgical instruments. Such a clean break could not have been caused by trauma. In our private discussion the specialist explained that there was no reason for the doctor who performed the hernia surgery to be "poking around" in the area of the vas deferens. If Troy's parent had known at the time what had happened, they ought to have filed a malpractice lawsuit.

17. Greil 2002.

18. Ibid., 105–106.

19. In contrast to Kevin, two infertile women in a study by anthropologist Gaylene Becker (2003, 53) were profoundly distressed to have missing fallopian tubes, the female parts that are analogous to the male vasa deferentia. In Becker's study, one woman lost her fallopian tube in an ectopic pregnancy, and another woman had to have both fallopian tubes removed surgically. The first woman said, "I felt like my body had betrayed me." The second woman claimed that not having her fallopian tubes was "devastating" and left her feeling "not whole."

20. Gray et al. (2002, 46), scholars of prostate cancer patients, note that "current crises are linked to past personal history."

21. Becker (2000, 83) observed that women and men with preexisting health issues were more likely to raise questions about risks associated with IVF than were others. She argues that "prior experiences with medical care socialized them to think in such terms." My point here is not that patients were more risk-oriented but just that, as Becker says, prior experience with medical

care socialized them to all aspects of patienthood: willingness to visit doctors regularly, compliance with doctors' orders, and so forth.

22. In her study of male infertility in Israel, Helene Goldberg (2009, 214) recounts the experiences of one subject who, like the men in my study, was able to separate his self-image from his sperm quality. However, Goldberg notes, he was not able to do this until after he learned that other men suffer from fertility problems too.

23. Lee 2003.

24. Connell 1995; Goffman 1959; Kaufman 1994; Kimmel 1994.

25. Connell 1995; Ridgeway and Correll 2004.

26. Webb and Daniluk 1999, 21.

27. Kimmel 1994, 129.

28. Allison 2011; Birenbaum-Carmeli 2009; Dyer et al. 2004; Greil 1991; Hjelmstedt et al. 1999; Lee and Chu 2001; Letherby 1999; Miall 1986; White-ford and Gonzalez 1994.

29. Williams 1989.

30. A white middle-class male subject in Becker's infertility study made a similar observation. He explained that he was willing to talk about his infertility with his friends, but he would not discuss his infertility at work, "a fairly blue-collar environment," for fear of being ridiculed. These examples reflect "class differences associated with cultural dialogues on masculinity" and infertility (Becker 2000, 47).

31. Kaufman 1994, 145.

32. Bordo 1989. For additional discussion of male/female duality, see Chapter 2.

33. Greil 1991, 65.

34. Because of the highly sensitive nature of this issue, I refrain from using this man's real name or his regular pseudonym to ensure absolute anonymity. I do not want this information to be connected with any other identifying information (age, occupation, diagnosis) presented in the other chapters.

35. This research project was tightly monitored by the institutional review boards (IRBs) that oversaw it. I was warned that the subject matter, male infertility, was "too sensitive" a topic to study, and it was not easy to get approval to conduct the research study. I reassured IRB committees that I would be very gentle with the people I interviewed. During the study, I constantly worried that if any participants had a negative interview experience and complained about it to the IRBs, the entire study would get shut down. I tried to be clear with patients that I was not asking for details about their sexual activity. This was not a study about sexuality or sex behaviors; that is an altogether different field of scholarship. In retrospect, however, my one regret is that I did not probe more deeply in asking about sex and sexuality. Patients provided some provocative answers, and I wish that I had asked them to clarify and elaborate their ideas more thoroughly. Despite the brevity of responses, these data are too rich and relevant not to include.

36. Becker 2000; Hammarberg, Baker, and Fisher 2010; Keylor and Apfel 2010; Peterson, Newton, and Feingold 2007; Smith et al. 2009.

37. Thompson 2005, 136.

38. Similarly, 85 percent of the women in Sarah Franklin's (1997) study of infertility reported that infertility had affected their marriage positively.

39. Mazor 1985, 31–32.

40. Greil 1991; Greil, Leitko, and Porter 1988; Tjørnhøj-Thomsen 2009, 237.

41. Davis-Floyd 1992; Martin 1987.

42. Becker 2000; Greil 2002; Letherby 1999.

43. Han 2009.

44. Drawing on the work of psychoanalysts such as Sigmund Freud, Nancy Chodorow, Dorothy Dinnerstein, and Jessica Benjamin, sociologist Michael Kaufman (1994, 146–147) points out that manhood is learned in the home, beginning in childhood, and that masculinity is represented by fathers.

45. Kimmel 1994, 131.

46. At the 2007 meeting of the American Society for Reproductive Medicine, a group of mental health professionals gathered for a two-day seminar entitled "Men and ART: The Missing Voice," which focused on men's experiences with infertility and assisted reproductive technologies. Seminar speakers lamented the dearth of research on the topic of male infertility and repeatedly encouraged the audience, made up of members of the mental health community, to conduct more research on men's emotional and social experiences with infertility. During one question-and-answer period, a clinical therapist in the audience stepped to the microphone and declared with some exasperation, "We are *trying* to study male infertility, but it is impossible to recruit men for our studies. Men don't want to talk about their infertility!"

47. Thompson 2005, 120.

48. Goldberg 2009, 205.

49. Webb and Daniluk's (1999) research subjects had all experienced infertility several years before the study. By the time they were interviewed, five of them had adopted children, and one had a child from donor sperm. Webb and Daniluk acknowledge that the subjects may have been unique in their willingness to discuss such an intimate aspect of their lives, and their stories likely do not reflect the early experiences of men dealing with infertility. Furthermore, their study was conducted before IVF-ICSI had gained popularity, a time when infertile men were particularly invisible and had little to share in the way of medical experiences.

50. Words in quotations are taken verbatim from the IRB-approved informed consent forms used for this research study.

51. Lorber and Bandlamudi 1993; Webb and Daniluk 1999.

52. Letherby 1999, 177.

53. In this study, a few wives and only one man had ever attended a support group, and only one woman attended a support group on a regular basis. The one man who had attended the support group with his wife noted

that they were the only couple in attendance dealing with male factor infertility.

54. Furman et al. 2010; Haagen et al. 2003; Huang et al. 2003; Lee 2003; Schmidt et al. 2003; Wischman et al. 2013.

55. Inhorn et al. 2009a.

56. Mason 1993; Webb and Daniluk 1999.

Chapter 5

1. Jack's experiences highlight two important points made in Chapter 2: (1) Male infertility specialists are not easy to locate, and patients often must travel a winding road to reach a qualified doctor. (2) In contrast to male infertility specialists, general urologists often lack sufficient training to properly diagnose and treat male infertility.

2. The wife had a bicornuate uterus, for which she was seeing a specialist to help determine her chances for success with treatment.

3. Arditti, Klein, and Minden 1984; R. Klein 1989; Solomon 1986.

4. Thompson 2005, 60.

5. Thompson 2005.

6. Sandelowski 1990.

7. Greil 2002, 103.

8. Thompson 2005, 185.

9. Rosenfeld and Faircloth 2006, 3.

10. Conrad 1992; Conrad and Schneider 1980; Freidson 1970; Zola 1972.

11. Courtenay 2000; Rosenfeld and Faircloth 2006, 1, 18–19.

12. Charmaz 1995; Courtenay 2000; Watson 2000.

13. Gray et al. 2002; Loe 2004; Potts 2000; Sabo 1995; Szymczak and Conrad 2006.

14. Becker 2000; Greil 2002; Thompson 2005; Whiteford and Gonzalez 1994, 36.

15. Loe 2004; Potts 2000, 97.

16. Cockburn and Ormrod 1993; Davis-Floyd 1992; Davis-Floyd and Dumit 1998; Ehrenreich and Ehrenreich 1978; Ehrenreich and English 2005; Harding 1986, 2004; Lohan and Faulkner 2004; Lorber 1975; Wajcman 2004.

17. Foucault 1973.

18. http://www.cdc.gov/art/. This definition is used in the 1992 Fertility Clinic Success Rate and Certification Act, which requires ART clinics in the United States to publicly report their success rates.

19. Davis-Floyd 1992; Davis-Floyd and Dumit 1998; Giddens 1990; Haraway 1990.

20. Davis-Floyd and Dumit 1998, 27.

21. Wajcman 2000, 454.

22. Inhorn 2009, 269

23. Becker 2000, 56.

24. See Franklin 1997, 97.

25. Two couples initially had reservations about the preliminary step of masturbation to provide semen for analysis on religious or moral grounds but chose to participate anyway.

26. For IVF, the woman's ovaries are stimulated to produce multiple eggs in one cycle. Some women produce as many as ten or even twenty eggs. All or most of the eggs are removed and fertilized as embryos, though not all embryos will survive. Technicians select the healthiest embryo or embryos to transfer into the uterus. The remaining embryos are frozen for possible future use. Couples who eventually choose not to use all of their embryos may donate the remainder to other infertile couples or discard them.

27. Wajcman 2000, 449.

28. Becker 2000, 6–7.

29. Franklin 1997, 137.

30. Ibid., 188–189.

31. Throsby and Gill 2004, 336.

32. Ibid., 336–337.

33. Thanks to their comprehensive health insurance, both Greg's surgery and the IVF-ICSI procedure were performed at minimal costs to Greg and Jane, so there were no economic incentives to postponing IVF-ICSI and no financial reasons to regret their treatment decisions.

34. I can think of two possible reasons why Kevin's specialist chose to do the second testicular extraction in the clinic with simple local anesthetic. One explanation may be that because egg retrieval dates are difficult to predict and schedule weeks in advance, a hospital operating room could not be scheduled ahead of time for the sperm extraction. Another explanation may be that some experts believe that general anesthesia can negatively affect the motility of sperm.

35. Morris 1993.

36. Benjamin and Ha'elyon 2002.

37. Ibid., 673

38. Lorber and Bandlamudi 1993.

39. Ibid., 40. A study by Bahman Baluch, Marian Nasseri, and Malek Mansour Aghssa (1998) on male infertility in Iran argues that men have greater household control but that once men are diagnosed with infertility, wives gain more household control. So while Lorber and Bandlamudi see wives of infertile men as less powerful when it comes to treatment decisions, Baluch, Nasseri, and Aghssa find that infertile men become less powerful in household decisions.

40. When the low sperm count is unexplained, there are few male-focused treatment options. There are no surgical solutions. The only possible solution would be the less common hormone therapy, but since Teresa also had infertility issues, IUI was the most promising option.

41. Becker 2000, 134.

42. Before the innovation of IVF-ICSI in the mid-1990s, couples in which the man had extremely low sperm counts or zero sperm regularly resorted to sperm donation to achieve pregnancy. The availability and preference for IVF-ICSI has driven down the demand for donor sperm. However, demand for donor sperm among single and lesbian women has increased significantly over the past two decades, and this group now makes up more than half of the consumer base for sperm banks.

43. Becker 2000, 65.

44. Moore 2007; Moore and Schmidt 1999.

45. A. Klein 1995.

Chapter 6

1. This assertion is nearly impossible to test and is admittedly based on anecdotal evidence. During my fieldwork, I heard countless stories from doctors, scientists, and laboratory technicians about couples being treated for what was believed to be female or idiopathic infertility, only to discover later that a male issue was preventing conception. I presume that there are just as many cases in which a male infertility factor is impeding conception but it is never discovered. Cynics (usually medical professionals) have told me that semen analyses are routine and male infertility never goes undiagnosed. Yet in private conversations with colleagues, friends, and acquaintances, I regularly hear women's stories of being prescribed hormones by a primary care physician or gynecologist to get pregnant, while the male partner's fertility status is never even investigated. In 2012 a friend confided in me that she was going through a full infertility workup at a local infertility clinic, part of a large, prominent HMO hospital. The reproductive endocrinologist there encouraged her to begin hormone injections in preparation for in vitro fertilization. Her husband had never provided a semen sample for analysis or consulted with any medical doctors. When she asked whether her husband should be tested, the doctor told her not to worry, he was sure the husband was fine.

2. MacDorman, Matthews, and Declercq 2012.

3. Daniels, Mosher, and Jones 2013.

4. Mosher and Jones 2010.

5. Davis-Floyd 1992; Ehrenreich and Ehrenreich 1978; Martin 1987.

6. Cook and Dickens 2009; Luna and Luker 2013; Ross 2006.

7. Inhorn 2009, 2012.

8. The term "genital cutting" most often refers to the forced practice of clitoridectomy in young girls in some parts of Africa. Genital cutting, or "genital mutilation," as it is sometimes called, is no doubt painful and serves no known medical purposes. This hot-button issue has galvanized human rights advocates around the world, but in an unexpected twist, some of the most vocal proponents of the practice are women who endured clitoridectomy in childhood.

9. Casper and Moore 2009.

10. Haraway 1996; Sprague and Kobrynowicz 2004.

11. Becker 2000; Greil 1991.

12. Martin 1987.

13. Becker 2000, 32,41–43; Mazor 1985, 32; Webb and Daniluk 1999, 8,12.

14. Kübler-Ross 1969.

15. Webb and Daniluk 1999, 21.

16. Fausto-Sterling 1995; Halberstam 1998; Pascoe 2007; Zinn and Dill 1996.

17. Kaufman 1994; Kimmel 1994.

Glossary

Acronyms and Abbreviations

ABOG: American Board of Obstetrics and Gynecology

ASRM: American Society for Reproductive Medicine

AUA: American Urological Association

CDC: Centers for Disease Control and Prevention

FSH: follicle-stimulating hormone

ICSI: intracytoplasmic sperm injection

IUI: intrauterine insemination

IVF: in vitro fertilization

LH: luteinizing hormone

MESA: microscopic epididymal sperm aspiration

PESA: percutaneous epididymal sperm aspiration

RE or RE/I: Reproductive Endocrinologist/Infertility Specialist

SART: Society for Assisted Reproductive Technologies

TESE: testicular sperm extraction

Terms

artificial insemination: Manual insertion of sperm into the vagina, cervix, or uterus

embryo: First eight weeks of development after an egg is successfully fertilized by a sperm

intracytoplasmic sperm injection: Manual injection of one sperm into one egg, a process used in conjunction with in vitro fertilization

in vitro fertilization: Fertilization of an egg by a sperm outside of the human body

laparoscopy: Minimally invasive abdominal surgery performed through small incisions

pipette: Laboratory tool used to transport and measure liquids and cells

varicocele: Abnormally enlarged vein in the testicles

varicocelectomy: Surgical repair or removal of a varicocele

References

Acker, Joan. 1992. "From sex roles to gendered institutions." *Contemporary Sociology* 21 (5): 565–569. doi: 10.2307/2075528.

Agarwal, Ashok, Fnu Deepinder, Rakesh K. Sharma, Geetha Ranga, and Jianbo Li. 2008. "Effect of cell phone usage on semen analysis in men attending infertility clinic: An observational study." *Fertility and Sterility* 89 (1): 124–128.

Agarwal, Ashok, Nisarg R. Desai, Kartikeya Makker, Alex Varghese, Rand Mouradi, Edmund Sabahegh, and Rakesh Sharma. 2009. "Effects of radiofrequency electromagnetic waves (RF-EMW) from cellular phones on human ejaculated semen: An in vitro pilot study." *Fertility and Sterility* 92 (4): 1318–1325.

Allison, Jill. 2011. "Conceiving silence: Infertility as discursive contradiction in Ireland." *Medical Anthropology Quarterly* 25 (1): 1–21.

Almeling, Rene. 2011. *Sex Cells: The Medical Markets for Eggs and Sperm*. Berkeley: University of California Press.

Alukal, Joseph P., and Dolores J. Lamb. 2008. "Intracytoplasmic sperm injection (ICSI): What are the risks?" *Urologic Clinics of North America* 35 (2): 277–288.

American Board of Obstetrics and Gynecology. 2004. *Guide to Learning in Reproductive Endocrinology and Infertility*. Dallas, TX: American Board of Obstetrics and Gynecology.

American Urological Association. 2009. *2010 Information for Applicants and Candidates*. 57th ed. Charlottesville, VA: American Board of Urology.

Arditti, Rita, Renate Duelli Klein, and Shelley Minden. 1984. *Test-Tube Women: What Future for Motherhood?* London: Pandora Press.

Baluch, Bahman, Mariam Nasseri, and Malek Mansour Aghssa. 1998. "Psychological and social aspects of male infertility in a male dominated society." *Journal of Social and Evolutionary Systems* 21 (1): 113–120.

Becker, Gaylene. 2000. *The Elusive Embryo: How Women and Men Approach New Reproductive Technologies.* Berkeley: University of California Press.

Benjamin, Orly, and Hila Ha'elyon. 2002. "Rewriting fertilization: Trust, pain, and exit points." *Women's Studies International Forum* 25 (6): 667–678.

Benninghaus, Christina. 2012. "Beyond constructivism? Gender, medicine, and the early history of sperm analysis, Germany 1870–1900." *Gender and History* 24 (3): 647–676.

Birenbaum-Carmeli, Daphna, and Marcia C. Inhorn. 2009. "Masculinity and Marginality: Palestinian men's struggles with infertility in Israel and Lebanon." *Journal of Middle East Women's Studies* 5 (5): 23–52.

Bordo, Susan. 1989. *Gender/Body/Knowledge.* New Brunswick, NJ: Rutgers University Press.

———. 1999. *The Male Body: A New Look at Men in Public and in Private.* New York: Farrar, Straus, and Giroux.

Boston Women's Health Book Collective. 1973. *Our Bodies, Our Selves: A Course by and for Women.* Boston: Boston Women's Health Book Collective.

Bowles, Gloria, and Renate Duelli Klein. 1983. "Introduction: Theories of women's studies and the autonomy/integration debate." In *Theories of Women's Studies,* edited by Gloria Bowles and Renate Duelli Klein, 1–26. Boston: Routledge.

Brown, Robert D. 1987. *Lucretius on Love and Sex: A Commentary on De Rerum Natura IV, 1030–1287, with Prolegomena, Text and Translation.* New York: E. J. Brill.

Carlsen, Elisabeth, Aleksander Giwercman, Niels Keiding, and Niels E. Skakkebaek. 1992. "Evidence for decreasing quality of semen during the past fifty years." *British Medical Journal* 305:609–612.

Casper, Monica J., and Lisa Jean Moore. 2009. *Missing Bodies: The Politics of Visibility.* New York: New York University Press.

CDC, ASRM, and SART. 2012. *2010 Assisted Reproductive Technology: Fertility Clinic Success Rates Report.* Atlanta: U.S. Department of Health and Human Services.

Chachamovich, Juliana Rigol, Eduardo Chachamovich, Helene Ezer, Marcelo P. Fleck, Daniela Knauth, and Eduardo P. Passos. 2010. "Investigating quality of life and health-related quality of life in infertility: A systematic review." *Journal of Psychosomatic Obstetrics and Gynecology* 31 (2): 101–110.

Charmaz, Kathy. 1995. "Identity dilemmas of chronically ill men." In *Men's Health and Illness: Gender, Power and the Body,* edited by Donald Sabo and David Frederick Gordon, 266–291. Thousand Oaks, CA: Sage.

Chen, S., L. Sun, S. Li, M. Yin, X. Xiong, and J. He. 2007. "Birth defects of 1,397 newborns conceived by in vitro fertilization/intracytoplasmic sperm injection and embryo transfer." *Fertility and Sterility* 88 (S1): S115.

Christianson, M. S., M. M. Yates, Z. R. Hubayter, L. Reigart, Y. Zhao, and E. E. Wallach. 2009. "Intracytoplasmic sperm injection for male factor infertility: Effects on gender of offspring." *Fertility and Sterility* 91 (3): S12.

Clarke, Adele. 1998. *Disciplining Reproduction: Modernity, American Life Sciences, and "the Problems of Sex."* Berkeley: University of California Press.

Clarke, Edward. 1873. *Sex in Education: Or, A Fair Chance for the Girls.* Boston: Osgood.

Cockburn, Cynthia, and Susan Ormrod. 1993. *Gender and Technology in the Making.* Thousand Oaks, CA: Sage.

Connell, R. W. 1995. *Masculinities: Knowledge, Power and Social Change.* Berkeley: University of California Press.

Conrad, Peter. 1992. "Medicalization and social control." *Annual Review of Sociology* 18:209–232.

Conrad, Peter, and Joseph W. Schneider. 1980. *Deviance and Medicalization: From Badness to Sickness.* St. Louis: C. V. Mosby.

Cook, Rebecca J., and Bernard M. Dickens. 2009. "From reproductive choice to reproductive justice." *International Journal of Gynecology and Obstetrics* 106 (2): 106–109.

Courtenay, Will H. 2000. "Constructions of masculinity and their influence on men's well-being: A theory of gender and health." *Social Science and Medicine* 50 (10): 1385–1401.

Culley, Lorraine, Nicky Hudson, and Maria Lohan. 2013. "Where are all the men? The marginalization of men in social scientific research on infertility." *Reproductive Biomedicine Online* 27 (3): 225–235.

Daniels, Cynthia R. 2006. *Exposing Men: The Science and Politics of Male Reproduction.* Oxford: Oxford University Press.

Daniels, Kimberly, William D. Mosher, and Jo Jones. 2013. "Contraceptive methods women have ever used: United States, 1982–2010." In *National Health Statistics Report.* Hyattsville, MD: National Center for Health Statistics.

Davis-Floyd, Robbie. 1992. *Birth as an American Rite of Passage: Comparative Studies of Health Systems and Medical Care.* Berkeley: University of California Press.

Davis-Floyd, Robbie, and Joseph Dumit. 1998. *Cyborg Babies: From Techno-Sex to Techno-Tots.* New York: Routledge.

de Beauvoir, Simone. 1951. *The Second Sex,* translated by H. M. Parshley. New York: Knopf.

De La Rochebrochard, Elise, Jacques de Mouzon, Francois Thepot, and Patrick Thonneau. 2006. "Fathers over 40 and increased failure to conceive: The lessons of in vitro fertilization in France." *Fertility and Sterility* 85 (5): 1420–1424.

De La Rochebrochard, Elise, and Patrick Thonneau. 2002. "Paternal age and maternal age are risk factors for miscarriage: Results of a multicentre

European study." *Human Reproduction* 17 (6): 1649–1656. doi: 10.1093/humrep/17.6.1649.

Dewey, John. 1933. *How We Think.* New York: Heath Books.

Dooley, Maeve, Aonghus Nolan, and K. M. Sarma. 2011. "The psychological impact of male factor infertility and fertility treatment on men: A qualitative study." *Irish Journal of Psychology* 32 (1–2): 14–24.

Dyer, S. J., N. Abrahams, N. E. Mokoena, and Z. M. van der Spuy. 2004. "'You are a man because you have children': Experiences, reproductive health knowledge and treatment-seeking behaviour among men suffering from couple infertility in South Africa." *Human Reproduction* 19 (4): 96–97.

Ehrenreich, Barbara, and John Ehrenreich. 1978. "Medicine and social control." In *The Cultural Crisis of Modern Medicine,* edited by John Ehrenreich, 39–79. New York: Monthly Review Press.

Ehrenreich, Barbara, and Deirdre English. 2005. *For Her Own Good: Two Centuries of the Experts' Advice to Women.* Rev. ed. New York: Anchor Books.

El-Chaar, Darine, Qiuying Yang, Jun Gao, Jim Bottomley, Arthur Leader, Shi Wu Wen, and Mark Walker. 2009. "Risk of birth defects increased in pregnancies conceived by assisted human reproduction." *Fertility and Sterility* 92 (5): 1557–1561.

Elster, Nanette. 2000. "Less is more: The risks of multiple births." *Fertility and Sterility* 74 (4): 617–623.

Emslie, Carol, and Kate Hunt. 2009. "Men, masculinities and heart disease: A systematic review of the qualitative literature." *Current Sociology* 57 (2): 155–191.

Epstein, Yakov M., and Helane S. Rosenberg. 2005. "Depression in primary versus secondary infertility egg recipients." *Fertility and Sterility* 83 (6): 1882–1884.

Erogul, Osman, Emin Oztas, Ibrahim Yidirim, Tayfun Kir, Emin Aydur, Gokhan Komesli, Hasan Cem Irilata, Mehmet Kemal Irmak, and Ahmet Fuat Peker. 2006. "Effects of electromagnetic radiation from a cellular phone on human sperm motility: An in vitro study." *Archives of Medical Research* 37 (7): 840–843.

Fausto-Sterling, Ann. 1995. "How to build a man." In *Constructing Masculinity,* edited by Maurice Berger, Brian Wallis, and Simon Watson, 127–134. New York: Routledge.

Firestone, Shulamith. 1970. *The Dialectic of Sex: The Case for a Feminist Revolution.* New York: Morrow.

Fisher, Jane R. W., and Karin Hammarberg. 2012. "Psychological and social aspects of infertility in men: An overview of the evidence and implications for psychologically informed clinical care and future research." *Asian Journal of Andrology* 14 (1): 121–129.

Foucault, Michel. 1973. *The Birth of the Clinic: An Archaeology of Medical Perception.* New York: Vintage Books.

Frankl, Viktor. 1963. *Man's Search for Meaning*. Boston: Beacon Press.

Franklin, Sarah. 1997. *Embodied Progress: A Cultural Account of Assisted Conception*. London: Routledge.

Freidson, Eliot. 1970. *Professional Dominance: The Social Structure of Medical Care*. Chicago: Aldine Publishing.

Friedan, Betty. 1963. *The Feminine Mystique*. New York: Norton.

Furman, Irene, Leslie Parra, Ariel Fuentes, and Luigi Devoto. 2010. "Men's participation in psychologic counseling services offered during in vitro fertilization treatments." *Fertility and Sterility* 94 (4): 1460–1464.

Gera, P. S., M. C. Allemand, L. L. Tatpati, D. R. Session, M. A. Wentworth, and C. C. Coddington. 2006. "P-743: Ovarian hyperstimulation syndrome (OHSS): Steps to maximize success and minimize effect." *Fertility and Sterility* 86 (3): S408–S409.

Giddens, Anthony. 1990. *The Consequences of Modernity*. Stanford, CA: Stanford University Press.

Goel, Ashish, V. Sreenivas, Shinjini Bhatnagar, Rakesh Lodha, and Neerja Bhatla. 2009. "Risk of birth defects increased in pregnancies conceived by assisted human reproduction." *Fertility and Sterility* 92 (1): e7.

Goffman, Erving. 1959. *The Presentation of Self in Everyday Life*. Garden City, NY: Doubleday.

Goldberg, Helene. 2009. "The sex in the sperm: Male infertility and its challenges to masculinity in an Israeli-Jewish context." In *Reconceiving the Second Sex: Men, Masculinity, and Reproduction,* edited by Marcia C. Inhorn, Tine Tjørnhøj-Thomsen, Helene Goldberg and Maruska la Cour Mosegard, 203–225. New York: Berghahn Books.

Gray, Ross, Margaret I. Fitch, Karen D. Fergus, Eric Mykhalovsky, and Kathryn Church. 2002. "Hegemonic masculinity and the experience of prostate cancer." *Journal of Aging and Identity* 7 (1): 43–62.

Greil, Arthur L. 1991. *Not Yet Pregnant: Infertile Couples in Contemporary America*. New Brunswick, NJ: Rutgers University Press.

———. 2002. "Infertile bodies: medicalization, metaphor, and agency." In *Infertility around the Globe: New Thinking on Childlessness, Gender and Reproductive Technologies,* edited by Frank van Balen and Marcia C. Inhorn, 101–118. Berkeley: University of California Press.

Greil, Arthur L., Thomas A. Leitko, and Karen L. Porter. 1988. "Infertility: His and hers." *Gender and Society* 2 (2): 172–199.

Gurtler, Bridget. 2013. "Synthetic conception: Artificial insemination and the transformation of reproduction and family in nineteenth and twentieth century America." Ph.D. diss., Rutgers State University.

Gutmann, Matthew. 2009. "The missing gamete? Ten common mistakes or lies about men's sexual destiny." In *Reconceiving the Second Sex: Men, Masculinities, and Reproduction,* edited by Marcia C. Inhorn, Tine Tjørnhøj-Thomsen, Helene Goldberg, and Maruska la Cour Mosegaard, 21–44. New York: Berghahn Books.

Haagen, E. C., W. Tuil, J. Hendriks, R. P. J. de Bruijn, D. D. M. Braat, and J. A. M. Kremer. 2003. "Current Internet use and preferences of IVF and ICSI patients." *Human Reproduction* 18 (10): 2073–2078.

Halberstam, Judith. 1998. *Female Masculinity*. Durham, NC: Duke University Press.

Hammarberg, K., H. W. G. Baker, and J. R. W. Fisher. 2010. "Men's experiences of infertility and infertility treatment 5 years after diagnosis of male factor infertility: A retrospective cohort study." *Human Reproduction* 25 (11): 2815–2820.

Han, Sally. 2009. "Making room for daddy: Men's 'belly talk' in the contemporary United States." In *Reconceiving the Second Sex: Men, Masculinity, and Reproduction,* edited by Marcia C. Inhorn, Tine Tjørnhøj-Thomsen, Helene Goldberg, and Maruska la Cour Mosegaard, 305–326. New York: Bergahn Books.

Haraway, Donna. 1990. "A manifesto for cyborgs: Science, technology, and socialist feminism in the 1980s." In *Feminism/Postmodernism,* edited by Linda J. Nicholson, 190–233. New York: Routledge.

———. 1991. *Simians, Cyborgs and Women: The Reinvention of Nature*. London: Free Association Books.

———. 1996. "Situated knowledges: The science question in feminism and the privilege of partial perspective." In *Feminism and Science,* edited by Evelyn Fox Keller and Helen E. Longino, 249–263. New York: Oxford University Press.

Harding, Sandra. 1986. *The Science Question in Feminism*. Ithaca, NY: Cornell University Press.

———. 2004. "Rethinking standpoint epistemology: What is 'strong objectivity'?" In *Feminist Perspectives on Social Research,* edited by Sharlene Nagy Hesse-Biber and Michelle L. Yaiser, 39–64. New York: Oxford University Press.

Hawkins, M. M., C. L. R. Barratt, A. G. Sutcliffe, and I. D. Cooke. 1999. "Male infertility and increased risk of diseases in future generations." *Lancet* 354 (9193): 1906–1907.

Hjelmstedt, Anna, Lena Anderson, Agneta Skoog-Svanberg, Torbjörn Bergh, Jacky Boivin, and Aila Collins. 1999. "Gender differences in psychological reactions to infertility among couples seeking IVF- and ICSI-treatment." *Acta Obstetricia et Gynecologica Scandinavica* 78 (1): 42–48.

Hochschild, Arlie Russell. 1989. *The Second Shift*. New York: Harper Collins.

Huang, J. Y. J., H. Al-Fozan, S. L. Tan, and T. Tulandi. 2003. "Internet use by patients seeking infertility treatment." *International Journal of Gynecology and Obstetrics* 83 (1): 75–76.

Huhner, Max. 1942. *Diagnosis and Treatment of Sexual Disorders in the Male and Female Including Sterility and Impotence*. 2nd ed. Philadelphia: F. A. Davis.

Inhorn, Marcia C. 2009. "Male genital cutting: Masculinity, reproduction, and male infertility surgeries in Egypt and Lebanon." In *Reconceiving the Second Sex: Men, Masculinity, and Reproduction*, edited by Marcia C. Inhorn, Tine Tjørnhøj-Thomsen, Helene Goldberg, and Maruska la Cour Mosegard, 253–278. New York: Berghahn Books.

———. 2012. *The New Arab Man: Emergent Masculinities, Technologies, and Islam in the Middle East*. Princeton, NJ: Princeton University Press.

Inhorn, Marcia C., Tine Tjørnhøj-Thomsen, Helene Goldberg, and Maruska la Cour Mosegaard. 2009a. "Introduction: The second sex in reproduction? Men, sexuality, and masculinity." In *Reconceiving the Second Sex: Men, Masculinity, and Reproduction*, 1–20. New York: Berghahn Books.

———, ed. 2009b. *Reconceiving the Second Sex: Men, Masculinity, and Reproduction*. New York: Berghahn Books.

Inhorn, Marcia C., and Frank van Balen. 2002. *Infertility around the Globe: New Thinking on Childlessness, Gender, and Reproductive Technologies*. Berkeley: University of California Press.

Kampf, Antje. 2013. "Tales of healthy men: Male reproductive bodies in biomedicine from 'Lebensborn' to sperm banks." *Health* 17 (1): 20–36. doi: 10.1177/1363459312447251.

Kaufman, Michael. 1994. "Men, feminism, and men's contradictory experiences of power." In *Theorizing Masculinities*, edited by Harry Brod and Michael Kaufman, 142–163. Thousand Oaks, CA: Sage.

Kessler, Suzanne J. 1998. *Lessons from the Intersexed*. New Brunswick, NJ: Rutgers University Press.

Keylor, Rheta, and Roberta Apfel. 2010. "Male infertility: Integrating an old pscyhoanalytic story with the research literature." *Studies in Gender and Sexuality* 11 (2): 60–77.

Kidd, Sharon A., Brenda Eskenazi, and Andrew J. Wyrobek. 2001. "Effects of male age on semen quality and fertility: A review of the literature." *Fertility and Sterility* 75 (2): 237–248.

Kimmel, Michael S. 1994. "Masculinity as homophobia: Fear, shame and silence in the construction of gender identity." In *Theorizing Masculinities*, edited by Harry Brod and Michael Kaufman, 119–141. Thousand Oaks, CA: Sage.

———. 2008. *The Gendered Society*. 3rd ed. New York: Oxford University Press.

Klein, Alan M. 1995. "Life's too short to die small." In *Men's Health and Illness: Gender, Power, and the Body*, edited by Donald Sabo and David Frederick Gordon, 105–120. Thousand Oaks, CA: Sage.

Klein, Renate D. 1989. "Infertility: Women speak out about their experiences of reproductive medicine." In *Test Tube Babies: What Future for Motherhood?* London: Pandora Press.

Krauss, Steven Eric. 2005. "Research paradigms and meaning making: A primer." *Qualitative Report* 10 (4): 758–770.

Kübler-Ross, Elizabeth 1969. *On Death and Dying*. New York: Macmillan.

Lee, Sammy. 2003. "Myths and reality in male infertility." In *Inconceivable*

Conceptions: Psychological Aspects of Infertility and Reproductive Technology, edited by Jane Haynes and Juliet Miller, 73–85. New York: Brunner-Routledge.

Lee, Tsorng-Yeh, and Treu-Yen Chu. 2001. "The Chinese experience of male infertility." *Western Journal of Nursing Research* 23 (7): 714–725.

Letherby, Gayle. 1999. "Other than mother and mothers as others: The experience of motherhood and non-motherhood in relation to 'infertility' and 'involuntary childlessness.'" *Women's Studies International Forum* 22 (3): 359–372.

Loe, Meika. 2004. *The Rise of Viagra: How the Little Blue Pill Changed Sex in America.* New York: New York University Press.

Lohan, Maria, and Wendy Faulkner. 2004. "Masculinities and technologies: Some introductory remarks." *Men and Masculinities* 6 (4): 319–329.

Lorber, Judith. 1975. "Women and medical sociology: Invisible professionals and ubiquitous patients." In *Another Voice: Perspectives on Social Life and Social Science,* edited by Marcia Millman and Rosabeth Moss Kanter, 75–105. Garden City, NY: Anchor Books.

Lorber, Judith, and Lakshmi Bandlamudi. 1993. "The dynamics of marital bargaining in male infertility." *Gender and Society* 7 (1): 32–49.

Luke, Barbara, and Morton B. Brown. 2007. "Contemporary risks of maternal morbidity and adverse outcomes with increasing maternal age and plurality." *Fertility and Sterility* 88 (2): 283–293.

Luna, Zakiya, and Kristin Luker. 2013. "Reproductive justice." *Annual Review of Law and Social Science* 9 (1): 327–352.

MacDorman, Marian F., T. J. Matthews, and Eugene Declercq. 2012. *NCSH Data Brief,* 84. Hyattsville, MD: National Center for Health Statistics.

Martin, Emily. 1987. *The Woman in the Body: A Cultural Analysis of Reproduction.* Boston: Beacon Press.

Martinez, Gladys, Kimberly Daniels, and Anjani Chandra. 2012. "Fertility of men and women aged 15–44 years in the United States: National Survey of Family Growth 2006–2010." In *National Health Statistics Reports.* Hyattsville, MD: National Center for Health Statistics.

Mason, Mary-Claire. 1993. *Male Infertility—Men Talking.* New York: Routledge.

Mazor, Miriam D. 1985. "Emotional reactions to infertility." In *Infertility: Medical, Emotional and Social Considerations,* edited by Miriam D. Mazor and Harriet F. Simons, 23–35. New York: Human Sciences Press.

Miall, C. E. 1986. "The stigma of involuntary childlessness." *Social Problems* 33 (4) : 268–282.

Mondat, Chevalier. 1844. *On Sterility in the Male and Female: Its Causes and Treatment.* Translated from the French. 5th ed. New York: J. S. Redfield, Clinton Hall.

Moore, Lisa Jean. 2007. *Sperm Counts: Overcome by Man's Most Precious Fluid.* New York: New York University Press.

Moore, Lisa Jean, and Matthew Allen Schmidt. 1999. "On the construction of male differences: Marketing variations in technosemen." *Men and Masculinities* 1 (4): 331–351.

Morris, David B. 1993. *The Culture of Pain*. Berkeley: University of California Press.

Moscucci, Ornella. 1990. *The Science of Woman: Gynaecology and Gender in England, 1880–1929*. Cambridge: Cambridge University Press.

Mosher, W. D., and J. Jones. 2010. "Use of contraception in the United States: 1982–2008." In *Vital Health Statistics*. Hyattsville, MD: National Center for Health Statistics.

Mosher, W. D., and W. F. Pratt. 1990. "Fecundity and infertility in the United States, 1965–88." In *Advance Data: From Vital and Health Statistics of the National Center for Health Statistics*. Hyattsville, MD: National Center for Health Statistics.

Moynihan, Ray, Iona Heath, and David Henry. 2002. "Selling sickness: The pharmaceutical industry and disease-mongering." *British Medical Journal* 324 (866): 1.

Nangia, Ajay K., D. S. Likosky, and D. Wang. 2007. "Distribution of male infertility specialists in relation to male population and ART centers in the USA: Are specialists appropriately located?" Poster presentation at the annual meeting of the American Society for Reproductive Medicine, October 13–17, Washington, DC.

Nicholas, Donald R. 2000. "Men, masculinity, and cancer: Risk-factor behaviors, early detection, and psychosocial adaptation." *Journal of American College Health* 49 (1): 27–33.

Nicolaidis, P., and M. B. Petersen. 1998. "Origin and mechanisms of nondisjunction in human autosomal trisomies." *Human Reproduction* 13 (2): 313–319. doi: 10.1093/humrep/13.2.313.

Niemi, Mikko. 1987. "Andrology as a specialty: Its origin." *Journal of Andrology* 8 (4): 201–202.

Olivennes, Francois. 2005. "Do children born after assisted reproductive technology have a higher incidence of birth defects?" *Fertility and Sterility* 84 (5): 1325–1326.

Olson, Christine K., Kim M. Keppler-Noreuil, Paul A. Romitti, William T. Budelier, Ginny Ryan, Amy E. T. Sparks, and Bradley J. Van Voorhis. 2005. "In vitro fertilization is associated with an increase in major birth defects." *Fertility and Sterility* 84 (5): 1308–1315.

Oudshoorn, Nelly. 2003. *The Male Pill: A Biography of a Technology in the Making*. Durham, NC: Duke University Press.

Pascoe, C. J. 2007. *Dude, You're a Fag: Masculinity and Sexuality in High School*. Berkeley: University of California Press.

Payne, Alma Smith. 1970. *The Cleere Observer: A Biography of Antoni van Leeuwenhoek*. New York: Macmillan.

Peterson, B. D., C. R. Newton, and T. Feingold. 2007. "Anxiety and sexual stress in men and women undergoing infertility treatment." *Fertility and Sterility* 88 (4): 911–914.

Potts, Annie. 2000. "'The essence of the hard on': Hegemonic masculinity and the cultural construction of 'erectile dysfunction.'" *Men and Masculinities* 3 (1): 85–103.

Practice Committee of the American Society for Reproductive Medicine. 2008a. *Definitions of Infertility and Recurrent Pregnancy Loss.* Birmingham, AL: American Society for Reproductive Medicine.

———. 2008b. "Report on varicocele and infertility." *Fertility and Sterility* 90 (5): S247–S249.

Prentice, Deborah A., and Erica Carranza. 2002. "What women and men should be, shouldn't be, are allowed to be, and don't have to be: The contents of prescriptive gender stereotypes." *Psychology of Women Quarterly* 26:269–281.

Ridgeway, Cecilia L. 2011. *Framed by Gender: How Gender Inequality Persists in the Modern World.* New York: Oxford University Press.

Ridgeway, Cecilia L., and Shelley J. Correll. 2004. "Unpacking the gender system: A theoretical perspective on gender beliefs and social relations." *Gender and Society* 18 (4): 510–531.

Riessman, Catherine Kohler. 2000. "Stigma and everday resistance practices: childless women in south India." *Gender and Society* 14 (1): 111–135.

Rosenberg, David J, and Stanton J Honig. 2007. "Patients are very uninformed about male infertility: A patient/partner questionnaire study." Paper presented at the annual meeting of the American Urological Association, Anaheim, California, May 19–24.

Rosenfeld, Dana, and Christopher Faircloth. 2006. *Medicalized Masculinities.* Philadelphia: Temple University Press.

Ross, Loretta. 2006. "Understanding reproductive justice: Transforming the pro-choice movement." *Off Our Backs* 36 (4): 14–19.

Rowe, Patrick J., Frank H. Comhaire, Timothy B. Hargreave, and Ahmed M. A. Mahmoud. 2000. *WHO Manual for the Standardized Investigation, Diagnosis and Management of the Infertile Male.* Cambridge: Cambridge University Press.

Sabo, Donald. 1995. "Testicular cancer and masculinity." In *Men's Health Illness: Gender, Power, and the Body,* edited by Donald Sabo and David Frederick Gordon, 246–265. Thousand Oaks, CA: Sage.

Sandelowski, Margarete. 1990. "Faultlines: Infertility and imperiled sisterhood." *Feminist Studies* 16 (1): 33–51.

Sandelowski, Margarete, and Sheryl de Lacey. 2002. "The uses of a 'disease': Infertility as rhetorical vehicle." In *Infertility around the Globe: New Thinking on Childlessness, Gender, and Reproductive Technologies,* edited by Marcia C. Inhorn and Frank van Balen, 33–51. Berkeley: University of California Press.

Schieve, Laura A., Sonja A. Rasmussen, and Jennita Reefhuis. 2005. "Risk of birth defects among children conceived with assisted reproductive technology: Providing an epidemiologic context to the data." *Fertility and Sterility* 84 (5): 1320–1324.

Schmidt, L., B. E. Hostein, J. Boivin, H. Sångren, Tine Tjørnhøj-Thomsen, J. Blaabjerg, F. Hald, A. Nyboe Anderson, and P. E. Rasmussen. 2003. "Patients' attitudes to medical and psychosocial aspects of care in fertility clinics: Findings from the Copenhagen Multi-Centre Psychosocial Infertility (COMPI) Research Programme." *Human Reproduction* 18 (3): 628–637.

Sloter, Eddie D., Francesco Marchetti, Brenda Eskenazi, Rosana H. Weldon, Joginder Nath, Debby Cabreros, and Andrew J. Wyrobek. 2007. "Frequency of human sperm carrying structural aberrations of chromosome 1 increases with advancing age." *Fertility and Sterility* 87 (5): 1077–1086.

Smith, James F., Thomas J. Walsh, Alan W. Shindel, Paul J. Turek, Holly Wing, Lauri Pasch, Patricia P. Katz, and Infertility Outcomes Program Project Group. 2009. "Sexual, marital, and social impact of a man's perceived infertility diagnosis." *Journal of Sexual Medicine* 6 (9): 2505–2515.

Snajderova, M., B. Petrak, T. Mardesic, M. Havlovicova, and D. Zemkova. 2009. "Is there any relation between paternal age and sporadic cases of neurofibromatosis Von Recklinghausen type 1?" *Fertility and Sterility* 92 (3): S199.

Solomon, A. 1986. "Sometimes perganol kills." In *Infertility: Women Speak Out about Their Experiences of Reproductive Medicine,* edited by Renate D. Klein, 46–50. London: Pandora Press.

Spar, Debora. 2006. *Baby Business: How Money, Science, and Politics Drive the Commerce of Conception.* Boston: Harvard Business School Press.

Sprague, Joey, and Diane Kobrynowicz. 2004. "A feminist epistemology." In *Feminist Perspectives on Social Research,* edited by Sharlene Nagy Hesse-Biber and Michelle L. Yaiser, 78–98. New York: Oxford University Press.

Squires, J. K., A. Carter, and P. F. Kaplan. 2001. "Developmental monitoring of children conceived by ICSI and IVF." *Fertility and Sterility* 76 (3): S145–S146.

Szymczak, Julia, and Peter Conrad. 2006. "Medicalizing the aging male body: Andropause and baldness." In *Medicalized Masculinities,* edited by Dana Rosenfeld and Christopher Faircloth, 89–111. Philadelphia: Temple University Press.

Thompson, Charis. 2005. *Making Parents: The Ontological Choreography of Reproductive Technologies.* Cambridge, MA: MIT Press.

Throsby, Karen, and Rosalind Gill. 2004. "It's different for men: Masculinity and IVF." *Men and Masculinities* 6 (4): 330–348.

Tjørnhøj-Thomsen, Tine 2009. "'It's a bit unmanly in a way': Men and infertility in Denmark." In *Reconceiving the Second Sex: Men, Masculinity, and Reproduction,* edited by Marcia C. Inhorn, Tine Tjørnhøj-Thomsen, Helene Goldberg, and Maruska la Cour Mosegard, 226–252. New York: Berghahn Books.

van der Ploeg, Irma. 1995. "Hermaphrodite patients: In vitro fertilization and the transformation of male infertility." *Science, Technology, and Human Values* 20 (4): 460–481.

———. 2004. "'Only angels can do without skin': On reproductive technology's hybrid and the politics of body boundaries." *Body and Society* 10 (2–3): 153–181.

Wajcman, Judy. 2000. "Reflections on gender and technology studies: In what state is the art?" *Social Studies of Science* 30 (3): 447–464.

———. 2004. *Techno Feminism*. Malden, MA: Polity.

Wang, Jim X., Monica Kwan, Michael J. Davies, Christine Kirby, Stephen Judd, and Robert J. Norman. 2003. "Risk of multiple pregnancy when infertility is treated with ovulation induction by gonadotropins." *Fertility and Sterility* 80 (3): 664–665.

Watson, Jonathan. 2000. *Male Bodies: Health, Culture and Identity*. Philadelphia: Open University Press.

Webb, Russell E., and Judith C. Daniluk. 1999. "The end of the line: Infertile men's experiences of being unable to produce a child." *Men and Masculinities* 2 (1): 6–25.

West, Candace, and Don Zimmerman. 2002. "Doing gender." In *Doing Gender, Doing Difference: Inequality, Power, and Institutional Change,* edited by Sarah Fenstermaker and Candace West, 3–23. New York: Routledge.

Whiteford, Linda M., and Lois Gonzalez. 1994. "Stigma: The hidden burden of infertility." *Social Science and Medicine* 40 (1): 27–36.

Williams, Christine L. 1989. *Gender Differences at Work: Women and Men in Nontraditional Occupations*. Berkeley: University of California Press.

Williams, D. H., S. A. Land, M. Han, P. D. Sutton, and R. E. Brannigan. 2004. "Paternity rates in the US 1993–2002: Analysis of birth rates by paternal age and race." *Fertility and Sterility* 82 (S2): S20.

Wilshire, Donna. 1990. "The uses of myth, image, and the female body in re-visioning knowledge." In *Gender/Body/Knowledge,* edited by Allison Jaggar and Susan R. Bordo, 92–114. New Brunswick, NJ: Rutgers University Press.

Wischmann, Tewes, and Petra Thorn. 2013. "(Male) Infertility: What does it mean to men? New evidence from quantitative and qualitative studies." *Reproductive Biomedicine Online* 27 (3): 236–243.

Zinn, Maxine Baca, and Bonnie Thornton Dill. 1996. "Theorizing difference from multiracial feminism." *Feminist Studies* 22 (2): 321–331.

Zola, Irving K. 1972. "Medicine as an institution of social control." *Sociological Review* 20 (4): 487–504.

Index

ABOG (American Board of Obstetrics and Gynecology): certification by, 32, 175n34; founding of, 22

Abortion, 155; abortion debates, 144

Abstaining from sex, 37, 109

Adoption, 97–98, 124, 132, 147, 148–149

Age, advanced parental, 41–43

Aghssa, Malek Mansour, 183n39

Almeling, Rene, 25

American Board of Obstetrics and Gynecology (ABOG): certification by, 32, 175n34; founding of, 22

American Board of Urology certification, 32–33, 175n34, 175–176n36

American Society for Andrology, 22, 26

American Society for Reproductive Medicine (ASRM): on definition of infertility, 9–10; on prevalence of male factor infertility, 3

American Urological Association (AUA) on male infertility subspecialty, 33

Anabolic steroids, 46–47, 153

Andrology, 22–26; no board certification for, 32

Andropause, 126

Anesthesia for male infertility surgery, 45, 138, 183n34

Animalcules, 20–21

Antioxidant supplements, 41

Appearance of genitals, 66–67

ART. See Assisted reproductive technologies (ART)

Artificial insemination, 24, 25, 27, 174n19

ASRM (American Society for Reproductive Medicine): on definition of infertility, 9; on prevalence of male factor infertility, 3

Assisted reproductive technologies (ART), 16; complications of, 36, 40, 176n42; cost of, 38–40; definition of, 128–129; vs. donor sperm, 31. See also In vitro fertilization (IVF)

AUA (American Urological Association) on male infertility subspecialty, 33

Automotive metaphors, 63–65

Azoospermia, 30, 34–35, 47–48. See also Zero sperm count

Baer, Karl Ernst von, 21

Balloon for semen collection, 60

Balls, big, 66–67
Baluch, Bahman, 183n39
Bandlamudi, Lakshmi, 140–141
Bargaining power in decision making, 140–141, 183n39
Baseball analogies, 64–65
Becker, Gaylene, 134, 146, 178n15, 179n19, 179–180n21, 180n30
Beer commercial, 76
Benjamin, Orly, 140
Benninghaus, Christina, 174n21
Bicornuate uterus, 182n2
Biological children, 146–152
Biological determinism, 8, 105, 107
Biomedicine, 2–3, 28, 50, 87, 125
Biopsy: to retrieve sperm, 30; testicular, 82
Birth, home vs. hospital, 156–157
Birth control: access to, 155; medicalization of, 157
Birth control pill, 157
Birth defect(s): infertility as, 92; with IVF, 30, 175n30; parental age and, 36; as potential risk, 133, 153
The Birth of the Clinic (Foucault), 127
Board certification, 32–33, 175n34, 175–176n36
Bodybuilding, 153
Body vs. self, 94–95, 107, 130, 160–161, 179n19
Bordo, Susan, 53
Boston Women's Health Book Collective, 24
Brain tumor, 90–91, 95
Bridge metaphor, 61–63
Brother as sperm donor, 150
Brown, Louise, 9, 10–11, 172n24
Buyer's remorse, 159

Cancer: hormone injections and, 132; prostate, 126; testicular, 95–96, 126
Capitalist metaphors, 61
Car metaphor, 63–65
Casper, Monica J., 159–160
CBAVD (congenital bilateral absence of the vas deferens), 92, 97–98, 138
Cell phones and male fertility, 41
Centers for Disease Control and Prevention (CDC): on definition of assisted reproductive technology, 128–129; on success rates for IVF, 39
Chastity, female, 152
Childlessness, stigma of, 12, 26, 80, 160
Chromosomal anomalies, 69–70
Circumcision, 159
Clarke, Adele, 7–8, 22
Class differences, 17, 64, 103–104, 180n30
Clinical encounters, terminology used in, 67–68
Clitoridectomy, 184n8
Clomiphene citrate (Clomid), 26–27
Cognitive aspects of infertility, 85
Conception: early understanding of, 20–21; "natural," 16, 19, 35, 128
Condom for semen collection, 60, 177–178n7
Congenital bilateral absence of the vas deferens (CBAVD), 92, 97–98, 138
Connell, R. W., 7
Consumers, informed, 126
Contraception: access to, 155; medicalization of, 157
Control: loss/lack of, 12, 89–90, 107; and masculinity, 65–66, 131–132; of medical technology, 126–127; reproductive, 156–159
Correll, Shelley, 5–6, 77
Cost calculation, 37–40, 176n43
Crisis of masculinity: feelings incited by, 93; and gender work, 79, 84; loss of control and, 107; and male infertility specialists, 80; medicalization and, 99, 101; zero sperm count as, 104, 106
Cultural milieu, masculinity and virility in, 4–8
Cultural taboos, 50
Culture: democratic, 145; and family life, 84; and gender ideology, 5–6; image-obsessed, 66–67; and impotence, 86, 101, 103; and male infertility, 80; and masculinity, 7, 75; of technology, 129, 140
The Culture of Pain (Morris), 140 •
Cyborg realm, 129
Cystic fibrosis, 97–98, 104, 110–111

Daniels, Cynthia, 5, 13
Daniluk, Judith, 118–119, 161, 181n49
Davis-Floyd, Robbie, 129
Decision making: bargaining power in, 140–141, 183n39; equal vote in, 141–143; interview questions about, 168–169; marital, 140–146; veto power in, 145–146
Democratic decision making, 141–143
Denial: of impact of infertility on masculinity, 99–107; as stage of grief, 161
Depression, 12
Developmental disorders with IVF, 30
Diabetes, erectile dysfunction due to, 96
Diagnosis, 67–70; interview questions about, 167–168
DINK (double-income, no kids) couples, 17
Disciplining Reproduction: Modernity, American Life Sciences, and "the Problems of Sex" (Clarke), 7–8
Disease, infertility as, 10–11
Divorce rates, infertility and, 68, 178n15
Doctors, doing gender by, 51–81
Doing gender, 51–81; in diagnosis, 67–70; by male infertility specialists, 51–81; in medical metaphors, 60–65; physical examination in, 65–67; in semen collection, 52–60; theory of, 51–52; and urology as masculine institution, 75–77; and wives as information keepers, 70–75
Donor sperm, 4, 31, 145–152, 175n24, 184n42
Doppler ultrasound of varicocele, 47
Double-income, no kids (DINK) couples, 17
Down syndrome, 155
Dumit, Joseph, 129

ED. *See* Erectile dysfunction (ED)
Edwards, Robert G., 8–9
Egalitarian approach: to addressing infertility, 133; to decision making, 141–143, 164
Egg(s): discovery of, 21; harvesting of, 27, 59
Ehrenreich, Barbara, 22–23

Ejaculation, 62
Ejaculatory duct in factory and bridge metaphor, 63
Electroejaculation, 43, 58, 60
Emasculation, sickness and, 126
Embodied politics, 159–161
Embryo(s), leftover (unused), 132, 145, 183n26
Embryo transfer, guidelines for, 36, 176n42
Emotional aspects: of impotence, 86; interview questions about, 168–169
Emotional distress, infertility and, 13
Emotional expression: cultural differences in, 7; gender stereotypes of, 79
Emotional impact: of female infertility, 107, 111, 112; of male infertility, 11, 85, 89, 92–93, 96, 103, 105–107
Emotional needs of infertile men, 100
Emotional processing in gender work, 6
Engine metaphor, 63–64
English, Deirdre, 22–23
Epididymis(ides) in factory and bridge metaphor, 62, 63
Equal vote, 141–143
Erectile dysfunction (ED): advanced paternal age and, 42; due to diabetes, 96; due to testosterone after pituitary tumor, 90–91; vs. infertility, 158–159; as medical condition, 69, 89; medical technology for, 126; and semen collection, 56; treatment of, 86–87
Erection, involuntary, 65–66
Ethnography, 16–17, 173n42
Etiologies, focusing on, 91–95
Exploratory surgery, 128
Exposing Men: The Science and Politics of Male Reproduction (Daniels), 5
Extramarital affairs, 11, 108, 111, 151–152

Factory metaphor, 61–63
Failure: childlessness as, 80; infertility as, 12; role failure, 84–85
Faircloth, Christopher A., 125
Fallopian tubes, surgical removal of, 179n19
Family tree of urology, 76–77
Father, 114–115, 116–117, 181n44

Fatherhood, 114–118; interview questions about, 169–170
Fatherhood rights, sperm in, 4
FDA (Food and Drug Administration) on clomiphene citrate, 26
Female infertility specialists, 32. *See also* Reproductive endocrinologists (REs) vs. male infertility specialists
Female power and sperm counts, 5
Femininity: culturally defined, 6; interview questions about, 169–170
Feminist activism, 24
Feminization of infertility medicine, 26–29
Fertility status, inheritance of poor, 43–45, 177n55
Fetus, gender of, 155
Financial resource, 163
Food and Drug Administration (FDA) on clomiphene citrate, 26
Forensics, sperm in, 4
For Her Own Good: Two Centuries of the Experts' Advice to Women (Ehrenreich and English), 22–23
Foucault, Michel, 127
Framed by Gender: How Gender Inequality Persists in the Modern World (Ridgeway), 52
Franklin, Sarah, 134–135
Freud, Sigmund, 66, 100, 130
Frustration: with getting diagnosis and treatment, 121, 159, 182n1; with infertility, 93; with low sperm count, 89, 90; with pain of treatment, 137–138; with semen collection, 56, 60

Gay couples, 14–16, 164, 172–173n41
Gender: doing, 51–81; of fetus, 155; preconceived notions of, 3; as social category, 2
Gender beliefs, hegemonic, 77, 162–163; language of, 52. *See also* Stereotypes, gender
Gender binary, 8
Gender Differences at Work (Williams), 103
Gender discrepancy in infertility and childlessness, 107, 115

Gendered identity, loss of, 161
Gendered institutions, 78
Gendered scripts, 135
Gender hierarchy, 7
Gender identity, infertility and, 12, 70
Gender ideology: construction and perpetuation of, 51–52; traditional, 77–80
Gender inequality, 77
Gender norms: construction and perpetuation of, 51–52; culturally defined, 6; negotiating, 8; redefinition of, 164. *See also* Norms
Gender stereotypes, 52, 53, 72–73, 78–79
Gender system, 5–6, 77–81
Gender work, 6–7, 82–120; denying infertility's impact on masculinity as, 99–107, 180n22, 180n30; on fatherhood, 114–118; how men engage in, 84; making sense of male infertility as, 86–99, 163; on sex and marriage, 108–114
General anesthesia for male infertility surgery, 138, 183n34
General information, interview questions about, 167
Genital(s), size and appearance of, 66–67
Genital cutting, male, 159, 184n8
Genital mutilation, 184n8
Gill, Rosalind, 135
God, punishment from, 83
Goldberg, Helene, 173n42, 180n22
Greil, Arthur, 94–95, 125
Grief, 11–12, 161–162
Growth of American Families Surveys, 171n5
Guilt, 12
Gurtler, Bridget, 25
Gutmann, Matthew, 53

Ha'elyon, Hila, 140
Harvesting of mature eggs, 27
Health, interview questions about, 169–170
Health insurance: and infertility as disease, 10; for infertility treatments, 38–39, 176–177n44
Heartache, 45, 85, 136
Hegemonic gender beliefs, 77, 162–163

Hegemonic masculinity, 7, 8, 52, 101, 126, 162
"Hermaphrodite patients," 175n25
Heteronormativity, 14–15, 70, 172–173n41
Heterosexual paradigm, 14–16
Hinman, Frank, 175n32
Historical overview of emergence of male infertility medicine, 20–50, 174n3
Hochschild, Arlie, 74
Home birth, 156
Home semen analysis kit, 130–131
Homoerotic aspects of physical examination, 66
Homosexual couples, 14–16, 164, 172–173n41
Hooke, Robert, 174n4
Hormone injections and cancer, 132
Hospital birth, 156–157
Hot man thesis, 53, 65
Hot tubs and sperm count, 40–41
Household control, 183n39
Huhner, Max, 24–25, 177–178n7
Humor, 66–67, 76–77
Hypermasculine milieu of urology, 75–77

IBF (in bed fertilization), 35, 78, 129
ICSI. *See* Intracytoplasmic sperm injection (ICSI)
Image-obsessed culture, 66–67
Impotence, 69; medicalization of, 86–87
Inadequacy, 12
In bed fertilization (IBF), 35, 78, 129
Individual analysis, 2
Individual(s) and gender ideology, 5–6
Industrial metaphors, 61
Industrial Revolution: and man/woman dichotomy, 28; medical metaphors in, 61
Infertility: causes of, 9; defined, 9–10, 83–84; as disease, 10–11; and gender identity, 12; invention of, 8–14, 172n24; as life-defining, 12; media coverage of, 12–13; medical and social context of, 9; medicalization of, 86–91; as process, 11–12; use of term, 67; as women's issue, 3. *See also* Male infertility
Infertility clinic: history of, 28. *See also* Male infertility clinics

Infertility journey, 162
Infertility: Medical, Emotional, and Social Considerations (Mazor), 114
Infertility medicine, feminization of, 26–29
Infertility research, 124–125
Infertility services, use of, 3–4
Infertility support groups, 16, 119–120, 181–182n53
Infertility workup, 51–81; diagnosis based on, 67–70; medical metaphors in, 60–65; physical examination in, 65–67; semen collection in, 52–60; and urology as masculine institution, 75–77; and wives as information keepers, 70–75; for women, 54, 177n6
Infidelity, 11, 108, 111, 151–152
Information keepers, wives as, 70–75
Information management by male infertility specialists, 41–46
Informed consumers, 126
Inhorn, Marcia, 130, 159
Institution(s): gendered, 78; and gender ideology, 5–6
Institutional analysis, 2
Institutional review boards (IRBs), 180n35
Insurance: and infertility as disease, 10; for infertility treatments, 38–39, 176–177n44
Intersexuality, 69–70, 178n16
Interview guide, 167–170
Intracervical insemination, 27
Intracytoplasmic sperm injection (ICSI): development of, 29–31; after male infertility surgery, 135–136, 183n33; as phenotypic time bomb, 43–45, 177n55; preference for male infertility treatment over, 124; role of reproductive endocrinologist vs. male infertility specialist in, 34; sperm extraction for, 45–46
Intrauterine insemination (IUI), 27; complications of, 36, 40, 176n42; cost of, 38–40; role of reproductive endocrinologist vs. male infertility specialist in, 34–35; semen collection for, 59
Invisibility, 159–160

In vitro fertilization (IVF): birth defects or developmental disorders with, 30, 175n30; complications of, 36, 40, 176n42; cost of, 38–40; decision making about, 141–146; development of, 8–9, 10; with intracytoplasmic sperm injection, 29–31; after male infertility surgery, 135–136, 183n33; as normal path to pregnancy, 133–137; as phenotypic time bomb, 43–45, 177n55; preference for male infertility treatment over, 124; procedure for, 27–28; religious concerns about, 128, 132; role of reproductive endocrinologist vs. male infertility specialist in, 34–36; semen collection for, 59; sperm extraction for, 45–46

In vitro fertilization (IVF) clinics, recruiting research participants from, 16, 173n42

Involuntary erection, 65–66

IRBs (institutional review boards), 180n35

"It's her body" rhetoric, 144

IUI. *See* Intrauterine insemination (IUI)

IVF. *See* In vitro fertilization (IVF)

Jokes, 66–67, 76–77

Kamrava, Michael, 176n42

Kaufman, Michael, 104, 181n44

Kimmel, Michael, 7, 102, 118

Kinship, 12

Klein, Alan M., 152–153

Klinefelter's syndrome, 69–70, 178n16

Kübler-Ross, Elizabeth, 161

Laptop computers and sperm count, 40–41

Leadership skills, 104

Lee, Sammy, 100

Leeuwenhoek, Antonie van, 20–21, 174n4

Lesbian women, 14–16, 172–173n41, 175n24

Lifestyle, interview questions about, 169–170

Local anesthesia for male infertility surgery, 138, 183n34

Lorber, Judith, 140–141

Loss: of control, 12; of normalcy and gendered identity, 161

Lucretius, 20

Machine, uterus as, 61

Making Parents (Thompson), 173n42

Male/female duality, 28–29, 106–107, 160–161

Male fertility status, upgrading of, 35

Male genital cutting, 159, 184n8

Male infertility, 86–99; dearth of research on, 118–120, 181n46, 181n49, 181–182n53; denying impact of, on masculinity, 99–107, 180n22, 180n30; focusing on etiologies of, 91–95; heterosexual paradigm of, 14–16; making sense of, 86–99; and masculinity, 7–8, 13; prevalence of, 3; as symptom of something bigger, 95–99, 179–180n21; treatment of women for, 13–14, 156; undiagnosed, 156, 184n1. *See also* Infertility; Sterility

Male infertility clinics: history of, 26, 28, 31; recruiting research participants from, 16–17; referrals to, 33–34, 36, 176n38, 176n39

Male infertility medicine, historical overview of emergence of, 20–50, 174n3

Male infertility practice, variations in, 40–48

Male infertility procedures: cost of, 38; insurance coverage for, 39

Male infertility specialists: certification of, 32–33, 175n34, 175–176n36; diagnosis by, 67–70; difficulty in finding, 121–122, 182n1; doing gender by, 51–81; harm caused by, 46–48; information management by, 41–46; medical metaphors of, 60–65; number of, 33–34, 176n41; physical examination by, 65–67; vs. reproductive endocrinologists, 31–37; semen collection by, 52–60; and urology as masculine institution, 75–77; and wives as information keepers, 70–75

Male infertility subspecialty, 31

Male infertility treatment(s), 121–154; and IVF, 133–137; marital decision making on, 140–146; as natural approaches, 127–133; pain of, 137–140; preference for, 123–124; sperm donation for, 146–152. *See also* Treatment plan

Male reproductive health center, 28. *See also* Male infertility clinics

Male vulnerability, 66

Manual egg fertilization technique, 29–31

Man/woman dichotomy, 28–29, 106–107, 160–161

Mapping procedure, 82

Marital decision making, 140–146, 164

Marriage, impact of infertility on, 108–114, 180n35

Martin, Emily, 61, 62, 160

Masculine institution, urology as, 75–77

Masculine metaphors, 60–65

Masculine milieu of urology, 75–77

Masculine stereotypes, 52, 53, 78–79

Masculine traits, 104

Masculinity: and access to power and resources, 103; aging and, 102; alternative forms of, 101; conceiving, 162–164; control and, 65–66, 131–132; crisis of, 79, 80, 84, 93, 99, 101, 104, 106, 107; culturally defined, 6; in cultural milieu, 4–8; denying impact of infertility on, 99–107, 180n22, 180n30; hegemonic, 7, 8, 52, 101, 126, 162; interview questions about, 169–170; male infertility and, 7–8, 13; multiple forms of, 7; norms around, 57, 58, 60, 78, 81; pain and, 137–140; proving one's, 102; and rationality, 106; virility and, 84–85

Masturbation for semen collection, 54–60, 177–178n7, 183n25

Maternal age, advanced, 41–43

Mazor, Miriam, 114

Meaning making, 84

Mechanical metaphors, 61–64

Media coverage of infertility, 12–13

Medical condition, infertility as, 86–91

Medical encounter, interview questions about, 167–168

"Medical gaze," 127

Medical interventions, 126–127

Medicalization: of male infertility, 86–91; men and, 124–127; of reproduction, 157

Medical metaphors, 60–65, 178n12

Medical system, previous experience with, 98–99, 179–180n21

Medical technology, 121–154; IVF as, 133–137; marital decision making on, 140–146; men and medicalization in, 124–127; men as controllers of, 126–127, 129–131; and natural approaches to male treatments, 127–133; pain and masculinity with, 137–140; sperm donation as, 146–152

Medicine as social category, 2–3

Men and medicalization, 124–127

Menopause as failed business, 61

Men's health research, 125–127

Menstruation as failed production, 61

MESA (microscopic epididymal sperm aspiration), 45–46

Metaphors, medical, 60–65, 178n12

Microscope in home semen analysis kit, 131

Microscopic epididymal sperm aspiration (MESA), 45–46

Microscopic testicular sperm extraction (Micro-TESE), 45–46

Microscopy, 20–21

Micro-TESE (microscopic testicular sperm extraction), 45–46

Middle East, male infertility in, 130, 159

Midwifery, 24

Mind/body duality, 106–107. *See also* Male/female duality

Minorities, underrepresentation of, 17–18, 163–164

Miracle: of birth, 20, 49; of reproductive technology, 98, 122, 134, 151

Missing Bodies: The Politics of Visibility (Casper and Moore), 159–160

Moore, Lisa Jean, 4–5, 151, 159–160

Moral hierarchy of norms, 152–154

Morris, David, 140

Moscucci, Ornella, 23

Motherhood mandate, 13

Motherhood vs. fatherhood, 115

Motorcycle metaphor, 63–64

Nasseri, Mariam, 183n39
National Center for Health Statistics
 (NCHS) on use of infertility services, 3
National Fertility Study, 171n5
National Survey for Family Growth
 (NSFG), 171n5
National virility, sperm counts and, 5
Natural, what is, 129
Natural approaches, male infertility treat-
 ment as, 127–133
Natural childbirth, 134
"Natural" conception, 16, 19, 35, 128
Natural foods, 41
Natural process, IVF as, 133–137
Natural selection, circumvention of,
 43–45, 177n55
NCHS (National Center for Health Statis-
 tics) on use of infertility services, 3
Nineteenth century, reproductive medi-
 cine in, 22–24
Norm(s): around masculinity, 57, 58, 60,
 78, 81; moral hierarchy of, 152–154. *See
 also* Gender norms
Normalcy, loss of, 161
Normal pregnancy via IVF, 133–137
NSFG (National Survey for Family
 Growth), 171n5
Nutraceuticals, 41

Objectification, 125
Obstetrician/gynecologists (OB/GYNs) in
 infertility clinics, 28
Obstruction between testicles and semi-
 nal vesicles, 121–122
"Octo-Mom," 176n42
Offspring, risks to, 133
Olympic metaphor of sperm counts, 5
Orgasm for semen collection, 60
Oudshoorn, Nelly, 23
Ovarian hyperstimulation syndrome, 39

Pain: of male reproductive surgery,
 122–123, 137–140; and masculinity,
 137–140; narratives of, 140
Pain threshold, 139, 154
Palermo, Gianpiero, 29–30
Parentage Act (1978), 174n19
Parental age, advanced, 41–43

Participants in study, 17, 173n44
Paternal age, advanced, 41–43
Pathologization: of menstruation and
 menopause, 61; of women's bodies,
 22–24
Patriarchal lineage of urology, 76–77
Patriarchal relationship, 141
Penile implants, 86
Penis, size and appearance of, 66–67
Percocet, 123
Percutaneous epididymal sperm aspira-
 tion (PESA), 45–46
Personhood status of embryos, 145
PESA (percutaneous epididymal sperm
 aspiration), 45–46
Phallocentricity of Western thought, 160
Phallus in Freudian interpretation, 66
Phenotypes, 177n54
Phenotypic time bomb theory, 43–45,
 177n55
Physical examination, 32, 33, 65–67,
 175n35, 176n38
Pituitary tumor, 90–91, 95
Plane metaphor, 63–64
Plumbing, messed up, 94, 95, 99, 120, 161
Politics of reproduction, 155–164; con-
 ceiving masculinity in, 162–164; crisis
 interrupted in, 161–162; embodied
 politics in, 159–161; technology,
 progress, and reproductive control in,
 156–159
Polycystic ovarian syndrome, 144–145
Pornography, sperm and semen in, 4
Potts, Annie, 87
Power: and masculinity, 65–66; mascu-
 linity and access to, 103
Powerlessness, 12, 25
Pregnancy: experience of, 148–151; IVF as
 normal path to, 133–137
Pregnancy-on-demand, 157
Prenatal bonding, 115
Prescriptions in gender stereotypes,
 72–73
Pricing of treatment options, 37–40
Progress and reproductive control,
 156–159
Progressive social scripts, 144
Proscriptions in gender stereotypes, 72–73

Prostate cancer, 126
Prosthetic penile implants, 86
Protection: of family, 133, 139; of masculinity, 13, 29, 64–67, 70, 76–77, 79, 80, 103, 106, 145, 148, 151–152; of wives, 123, 127, 130, 133, 147, 153–154
Providers, men as, 88
Proxeed, 41
Public/private dichotomy, 28–29
Punishment from God, 83

Rationality, masculinity and, 106–107
RE(s) (reproductive endocrinologists) vs. male infertility specialists, 31–37
Reconstructive surgery, 128
Recruitment of research subjects, 118–120, 181n46, 181n49, 181–182n53
Referral to male infertility clinic or urologist, 33–34, 36, 176n38, 176n39
Regrets: about invasive surgery, 134, 135, 136–137, 159; about IVF, 136; about marriage, 104–105, 113
Religion: and infertility as punishment from God, 83; and IVF, 128, 132; and semen collection, 56
Reproduction: biological reality to, 172–173n41; medicalization of, 157; politics of, 155–164
Reproductive control, technology, and progress and, 156–159
Reproductive endocrinologists (REs) vs. male infertility specialists, 31–37
Reproductive endocrinology, 28; vs. urology, 31–37
Reproductive medicine, development of, 22–26
Reproductive technology, 121–154; IVF as, 133–137; marital decision making on, 140–146; men and medicalization in, 124–127; men as controllers of, 126–127, 129–131; and natural approaches to male treatments, 127–133; pain and masculinity with, 137–140; sperm donation as, 146–152. *See also* Technology
Research, dearth of, 118–120, 181n46, 181n49, 181–182n53
Research methods, 16–18

Research participants, 165
Resources, masculinity and access to, 103
Ridgeway, Cecilia, 5–6, 52, 77, 78
Risk calculation, 37–40
Role failure, infertility as, 84–85
Rosenfeld, Dana, 125

SART (Society for Assisted Reproductive Technologies) on price comparison, 38
Schmidt, Matthew Allen, 151
Scripts: gendered, 135; progressive social, 144
Seeds, sperm and, 21
Self vs. body, 94–95, 107, 130, 160–161, 179n19
Semen analysis test, 52–60; home kit for, 130–131; results of, 67–68; with varicocele, 127
Semen and masculinity, 4–5
Semen collection, 52–60
Semen collection cup, 53, 60
Seminal enterprises, 4–5
Seminal vesicles: in factory and bridge metaphor, 63; obstruction between testicles and, 121–122
Sex lives: impact of infertility on, 108–114, 180n35; interview questions about, 169–170
Sexual power, 65–66
Shooting blanks, 4, 94
Sickness as emasculating, 126
Single-sperm injection technique, 29–31. *See also* Intracytoplasmic sperm injection
Single women, donor sperm for, 175n24
Size of genitals, 66–67
Social construction of gender, 51–52
Society for Assisted Reproductive Technologies (SART) on price comparison, 38
Socioeconomic status, 17; and masculinity, 103–104
Sociological approach, 2–4
Sperm: discovery of, 21; donor, 4; and masculinity, 4–5; reproduction without, 172–173n41; "saving up," 37, 109; washing of, 27
Spermatogenesis, 62

Sperm banks and banking, 11, 14, 59, 151–152

Sperm counts: anabolic steroids and, 46–47; in delivering diagnosis, 68; and donor sperm, 147–150; and female power, 5; and national virility, 5; Olympic metaphor of, 5; and sexuality, 111–112; theories about factors affecting, 40–41; unexplained low, 144–145, 183n40; WHO "gold standard" for, 30; worldwide decrease in, 5. *See also* Azoospermia; Zero sperm count

Sperm Counts: Overcome by Man's Most Precious Fluid (Moore), 4–5

Sperm donation, 4, 31, 145–152, 175n24, 184n42

Sperm extraction, 30–31, 43, 45–46, 59

Sperm quality: age and, 42; denying impact of, on masculinity, 99–100, 101; and IVF, 135; nineteenth-century understanding of, 23; in sharing diagnosis, 67; varicocele and, 111

Spinal cord injury, 96–97

Sports analogies, 64–65

Stepfathers, 95–96, 114, 117–118

Stereotypes, gender, 52, 53, 72–73, 78–79. *See also* Gender beliefs, hegemonic

Sterility, 9, 23–25, 110, 172n24; perceptions of, 120; and powerlessness, 25; secrecy over, 25, 174n21. *See also* Male infertility

Steroids, anabolic, 46–47, 153

Stigma: of disease, 12; of impotence and male infertility, 87; of infertility, 102; of infidelity, 151; medicalization and, 86

Subfertility, 67

Success rates: calculation of, 37–40; of specialists, 47

Suicide, fertility and, 68

Suleman, Nadya, 176n42

Support groups, 16, 119–120, 181–182n53

Surgeries, exploratory and reconstructive, 128

Taboos, cultural, 50

Technobirth, 129

Technology: as alienating, 160; men as controllers of, 126–127, 129–131; and reproductive control, 156–159; women and, 160. *See also* Reproductive technology

Technology hierarchy, 35

Technosemen market, 151

Telephone interviews, 17, 173n43

Terminology used in clinical encounters, 67–68

TESE (testicular sperm extraction), 45–46

Testicles: as engines, 63–64; examination of, 66; as factories, 62; obstruction between seminal vesicles and, 121–122; size and appearance of, 66–67

Testicular biopsy, 82

Testicular cancer, 95–96, 126

Testicular sperm extraction (TESE), 45–46

Testosterone and sperm count, 46–47

"Test tube baby," 9, 27

Thompson, Charis, 111, 125, 173n42

Throsby, Karen, 135

Time limit in definition of infertility, 10

Treatment plan: interview questions about, 167–168; marital decision making on, 140–146. *See also* Male infertility treatment(s)

Tumor, pituitary, 90–91, 95

Underwear and sperm count, 40–41

Unprotected intercourse, 9–10, 67

Urethra in factory and bridge metaphor, 63

Urologists: harm caused by, 46–48; referrals to, 33–34, 36, 176nn38–39; women as, 76, 178n20

Urology, 31, 175n32; as masculine institution, 75–77; vs. reproductive endocrinology, 31–37

Uterus: bicornuate, 182n2; as machine, 61

Valium for male infertility surgery, 138

Van der Ploeg, Irma, 175n25

Varicocele(s), 47–48, 68, 111–112, 127–128, 130–132

Varicocelectomy, 38–39, 47–48, 127–128, 130, 135–136

Vas deferens (vasa deferentia): as bridges, 62; congenital bilateral absence of,

92, 97–98, 138; severed, 94, 136–137, 179n16
Vasectomy, 62, 159
Vasectomy reversals, 42, 177n53
Veto power, 145–146
Viagra, 86, 87, 158
Virility: in cultural milieu, 4–8; and masculinity, 84–85
Visibility, politics of, 159–160
Vitamins, 41
Vote, equal, 141–143
Votive offerings, 20
Vulnerability, 66

Wajcman, Judith, 7, 129, 133
Washing sperm, 27
Weakness, sickness and, 126
Webb, Russell, 118–119, 161, 181n49
West, Candace, 51–52
Whiteness: and masculinity, 7; of subject pool, 17–18, 163–164
WHO. *See* World Health Organization (WHO)
Williams, Christine, 103
Wives: as decision makers, 143–145; as information keepers, 70–75

The Woman in the Body: A Cultural Analysis of Reproduction (Martin), 61
Women as informed consumers, 126
Women's bodies, pathologization of, 22–24
Working-class background, 17, 64, 103–104, 163–164, 180n30
World Health Organization (WHO): on definition of infertility, 9–10; on prevalence of male factor infertility, 3; on sperm count, 30
World War II, artificial insemination after, 25

Zero sperm count: and assisted reproductive technologies, 30; and donor sperm, 147–150; and fatherhood, 114; feelings about, 91–92, 104–106; focusing on etiology of, 91–92; vs. infertility, 93–94; in Klinefelter's syndrome, 69; and male infertility specialists, 48; and masculinity, 104–106; as medical condition, 92–94, 120; rarity of, 63; due to severed vas deferens, 94, 136–137, 179n16; sharing diagnosis of, 68. *See also* Azoospermia
Zimmerman, Don, 51–52

Liberty Walther Barnes is a Research Associate in the Department of Sociology at the University of Cambridge.